THE MORALS AND POLITICS OF PSYCHOLOGY

SUNY Series, Alternatives in Psychology
Michael A. Wallach, Editor

THE MORALS AND POLITICS OF PSYCHOLOGY

Psychological Discourse and the Status Quo

ISAAC PRILLELTENSKY

STATE UNIVERSITY OF NEW YORK PRESS

Published by
State University of New York Press, Albany

© 1994   State University of New York

For information, address State University of New York
Press, State University Plaza, Albany, N.Y., 12246

Production by E. Moore
Marketing by Bernadette LaManna

Library of Congress Cataloging-in-Publication Data

Prilleltensky, Isaac, 1959-
    The morals and politics of psychology : psychological discourse
and the status quo / Isaac Prilleltensky.
        p.   cm. — (SUNY series, alternatives in psychology)
    Includes bibliographical references and index.
    ISBN 0-7914-2037-X (alk. paper). — ISBN 0-7914-2038-8 (pbk. :
alk. paper)
    1. Psychology—Moral and ethical aspects. 2. Psychology, Applied-
-Moral and ethical aspects. 3. Psychology—Social aspects.
4. Psychology, Applied—Social aspects. 5. Social ethics-
-Psychological aspects. 6. Social change—Psychological aspects.
I. Title. II. Series.
BF76.4.P75 1994
150′.1—dc20   93-37494
                                                              CIP

10 9 8 7 6 5 4 3 2 1

Dedicated to the memory of my parents,
Betty and Jacobo Prilleltensky,
who died at a young age

and to the memory of my aunt,
Eusebia Kotliroff,
who under great hardship
provided me with the best possible home
after the tragic death of my parents

CONTENTS

PART III.
PSYCHOLOGY AND SOCIAL ETHICS

PREFACE

This is an important book. It will startle and challenge the various fields of applied psychology, but it will also challenge the scientists in the field as well. It will force its readers to reconsider the historic, slavish, ongoing preoccupation of psychology with attempts at changing the individual to the neglect of changing the social environmental factors that play a crucial role in determining human behavior. There is an old saying in psychoanalysis that the major task in working with neurotics is to make the unconscious conscious. The rule applies equally well to everyone who has unconsciously neglected the powerful influences of social class in determining behavior.

One of the delightful things about this book is the way Prilleltensky organizes the extensive literature, illuminating the ideological components of seven separate fields of intervention with human problems. He clarifies the inherent conservatism of the Skinnerians, the Freudians, and the humanists. He indicts the emerging enthusiastic supporters of cognitivism as well as those in the older fields of abnormal, industrial, and school psychology. Throughout the volume his scholarship challenges idealism, explains oppression, and illuminates the ever-present efforts at blaming the victim, all of which so dominate the field. Psychologists have been political innocents, in large measure because their education has completely neglected political theory and economics. As a consequence we have accepted uncritically the assignment to preserve the status quo. Prilleltensky forces us to confront our biases and our narrow understanding of the social world—whether our identification with management in industrial psychology, or our acceptance of the belief that school failures result from the child's individual defect rather than from problems in the school's social environment.

For the past several years I have been reading extensively on the topics of social class influences and the power of patriarchy. For the past 150 years British scientists have formulated psychological theory that explains how the white male upper-class British elite managed to dominate much of the world and to exploit mercilessly the poor in their own country, and the masses in their colonial empire. Social Darwinism as developed and elaborated by Herbert Spencer was rooted in the belief that superior genes account for the success and power of the upper classes; British scientists, including Galton, Darwin, Pearson, Burt, and Eysenck, formulated a genetic theory supporting class structure. Spencer was the favorite theorist of the American robber-barons, and William McDougall came to America to help psychology give scientific justification for racism, classism, and political conservatism. American psychologists have been educated by a succession of intellectual leaders whose conservative view of humankind has dominated the field. Prilleltensky manages to demonstrate their continuing influences, and he also clarifies for us the urgent need for a new force in the field, for people who are outspoken critics of the powerful conservatives.

It is my hope that this book will be read by young people coming into the field, that their unconscious biases will be made conscious, that they will realize that it is social class, with attendant powerlessness, racism, sexism, and the pervasive influence of "scientific capitalism," that is far more responsible for human suffering than internal defects and genetic diseases of the brain.

GEORGE W. ALBEE

ACKNOWLEDGMENTS

Fredy Marcuse, now a Senior Scholar at the University of Manitoba, has many wonderful qualities. I benefited tremendously from two. The first one is the courage to pursue his convictions in less-than-favorable climates. When he was my Ph.D. advisor, he fought not only for his convictions, but for mine as well. He made every possible effort to ensure that I be allowed to write a dissertation on the topic of this book. The second quality I greatly enjoyed was the sense of humor with which he helped me overcome the many barriers I encountered in exploring the morals and politics of psychology.

George Albee, now Professor Emeritus at the University of Vermont, continues to be an exemplary role model for me, both as a person of morals and compassion, and as a psychologist. He never failed to be there for me when I needed his help. I feel honored to have had his support.

Geoff Nelson, Professor of Psychology at Wilfrid Laurier University and my closest mentor, helped me at the beginning stages of my career in more ways than I can remember. His intellect, humor, and personal integrity make our friendship a cherished source of pride for me. I am thankful to him for hours of academic talk and many healthy laughs. I feel immensely fortunate to have received the encouragement of these three great psychologists.

Other associates and relatives assisted in unique and wonderful ways. I wish to thank my friends and colleagues Dan Burston, Dennis Fox, and Lev Gonick for the interest they showed in this project. They listened attentively and sympathetically to my doubts, fears, and excitement. Leslea Peirson, my student, research assistant, and editorial assistant, performed all her duties exceptionally well. Her unmatched academic skills and delightful predisposition made our work together very enjoyable. Linda Potter, Administrative Assistant in the Department of Psychology, spent several days merging and alphabetizing computer files with hundreds of references. As always, she was most helpful.

Carola Sautter, Elizabeth Moore and Cari Goldberg Janice of SUNY Press made the production of the book easier than expected. Their "author-friendly" handling of the publication process was both cordial and professional.

My sister Cachi in Israel and my brother Mario in Mexico affectionately expressed their support for my work, as did my father-in-law Nathan Rapoport. I am indebted to them all. My mother-in-law Rachel Rapoport, a remarkable woman, helped in many ways. Her contributions to this book are numerous and substantial.

No other person has been more understanding, supportive, and caring than Ora, my wife. As my closest critic and companion she shared with me the many stressful and exciting moments that are part and parcel of writing a book. Without her I could not have completed the book and have a rewarding life at the same time. My six-year-old son, Matan, is a marvelous source of pleasure. He provided much-needed relief from research and writing. I thank him also for tolerating my long working hours.

A book preparation grant from the Research Office of Wilfrid Laurier University assisted in the completion of the work. Their help is gratefully acknowledged.

Some of my earlier publications have been adapted for this book. I wish to thank the publishers listed below for allowing me to use this material. Chapters 7, 8, 9, 10, 11, 12, 14, and 15 have been adapted, respectively, from:

"On the Social Legacy of B. F. Skinner: Rhetoric of Change/ Philosophy of Adjustment." *Theory and Psychology*, 4(1). Copyright (1994) Sage publications. Reprinted with permission.

"Humanistic Psychology, Human Welfare, and the Social Order." *Journal of Mind and Behavior*, 13(4). Copyright (1992) The Institute of Mind and Behavior. Reprinted with permission.

"On the Social and Political Implications of Cognitive Psychology." *Journal of Mind and Behavior*, 11(2). Copyright (1990) The Institute of Mind and Behavior. Reprinted with permission.

"The Politics of Abnormal Psychology: Past, Present, and Future." *Political Psychology*, 11(4). Copyright (1990) Plenum Press. Reprinted with permission.

"Psychology in Industry: Origins and Sociopolitical Implications." *Critical Sociology*, 17(2). Copyright (1990) Critical Sociology. Reprinted with permission.

"The Social Ethics of School Psychology: A Priority for the 1990's." *School Psychology Quarterly*, 6(3). Copyright (1991) Guilford Press. Reprinted with permission.

"Enhancing the Social Ethics of Psychology: Toward a Psychology at the Service of Social Change." *Canadian Psychology*, 31(4). Copyright (1990) Canadian Psychological Association. Reprinted with permission.

"Empowerment in Mainstream Psychology: Legitimacy, Obstacles, and Possibilities." *Canadian Psychology*. Copyright (in press) Canadian Psychological Association. Reprinted with permission.

PART I

PSYCHOLOGY AND THE STATUS QUO

This book is based on the assumption that psychological theories and practices are simultaneously constituted by, and formative of, the cultural and social order. Beyond the positive or negative effects of diagnosis and therapy on private individuals, modern psychology has considerable repercussions at the social level as well. These implications, which are both moral and political, are only minimally, if ever, addressed in the professional training of psychologists and mental health practitioners. However innocent, this neglect results in a very consequential moral illiteracy regarding the role of psychology in Western society. This is a blind spot that neither consumers nor providers of psychological services should ignore.

This part of the book places psychology in its sociohistorical context. Furthermore, it provides the necessary background for the argument that psychological discourse upholds the societal status quo. I discuss how the present state of social affairs is maintained by cultural and ideological means. These means inform, as well as benefit from, psychological constructs such as the "supreme self" and the conventional wisdom that most social problems can be solved by scientific and technical tools. Ideological elements inherent in psychological postulates are identified, with the purpose of setting the stage for part II. Part I concludes with a succinct statement of the analytical framework to be employed.

Chapter 1

INTRODUCTION

"It is a challenge," Harding argues in her book *Whose Science? Whose Knowledge?* (1991), "to figure out just which are the regressive and which the progressive tendencies brought into play in any particular scientific or feminist project, and how to advance the progressive and inhibit the regressive ones" (p. 11). The present work undertakes this challenge with respect to psychological theories and practices. In this introductory chapter I present some of the thoughts and aspirations that led me to write this book. This introduction should help to situate the text in the context of the social sciences in general, and of psychology in particular.

First, I would like to say a few words about the book's title. By "the morals and politics of psychology" I mean primarily the implicit social ethics of psychology, and the moral consequences of the discipline for the acceptance and transformation of power relations in society. The subtitle defines the contents of the book more specifically. By "psychological discourse and the status quo" I allude simply to the relationship between psychological theories and the current state of societal affairs. Implied in the expression *psychological discourse* is the assumption that this particular kind of language is saturated with social and political meanings that have serious repercussions for those directly and indirectly affected by it (Edwards and

Potter 1992; Parker 1992). The moral nature of these implications for the preservation of the societal status quo is the major concern of this work.

CRITICAL STANDPOINTS

When the expression *critical thinking* is invoked in psychology, it is used almost exclusively to refer to epistemological considerations such as methodological rigor, logical reasoning in deriving conclusions, and adequacy of generalizations. In essence, the term *critical thinking* is reserved for questioning the "scientific" grounds of psychological postulates. However, there is another possible and neglected use of this concept. It refers to the critical thinking involved in examining the social, political, and moral assumptions implicit in psychological theories and practices. Psychologists, for the most part, receive thorough training in critical thinking as it applies to the analysis of empirical positivist research. What psychologists do not receive during their preparation are the skills necessary to scrutinize the ideological repercussions of particular forms of theorizing. This contrast is evidenced in just about any psychology undergraduate or graduate program.

One of my goals here is to advance the political critical standpoint. The need to be educated in the political, social, and moral dimensions of psychology is just as important as being taught how to evaluate the methodology and research design of a study in human behavior. Nevertheless, the moral and political critical standpoint is still foreign to applied mainstream psychology (Bulhan 1985; Howitt 1991; Ussher and Nicolson 1992). If current training in psychotherapy fails to educate students on crucial moral aspects of their work directly affecting their clients (London 1986), then the problem is even deeper when it comes to the more distant social ramifications of their endeavors. Kovel (1988) argues that

> the prevailing 'psy' professions . . . of psychiatry, psychology, psychoanalysis, psychiatric social work, and so forth, consistently refuse to carry out this examination. Indeed, an opacity to the actual social basis of psy practice is one of the defining features of these professions. Generally speaking, this deficit is covered by a thick membrane of technocracy, which deflects any questioning in advance, indeed, rules out the possibility of questioning, the 'pure, value free, and scientific' pursuit of Mental Health. (p. 119)

Literature concerning the traditional scientific critical standpoint abounds. By contrast, material pertaining to the moral and political standpoint, while increasing, is less plentiful and rarely reaches students and mainstream psychologists. This is largely because, among other things, political and ethical critiques are written for small, specialist audiences. My hope is to stimulate discussion in wider circles as to the merits of the moral and political critical standpoint. Here, this approach is employed primarily to examine the moral and sociopolitical repercussions of central theories of personality and their respective use in the applied branches of the profession. The focus will be primarily on mental health concepts derived from various theories and their translation into common practice. As a consequence, this study will concern itself mainly with the applied and clinical aspects of such theories as behavioral, cognitive, humanistic, and psychoanalytic psychology. Practice informed by these and other bodies of knowledge will also be examined. The chapters dealing with abnormal, school, and industrial/organizational psychology explore the unquestioned ideologies of these professions.

My primary objectives, then, are to promote the political critical standpoint in psychology and to share certain insights concerning the social and moral ramifications of some influential theories and practices. To be sure, the political critical standpoint has a well-respected history in psychology, but this critical culture suffers, in my opinion, from two debilitating problems. First, as intimated above, it is written for exclusive audiences; and second, it has failed to produce cogent calls for action deriving from its critiques. I can only hope that this book makes at least a small contribution toward the correction of these shortcomings.

A critical standpoint of the kind advocated here cannot be oblivious to the standpoint of the author. In contrast to the traditional positivist critical standpoint, which assumes that the observer is value-neutral and devoid of personal projects other than the pursuit of truth, the political critical standpoint acknowledges the inevitable and ubiquitous presence of personal factors in the development of theory. All knowledge is situated in the writers' social contexts and is bounded by the interpretive horizons of its producers (Gergen 1992; Harding 1991; Reinharz 1992). Hence, I would like to disclose a few personal points of departure from which my arguments are derived. Although I am presently teaching undergraduate and graduate students in community psychology, I formerly worked as a child and family clinician in school settings. The critique to be elaborated in these pages emanates not from a detached intellectual interest in applied psychology, but rather from concern that grew out of eight years of experience working with children and their parents. Presently I work mainly in a university setting but maintain a measure of community involvement through consultation with mental health agencies and prevention activities with school personnel, children, and immigrant families. The research that follows, even if hurtful at times to the "psy" professions, is written in a spirit of constructive criticism. I write as an insider.

Another point of departure for me, as an author, concerns the audacity of engaging in moral critique. In writing about public philosophy, distributive justice, democracy, and social change, I wish to admit and face the vast distance that separates the written word from the transformational act of promoting justice. I am painfully aware that in my activities in the community and the university I may not always be able to enact the proactive ethical precepts discussed in the last part of the book. Am I doing enough? Am I investing my efforts in the best and most productive way? Am I forever upholding the values of self-determination, distributive justice, and collaborative and democratic participation, even at the expense of organizational efficiency? I am admittedly unable to answer yes to all of the above. Yet I believe in the intrinsic merit of struggling with one's values. Attaining a higher degree of morality is a process both nurtured by and ridden with personal conflict. Personal conflict, however, need not devolve into ethical relativism or political inaction. In fact, the entire book may be seen as a prescription for the opposite.

Important as it might be, writing is only a small commitment toward changing unjust social structures. In my case, at least, writing is largely an act of privilege. There is, and there must always be, a tension in the process of denouncing dehumanizing social conditions from the comfort of your office, particularly when one belongs to a privileged group. Commitment to human welfare and social justice must mean more than writing about implicit ideologies; it must mean helping groups and individuals who don't have the luxury to write about their own misery. I admit, I write this confessional for myself as much as for the reader. Academic talk, to which I willfully contribute, can be intoxicating at times. It is because of this fear of intoxication that I feel impelled to guard against the illusion of moral rectitude inherent in composing a book-long essay about the morality of psychology. Growing up in Argentina in rather turbulent times, I learned that oppression, violence, and ideological deception are more than academic words. They are human practices with high human costs attached to them. Suffering and pain were the lived expression of these words. Torture and political repression could not be eliminated through mere rhetoric. Perhaps as a result of this realization I grew up suspicious of written or spoken discourses that are not accompanied by committed actions. Whatever it is, the test of integrity cannot be the altitude of one's words. Concomitant actions supporting moral pronouncements must follow. Writing can be a version of complacency, and although I know it takes much more than a public confession, it is because of my profound desire to avoid this danger that I share these personal deliberations. These disclosures should also give readers an inkling as to what motivates me to keep their attention.

But if growing up in a so-called developing country instilled in me moral exigencies that are suspect in academic orations, it also made the writing of this book relatively simple. In "developing" countries, the political meanings of discourses, scientific or otherwise, are not necessarily studied in the university. Rather, they are the substance of everyday talk. The subordinated position of these countries in the world has generated a culture of skepticism toward political or scientific authoritative declamations. For individuals with even a minimal sense of cultural resistance, the question of whose interests are being served by intellectual enterprise X or Y is second nature. In this tradition, questioning the unarticulated ideology of modern psychology came to me without much effort.

Political Critiques of Psychology

Having presented the general orientation and attitudes I brought to this project, I would like to show some of the scholarly antecedents of the critical standpoint proposed here. I would claim that, however powerful, these critiques tend to remain peripheral in the discipline. While this may very well be the fate of this treatise, I think we can improve the political education of the profession by formulating a more integrated critique.

There is little doubt that psychology has left its imprint on twentieth-century society. There should also be little doubt that socioeconomic, cultural, and political trends have shaped, to a large extent, the methods and content of the discipline (e.g., Anderson and Travis 1983; Chorover 1985; Danziger 1990; Deese 1985; Jacoby 1975; Sampson 1977; Sarason 1981b). Nevertheless, a tradition of alleged *value-neutrality* in political matters and pseudoimmunity to ideological influences within the profession have obstructed an in-depth examination of the interaction between social forces and psychology. To gain a better understanding of this interplay, an inquiry into the ideological elements that might have permeated psychological theories and practices is necessary.

In our era, depicted as "the age of psychology" (Haverman 1957) and "the psychological century" (Koch and Leary 1985, p. 33), the practice of behavioral science has far-reaching social and ethical implications. Is psychology promoting human welfare, as prescribed by most codes of ethics for psychologists? Or is it perhaps hindering the betterment of social conditions by guarding the interests of the status quo? An analysis of the moral, sociopolitical, and cultural values involved in psychological theories and practices will enable us to provide some answers to these crucial questions.

In view of the importance attributed in North America to psychology's position in a wide array of social issues (Koch and Leary 1985; Sarason 1984b, 1986), an investigation of its ideological biases is called for. Such an examination will bring us closer to determining the nature of the relationship between psychology and the social order. The main proposition to be advanced is that ideological elements supportive of the social order outweigh those conducive to social changes.

Although there has been a noticeable increase in the number of investigations dealing with the ideological aspects involved in the applications of modern psychology (e.g., Albee 1990; Butcher 1983; Gergen 1985; Ingleby 1972, 1981c; Jones 1986; Kitzinger 1991b; Nahem 1981; Parker 1992; Roffe 1986; Sampson 1991; Sarason 1981b; E. V. Sullivan 1984; Ussher and Nicolson 1992; Wilkinson 1991), the literature has not yet reached mainstream psychologists. To be sure, the thesis being advanced here, namely, that psychology is instrumental in reproducing the societal status quo, has already been suggested by other psychologists. However, I contend that the existing critical literature (a) still awaits integration; (b) remains mostly, with a few noticeable exceptions (Albee 1981, 1986; Anderson and Travis 1983; Billig 1979; Chesler 1989; Gilligan 1982; Halleck 1971; Sarason 1981b) at an abstract level without proper argumentation; (c) by and large, does not address the vast social implications of psychology's highly influential function in social reproduction; and (d) fails to consider how psychologists can deal, from an ethical point of view, with their witting or unwitting roles as social reproducers or reformers. This last shortcoming deserves special mention in view of the current proclivity of certain forms of postmodernist discourse to slide into ethical relativism and political paralysis (Burman 1990; Parker 1992; C. Taylor 1991).

Several authors (e.g., Braginsky and Braginsky 1974; Braginsky 1985; Deese 1985) have dealt with the social reproductive functions of psychology, but that has not been their principal locus of attention. Others have dealt with this issue from the perspective of a particular field. Albee (1970, 1981, 1986) and Sarason (1981a, 1981b), for instance, focused mainly on preventive and clinical psychology; Ingleby's *Critical Psychiatry* (1981a) analyzed the connection between psychiatry and social control; and Sedgwick (1982) examined conventional theories of abnormal psychology and their inability to seriously challenge the hegemony of the conservative medical model.

Jacoby's *Social Amnesia* (1975), undoubtedly one of the major and seminal works written on conformist psychology, is mostly devoted to arguments internal to the psychoanalytic school of thought, and there is only brief mention of other influential trends such as behaviorism and humanism. Similarly, Frosh's *The Politics of Psychoanalysis* (1987) is devoted entirely to the political legacy of Freudian theory. Anderson and Travis (1983), on the other hand, are interested in the singular political impact of cognitive psychology.

The ideological implications of areas in applied psychology such as behavior modification (J. G. Holland 1978; Nahem 1981; Woolfolk and Richardson 1984), family therapy (James and McIntyre 1983; Poster 1978), and industrial psychology (Baritz 1974; Guareschi 1982; Ralph 1983) have been suggested but not fully developed.

In summary, various authors have observed the conforming influences of psychology, but they have treated the problem as a relatively isolated occurrence. No single treatise has been devoted to the *pervasiveness* of this phenomenon in psychology. By analyzing the ideological components present in central theories of human behavior, and in some widely used psychological services, I hope to show that psychology's retarding impact on social change is far from insignificant. Once this insight is available to wider sectors of the population, there might be hope that service providers and consumers alike will demand change.

Feminist psychologists, to be sure, have done much to expose the patriarchal and capitalist roots of multiple branches of mainstream modern psychology (Kitzinger 1991b; Ussher and Nicolson 1992; Zanardi 1990). Their powerful indictment of oppressive practices, however, has not yet reached the consciousness of the vast majority of providers and consumers of psychological services (Fine and Gordon 1991). When Chesler compared the state of affairs in 1989 to the situation in the early seventies, when she first published *Women and Madness*, she wrote: "Today, the mental health professions are the same patriarchal institutions I once described" (Chesler 1989, p. xx). I have little doubt that the dialogue between the opponents and the sometimes unwitting supporters of what Wilkinson (1991) calls "main/malestream" psychology needs to cultivated.

Perhaps the most politically scrutinized field in psychology is social psychology. Several books (e.g., Archibald 1978; Armistead 1974; Billig 1982; Parker 1989; Parker and Shotter 1990; Wexler 1983) and influential articles (e.g., Gergen 1973; Ibanez Gracia 1983; Sampson 1978) in the last two decades have reflected upon the political character of social psychology and its failure to promote human welfare. While the critique mounted by these authors is pertinent to the general theme of this volume, my specific objective is to examine fields with a more clinical orientation. Readers interested in the ideological dimensions of social psychology are referred to these insightful sources.

My second concern as to the present literature has to do with the lack of emphasis on the actual ways through which psychology performs its role of conformity promoter. Most of the reviewed studies remain at a rhetorical and rather abstract level, without elaborating on how a certain psychological activity is going to affect the individual's acceptance or rejection of society's values and norms. There is a conspicuous discrepancy between the number of allegations made against psychology for its role in preventing social change and the detailed argumentation offered to support these accusations. Allegations abound, but relatively little evidence is usually provided. Some extreme examples are found in Iaroshevskii's 1950 paper "The Eclipse of Consciousness in Contemporary American Psychology." He stated that "in the last stage of capitalism, the stage of stagnation and approaching collapse, bourgeois psychology increasingly assumes the function of plunging human consciousness into the abyss of the irrational, of depriving human life and activity of reason and meaning" (p. 34). He further regarded psychologists as *the* ideologists of capitalism and states that they "try to perpetuate capitalist exploitation, wars, inequality, oppression and to ascribe the ugliness of bourgeois society to 'human nature'" (p. 39).

Consider also the following statements: "Because mainstream psychology is embedded in the dominant political, economic, and religious ideologies, professional psychologists have upheld these ideologies rather than examining their impact upon the lives of others" (Braginsky 1985, p. 881). "Because psychology seems to be unique among the social sciences in its inability to reflect on its place in the social order, it will, in this unreflective stance, function as an apologist for the status quo" (E. V. Sullivan 1984, pp. 131-32).

> What we are witnessing now is, an attempt by psychologists to awake up from the trance of their own unquestioning profession-alism to a realization of who they are working for and what their real job is . . . and the answer is not, ultimately, to be found any-where in their contracts, even in the small print. My hypothesis is that their unwritten contract is to maintain the status quo. (Ingleby 1974, p. 317)

Although some of these assertions are, in my view, justified in principle, they are not always accompanied by an exposition of the mechanisms involved in the utilization of psychology in the mainte-nance or reproduction of the prevalent social system. Explaining these mechanisms will be the main concern of the second part of the book.

The third critical remark concerning the current literature is of a more general nature and has to do with the social implications of a con-formist psychology, particularly in view of the increasing authority attributed to the behavioral sciences in a wide array of issues. To wit:

> Our services and advice are now sought and accepted in practi-cally all fields of human activity. Newspapers describe the activi-ties and opinions of psychologists on marriage, love, child rearing, and other aspects of day-to-day life. In the fields of marketing, personnel, training, selection, and more, executives rely on the advice and opinions of consulting psychologists. To state it bluntly, psychologists have considerable power to influence the opinions and behavior of the public. (Kipnis 1987, p. 30)

Or in the words of Koch (1980), "throughout this century (and before), psychology *has* been under gracious dissemination—whether in school, bar, office, or bedroom; whether by book, magazine, electronic propa-gation, or word of mouth—to a voracious consumership" (p. 33). Considering the popularity of psychological theories in the public forum, and the large number of children and adults consuming one type of psychological service or another provided by an army of school and clinical psychologists, family therapists, psychiatrists, psychiatric nurses, industrial counselors, and the like, it is not difficult to realize the substantial impact psychology's message to conform might have upon society as a whole. At best, it may be preventing changes that could enhance the well-being of the population. At worst, it may be silently endorsing unjust social practices.

Considering the late arrival of formal ethical education in the social sciences (Warwick 1980), we should not be surprised to notice that there are few guidelines for psychologists on how to face a pressing moral dilemma. Are psychologists supporting a social system that may not promote human welfare, by furnishing it with ideological ammunition? And if so, what should be done about it? The literature on this question has been characterized by denunciation more than annunciation, in that there are many accusations but very few suggestions about how to face this moral dilemma. Sampson (1983) and E. V. Sullivan (1984), who have written eloquently about the ideological functions of psychology, speak of an *emancipatory* psychology that will not ratify the social order but facilitate the advent of greater freedom for those in disadvantaged positions. Similarly, some Marxist writers, such as C. I. Cohen (1986), Nahem (1981), and Seve (1978), conjecture about the use of psychology in bringing about macrosocial changes. Feminist psychologists appear to be the leaders in articulating political agendas for the discipline (Chesler 1989; Kitzinger 1991b; Unger and Crawford 1992; Wilkinson 1991). The nonconformist moral stance of these authors notwithstanding, an elaboration of daily practices that will avoid a purblind endorsement of prevailing power arrangements in society still needs to be developed. These issues will be addressed in the last section of the book, where the concepts of social and quotidian ethics are formulated.

Finally, a reading of the American and Canadian codes of ethics for psychologists reveals a lack of sensitivity to the question of ideological intrusions in our discipline. Although the Canadian code is much more definite than its American counterpart about the responsibility of psychologists toward society (as reflected in the statement that psychologists should "participate in the process of critical self-reflection of the discipline's place in society and in the development [of] . . . beneficial societal functioning and changes" [Canadian Psychological Association 1991, principle IV.5]), it does not provide specific guidelines as to how to advance this objective. In synthesis, the codes do not address the vulnerability of the discipline to ideological and political biases. Although this is not yet widely known, the Feminist Therapy Institute (1990) has developed a code that does address these imperfections. The degree of candor with which this code deals with issues of power differences, societal oppression, and potential victimization of clients is quite unprecedented in documents of this kind. Unfortunately, the chasm separating this instrument from mainstream codes of ethics is as profound, or deeper, than the one segregating feminist discourse from traditional psychological theories.

This study will attempt to deal with the ethical shortcomings mentioned above, with the hope of providing a coherent argument as to the function of psychology in social reproduction. A comprehensive understanding of the multifaceted aspects involved in social reproduction or the maintenance of the status quo would necessitate an interdisciplinary approach with contributions from economics, political science, sociology, psychology, history, and philosophy, among others. The present study is intended to investigate only a small segment of the total machinery involved in social reproduction—that is, the messages to conform operating in psychological theories and practices.

The psychological formulations to be analyzed are those representative of Western views in the twentieth century, with particular emphasis on current practices. The incursion of ideology in psychology is not unique to any particular time within the suggested period. Although the *phenotypical* manifestations of conforming messages in psychology change with the times and with the particular school of thought, the *genotype* remains largely the same. I will argue that different psychological paradigms have been constituted by, and constitutive of, the prevalent ideology.

From a methodological point of view, it can be argued that the multitude of changes that have taken place in the Western world since the beginning of the century precludes the treatment of this period as a unit of historical analysis. I would claim, however, that the capitalist socioeconomic system, throughout its various phases, has always resorted to ideological means in order to legitimate its existence (Addams 1902; Giddens 1979; Silva 1970; H. T. Wilson 1977). Moreover, the fundamental values embraced by capitalism have basically remained the same in the period to be discussed (Edwards, Reich, and Weisskopf 1986; George and Wilding 1976; Rand 1967; Sargent 1969; Webb and Webb 1923).

In general terms, this study is concerned with "the penetration of the social process into the intellectual sphere" (Mannheim 1936, p. 268), and more specifically with the role played by ideology in scientific knowledge (Abercrombie 1980; Berger and Luckmann 1967; Eriksson 1975; Mannheim 1936). The present analysis, which views ideas as being affected by, as well as affecting, the social order, is congruous with the dialectical sociology of knowledge advocated by Haru (1987), with the feminist approach to the sociology of knowledge proposed by D. E. Smith (1990), and with the sociology of psychological knowledge endorsed by Buss (1975). Buss (1975) argues that the scholar and his or her "ideas, in part, both reflect and influence the underlying social structure" (p. 990). In more specific terms, this book advocates the scrutiny of psychological theories and practices by examining implicit ideological assumptions supportive of the status quo, with a view toward infusing into psychology a concern for the values of self-determination, distributive justice, democracy, and compassionate caring in interpersonal and public affairs.

The book is divided into three main sections. Part I, of which this introduction is the first chapter, presents the basic conceptual framework. This section develops and formulates the tools necessary to examine the social context of psychological discourse. Part II is an analysis of the morals and politics of psychological discourse, in its various manifestations. Part III deals with the social and ethical implications of psychology. This discipline is viewed as devoted, unconsciously perhaps, to fortifying a decadent state of social affairs. A moral framework for pursuing social change within psychology and the social sciences is also offered in part III.

Chapter 2

THE STATUS QUO AND ITS PRESERVATION

According to the *Dictionary of American English Usage* (Nicholson 1957), the term *status quo* refers to "the position in which things are." In the particular context of this inquiry, *status quo* pertains to the power structure of the present social system.

The evolution of capitalism has witnessed numerous economic changes and social reforms. Yet the foundations of this mode of production, namely, the unequal distribution of resources with its concomitant division of classes, have remained largely unaltered. Inequality of power between producers and owners of the means of production is a constitutive feature of capitalism (Edwards, Reich, and Weisskopf 1986). This inequality of power is the specific status quo that will be addressed in this analysis. Capitalism, to be sure, manifests itself in numerous forms and levels that are beyond the scope of this study. For the purpose of this inquiry, we shall remain at a rather general level of analysis.

Needless to say there have been many changes under the umbrella of capitalism: From laissez-faire capitalism to the welfare state; from overt and unrestrained discrimination to legal protection of minorities; from technological ignorance to scientific miracles. Some observers point to these changes as proof of the dynamic and humane character of capitalism (e.g., Murchland 1984). Still others contend that even greater advances for the entire population could have been accomplished, had the power structure of society been challenged. For, as things stand right now, the fruits of progress are not being apportioned equitably (Edwards, Reich, and Weisskopf 1986; see also chapter 13). Moreover, the claim could be made that in the long run it is the dominant groups who benefit more from these accommodating reforms, simply because they serve as containers of bigger, more radical changes (cf. Wells 1987). Gross (1980) addressed this point very lucidly:

> If the establishment were a mere defender of the status quo, it would be much weaker. While some of its members may resist many changes or even "want to turn the clock back," the dominant leaders know that change is essential to preserve, let alone, expand power. "If we want things to stay as they are," the young nephew said to his uncle, the prince, in Lampedusa's *The Leopard*, "things have got to change." (p. 58)

The capitalist system has shown remarkable resilience. Its ability to survive crises may very well rest on its impressive adaptability in coping with ever-changing conditions by introducing new measures. Yet these innovations at the operational level do not necessarily transform the foundations of capitalism. These are changes of form rather than essence. Therefore, when applied to the governing principles of capitalism, the term *status quo* is not deemed inappropriate. Such will be the meaning ascribed to it henceforth.

The status quo is upheld either by force or by fostering hegemony. We shall concern ourselves only with the latter. *Hegemony* refers to the tacit consent given by the majority of the population to the established set of rules regulating communal life (e.g., Femia 1981; Gramsci 1971; Kiros 1985). According to Gramsci (1971), hegemony is promoted by the institutions of what he called "civil society": schools, churches, the media, etc. This is done by depicting the doctrines in which dominant groups believe—and from which they profit—as possessing universal value (for a more detailed discussion of hegemony, see chapter 14).

Every ruling group of an organized community requires the existence of cultural mechanisms designed to ensure, or at least facilitate, the perpetuation of its position. A variety of strategies are employed by these groups to persuade the public that the present social arrangement is not only the most desirable, but the only possible civilized one. It should not surprise us to learn that the repertoire of stratagems utilized by dominant groups to secure their position of privilege does not exclude deception and disguise as valuable resources. These mechanisms, usually referred to as "ideological," attempt to reproduce the prevailing system of *ideas* (Mannheim 1936; Ricoeur 1978; Silva 1970; H. T. Wilson 1977).

Dominant groups make efficient use of civil society in disseminating and promoting their sociopolitical beliefs. The mass media as well as many private agencies (e.g., mental health clinics) and public agencies (e.g., schools, the welfare system) can be considered, at least partially, as simultaneously constituted by, and constitutive of the reigning ideology (Therborn 1980; H. T. Wilson 1977). The collective name assigned to the agencies of civil society assisting in the reproduction of the existing social order is *ideological apparatuses* (Therborn 1980).

Ideological apparatuses operate on the basis of moral and legal restrictions, as well as persuasion. Their messages "so deeply penetrate the consciousness of a culture that people unquestioningly accept their premises without further thought. . . . People are typically unaware of the ideologies that govern their existence, at least as ideologies" (Sampson 1983, pp. 128-29). The person is led, through a series of distortions, to believe that the current state of social affairs is indeed the best possible one.

As we shall notice below, the characteristics of these apparatuses bear great resemblance to the dominant social philosophy. Thus, in the case of capitalism, the specific ideological mechanisms employed are likely to "capitalize" on such themes as the possibility of self-improvement through self-help and the ability of science to solve all human predicaments.

THE SUPREME SELF

Probably one of the most significant pillars of capitalist society, along with the right to private property, is the promotion of self-interest through self-help (e.g., Zaretsky 1986). The self is conceived as a supreme entity with magnificent powers. Both success and failure are attributed to it. This pervasive presupposition interferes, for the most part, with scrutiny and possible transformations of systemic causes of happiness and misery. In this worldview, self supersedes the system, and therefore changes ought to come from the former and not the latter. Such is the way in which the supreme self assists in the conservation of the structural status quo (e.g., Cushman 1990).

Macpherson's theory of possessive individualism provides an account of the economic conditions that contributed to the rise of this highly individualistic culture (Bellah et al. 1985). According to his theory, the market economy regards individuals simply as the proprietors of their manual or intellectual labor power, a possession they exchange for monetary remuneration from capital owners or the state after competition with other potential employees (Macpherson 1969). Macpherson (1969) claims that "possessive market *society* also implies that where labour has become a market commodity, market relations so shape or permeate all social relations that it may properly be called a market society, not merely a market economy" (p. 24).

Following Macpherson's reasoning, then, social life would be very much determined by its economic grounds. This notion is well captured in the concept of utilitarian individualism. Bellah et al. (1985) contend that "utilitarian individualism views society as arising from a contract that individuals enter into only in order to advance their self-interest. . . .Utilitarian individualism has an affinity to a basically economic understanding of human existence" (p. 336).

Self-interest was indeed promoted as an important ingredient of the capitalist system, but it was not meant to contradict or come at the expense of social order. Proponents of the market system "posit a society of individuals . . . who, acting in their own self-interest, advance the social purpose by expanding private wealth" (Zaretsky 1986, p. 40). It is claimed not only that social order would emerge from the market economy, but also that everyone would be able to foster his or her own individual welfare, for the system is to provide "equality of opportunity" (George and Wilding 1976). If everyone possesses at least one commodity to sell in the market, that is, labor power, and the system offers equal opportunities, then the path to prosperity is open to all. Israel argues that possessive individualism, as the predominant social philosophy of modern capitalism, manifests itself in the United States in the belief that

> American society contains opportunity for everyone to get ahead, to be successful, to reach the top. Even if these opportunities are not distributed in equal proportion, everyone receives some opportunities. Thus, people are responsible for their success and for the status they achieve. *Society cannot be blamed.* (Israel 1979, p. 251; italics added)

Later it will become apparent that this belief is of crucial importance in analyzing the place of ideology in psychology, particularly as it manifests itself in the *defect* model of human functioning, which has been implicitly adopted by more than one school of thought.

Having emphasized the individualistic nature of capitalism, we can pose the following legitimate question: Is a society based on an economic system that is driven by self-interest and minimal interference by the government able to meaningfully promote social welfare? This highly relevant moral question can hardly be avoided when dealing with the reproduction of the social order. Obviously, as can be expected, opinions on this issue can be found in favor as well as in opposition of the capitalist system. Murchland (1984), for instance, contends that "nowhere do individual efforts so quickly merge into public benefits" (p. 54) as in capitalism. George and Wilding (1976), on the other hand, contend that the capitalist system, based on values such as achievement and competition, individualism and self-help, "is in clear opposition to the values needed to underpin a successful public welfare system. If such a system is to flourish, the stress on the virtue of self-help must be replaced by stress on the need to help others" (p. 118).

While I would not claim to provide comprehensive answers to the intricate philosophical problems involved in this question, namely, what is the "good life" and the "good society," an attempt will be made in chapter 13 to delineate some parameters for the discussion of such issues. However, the main thrust of this work is not the moral appraisal of capitalism but rather the actual function of psychology in its reproduction.

SALVATION THROUGH SCIENCE AND TECHNOLOGY

Along with the primacy of the individual, a reverence for science—not just any science, but the Cartesian paradigm in particular—is at the core of modern society. In his *Reenchantment of the World* (1981), Berman is most persuasive in arguing that this specific scientific paradigm and capitalism are, "historically, inextricably intertwined" (p. 58): Capitalism proved to be a very fertile ground for the development of the Cartesian, mechanistic, atomistic world view. The present admiration of science "retains all the assumptions of the Industrial Revolution and would lead us to salvation through science and technology" (p. 189).

A central presupposition underlying the present social order is, indeed, the belief in the resolution of *all* social problems through science and technology (Alvesson 1985; Anderson and Travis 1983; H. T. Wilson

1977). The premise that science and technology will eventually alleviate human predicaments that fall beyond the realm of present-day science is deeply embedded in capitalist cultures and has been cultivated in the West since the seventeenth century (Berman 1981). The atomistic explanation of physical and human nature as bodies given to manipulation and mechanical cures gave rise to the attitude referred to as "scientism"—the process of ascribing to science powers that it lacks (Capra 1982; Mullaly 1980; Ross 1991).

There are basically two reasons why the dominant Cartesian scientific paradigm cannot solve all our problems. First, by its own definition this mode of inquiry excludes values from its realm of interest. Facts and values should not be confused or mixed. Cartesian science is devoted to conquering nature and unveiling its "facts." As Berman (1981) pointed out, its primary concern is with the "how" of the events explored, not with their "why" or "for what purpose." As a result, human welfare, ethics, and politics fall beyond the Cartesian field of attraction. Second, when this paradigm has been forced to look at social and human predicaments, it has done so in such an atomistic fashion that it was bound to fail. For instance, in appealing to university-based intellectuals for help, government agencies did not identify the

> real problem that underlies our crisis of ideas: the fact that most academics subscribe to narrow perceptions of reality which are inadequate for dealing with the major problems of our time. These problems are . . . systemic problems, which means that they are closely interconnected and interdependent. They cannot be understood within the fragmented methodology characteristic of our academic disciplines. (Capra 1982, p. 25)

No matter how equivocal and devoid of meaning the Cartesian mentality might be, it is an almost ineradicable feature of our culture (Berman 1981; Capra 1982). As Berman (1981) put it, "developments that have thrown this world view into question—quantum mechanics for example, or certain types of contemporary ecological research—have not made any significant dent in the dominant mode of thinking" (p. 2).

The tremendous progress achieved by science in many areas of our lives has fostered the conviction that social conflicts based on the political structure of the social order can also be given scientific remedies. This has led to the phenomenon described by Robinson (1985) as the "externalization" of scientific values.

What is a useful finding highly productive of illuminating research is offered to the public as equally useful for settling matters that are nonscientific in the first instance. More generally, this externalization takes the form of requiring nonscientific issues to be determined according to standards that are appropriate only to science itself. (p. 151)

Leibowitz (1985) cogently argues throughout his entire book that while science has proved extremely beneficial in solving innumerable problems, there are some ethical dimensions involved in the advancement of human welfare that cannot be approached by the methods of science.

Salvation through science—as the inquiry into and manipulation of natural, human, and social phenomena—is, by exclusion, an apolitical salvation. This is a formula for survival that, by its own definition, is supposed to challenge neither social values nor, by implication, the power structure of society.

Chapter 3

PSYCHOLOGY IN MODERN SOCIETY

Although psychology can be conceptualized as a rather minor subsystem within the larger social system, its ability to influence the latter is not inconsequential. The interdependence of scientific paradigms and society's cultural ethos has been well documented in the social sciences in general (e.g., Connerton 1976; Deese 1985; Sabia and Wallulis 1983; Wolfe 1989), and in psychology in particular (Buss 1979b; Danziger 1990; Henriques et al. 1984; Larsen 1986b; Sampson 1983; Sarason 1981b; and E. V. Sullivan 1984). I will now explore this network of mutual influences.

THE SOCIALIZATION OF PSYCHOLOGY

The regnant cultural ethos would seem to predispose academicians to embrace scientific paradigms and sociopolitical beliefs congruent with the predominant ideology (e.g., Arditi, Brennan, and Cavrak 1980; Rose, Lewontin, and Kamin 1984; Savan 1988). This process of scientific acculturation is conducted through direct institutional regulations and in a more indirect fashion through the dicta of the prevalent *weltanschauung* (Sarason 1981b). Within the realm of psychology—as the study of human behavior and the utilization of its postulates for the alleviation of individual and social predicaments—prevalent scientific, moral, and cultural doctrines are reflected both at the theoretical and applied levels. Spence gave official recognition to this postulate in her presidential address to the American Psychological Association in 1985:

> Contemporary analysts recognize that, whatever their intentions, scientists are the products of their society and time, and their construction of social reality is shaped by the world view and values of the culture in which they were reared. These belief systems can influence all phases of the research in which scientists engage, from choice of problem to interpretation of results. (p. 1285)

In spite of numerous warnings, such as Spence's, psychologists have persistently refused to elaborate upon the influence of nonepistemic convictions on their discipline. This attitude has clearly interfered with an understanding of psychology in social context (Deese 1985; Toulmin and Leary 1985).

Viewed from the perspective of what Capra (1982) named "the Cartesian-Newtonian paradigm," out of which psychology built its own framework and gained considerable inspiration (Capra 1982, chap. 6 in particular), the unwillingness expressed by psychologists to talk about intrusions of ideology into their scientific endeavors is hardly surprising, for in the Cartesian-Newtonian worldview, as its critics Berman (1981) and Capra (1982) so aptly point out, there is no relationship between "fact" and "value." Such an association would be a disgrace for science. Science, Cartesian disciples claim, is first and foremost "value-free."

Faithful adherence of the scientific community to the Cartesian mode of thinking has made the acceptance of new paradigms very difficult. Thus, for instance, in the case of quantum mechanics and its philosophical implications, Berman comments that "we should not be surprised that the scientific establishment has managed to ignore the embarrassing intruder for more than five decades . . . for once these implications are fully accepted, it becomes unclear just what is involved in 'doing science'" (Berman 1981, pp. 136-38).

But as the urgency to acknowledge value dilemmas in science has increased steadily, resistance to consider such issues has, reluctantly, decreased. This trend has apparently led Robinson (1985) to state that "where the social sciences once defensively insisted they were 'value-neutral,' they now tend to present themselves as unavoidably 'value-loaded'" (p. 142). As one psychologist wrote: "Although philosophers of science still debate the role of values in scientific research, the controversy is no longer about *whether* values influence scientific practice, but rather about *how* values are embedded in and shape scientific practice" (Howard 1985, p. 255).

Before we proceed with our discussion on values in psychology and their sociopolitical ramifications, a few conceptual clarifications ought to be made. Numerous meanings have been attached to the concept of value in the social sciences (see Robinson 1985, chap. 5). Baier's article "What Is Value? An Analysis of the Concept" (1969) provides several useful distinctions. The value attributed to things must be distinguished from the values held by people. The former is an

> *evaluative property* whose possession and magnitude can be ascertained in appraisals. The latter are *dispositions* to behave in certain ways which can be ascertained by observation. The former are *capacities* of things to satisfy desiderata. The latter are *tendencies* of people to devote their resources . . . to the attainment of certain ends. (p. 40)

According to Baier's terminology, then, when studying the capacity of something to make a favorable difference in the life of the individual, we are engaged in *assessing* value; when considering tendencies of individuals to advance certain ends, we are *imputing* value. Part II of the present study will focus on the imputation of a specific value (perpetuation of the social order) to a particular professional community (psychologists). Part III will assess the values of psychology in promoting human welfare.

A possible objection that could be raised to the imputation of values to a group is that most or even all of its members may be unaware that they espouse such values. Indeed, as Martin (1977) points out, "there are connections within the world view of a people, just as there are happenings in its social institutions or in its ecosystem, of which individual persons are largely, perhaps wholly, unconscious" (p. 15). In our case, many psychologists may not realize that they value the social status quo. Hence, the following question can be raised: Can a person who is not aware of his or her values be said to promote these values? A negative answer would imply that a value can be promoted by a person only if he or she is *aware* of it and engages in *deliberate* actions to advance it. Lack of awareness of a value does not, however, logically preclude the possibility of engaging in activities that promote the value in question. In the present context, even if psychologists were totally unaware of their endorsement of the present social system, their very lack of awareness, in conjunction with their passivity, can be said to *maintain* the existing state of affairs. The very fact that psychologists do not question or think about the status quo can be considered an ideological victory for those interested in perpetuating the predominant social system; for as the Latin maxim advises: *Qui Tacet Consentit.* At any rate, I would like to make clear that my primary concern is with the actions of psychologists and their ideological consequences, and not so much with psychologists' recognition of holding certain values. This debate can also be approached from the point of view of the distinction between function and intent. My concern is with actual function and not with intent.

It can also be argued against the imputation of a set of values to an entire professional community that it neglects differences in value preferences within various sectors of the discipline. This is not an entirely invalid claim. However, as Krasner and Houts (1984) demonstrated, while groups of different theoretical orientations in the behavioral sciences differ in their discipline-specific epistemological assumptions, basically most of them share similar sociopolitical values.

According to Krasner and Houts (1984), most behavioral scientists make statements in favor of social Darwinism (vs. social altruism), conservatism (vs. liberalism), and a value-neutral as opposed to value-laden view of science. The last one, as indicated, is of particular interest to the present discussion. The notion of a "value-neutral psychology" is pivotal in our investigation, for it lends itself to various ideological uses. First and foremost, it has the power to portray psychology as depoliticized and to use this image to promulgate the regnant ideology. Psychology "has shown a clear bias in supporting the interests of the powerful and the status quo, many times in the name of scientific objectivity" (Steininger, Newell, and Garcia 1984, pp. 216-17). By portraying itself as a strictly "objective" endeavor, psychology erroneously interprets many of its *prescriptive* biases as merely *descriptive* assertions about human behavior. "Value commitments are almost inevitable by-products of social existence, and as participants in society we can scarcely dissociate ourselves from these values in pursuing professional ends" (Gergen 1973, p. 312). Consequently, it is highly unlikely that we, as psychologists, strictly describe what appears to be, without at the same time subtly prescribing what we regard as desirable. Our definition of "desirable," as will be argued below, is usually in conformity with that of the ideological apparatuses whose main function is to effect a successful socialization.

In addition, the idea that psychology is value-neutral predisposes the public to accept psychology's assertions unquestioningly and to regard them as apolitical truisms rather than sociohistorically conditioned statements. Although there is enough evidence to indicate that this notion has been widely used for ideological purposes (see, for example, Billig 1979; W. Ryan 1971; Ussher 1992; Wilkinson 1991), its popularity should be attributed not only to sociopolitical interest but also to the hegemony of the positivistic-empiricist scientific paradigm (Sampson 1978; Toulmin and Leary 1985). The initial epistemic value ascribed to the concept of "value-neutral psychology" by positivism may have opened the door for its use as an ideological nonscientific value. Whatever the precise degree of influence ideological interests might have exerted upon the development of the positivistic-empiricist scientific paradigm, it should be clear that, once established, the concept of value-neutral psychology has been utilized to advance ideological objectives. This apparent misuse of psychology motivated Sullivan to contend that "depoliticized at the level of theory and theory language, the effectively neutral position masks political intentions" (E. V. Sullivan 1984, p. 25-26). E. V. Sullivan (1984) further claims that a critical analysis of different orientations such as behaviorism and psychometric psychology

> gives ample evidence that social science theories are intricately involved in value issues and have broad social policy implications. . . . Social science theories are "legitimators" of the status quo, that is, they render interpretations which back up or legitimate a certain socio-political constellation of power. (p. 26)

Sarason, who dealt extensively in his *Psychology Misdirected* (1981b) with the socialization of psychologists, contended that psychologists are, by and large, successfully conditioned not to deviate from the intellectual order prescribed by the contemporary predominant ideological atmosphere. Furthermore, he demonstrated how theoretical innovations in the field were frequently promoted by the establishment of new social policies. In Sarason's opinion, not only do psychologists rarely challenge the existing social beliefs, but they actively endorse and facilitate their reproduction.

It should not be forgotten that most social scientists belong to a social class whose political and economic interests are usually in accordance with those of the dominant sectors (J. G. Holland 1978; E. V. Sullivan 1984). It is not my intention to reduce the scientific endeavors of psychologists to only legitimating the status quo, and their professional practice to a class weapon, as some Marxist writers would seem to do (e.g., Nahem 1981; see also A. Ryan 1970), but the potential impact of their class background on their practice has been seriously underestimated (J. F. Brown 1936).

No conspiracy theory should be inferred from the above argument that psychologists contribute to the confirmation of cultural practices that help strengthen the underlying principles of social organization. I am not claiming that psychologists *deliberately* mislead the public in an attempt to guard social stability. Their assistance in perpetuating the current state of affairs does not derive, in my opinion, from a conscious effort to serve themselves by deceiving the population as to the nature of power relations in society. Their assistance derives mainly from a very efficient socialization that taught them not to question, to any threatening degree, the existing social system (Chorover 1985; Howitt 1991). As Sarason (1981b) put it:

> To be socialized means that one has absorbed and accommodated to predetermined conceptions of the way things are and ought to be. One may resist and resent the process but if one wants to occupy a certain place and role in society (e.g., lawyer, physician, psychologist) one has to traverse successfully the rites of passage. The socialization may be partial but its effects are never absent. For most people the process is far more than partial; it is so successful that for all practical purposes there is no questioning, no self-consciousness, about the forces that shaped them and their conception of society. (p. 148)

The partial attribution of their conservative attitudes to the process of socialization does not exempt psychologists from facing the ethical dilemma implicit in this practice. Lack of intent does not free individuals from confronting the moral consequences of their actions (cf. Singer 1993). The first step in approaching this dilemma is to explore how psychologists help solidify the social system.

THE PSYCHOLOGIZING OF SOCIETY

Psychology has a place of privilege in society. As it is intermingled in social life in countless forms, psychology's potential to exercise an enduring impact upon society's institutions is substantial. This has been the case since the beginning of the century. Historically, North America offered psychology a unique opportunity: to come out of academe into the practical world of business, government, education, and the military; and to dissociate itself from philosophy to become an independent discipline (Danziger 1979, 1990; Samelson 1979). In the early 1900s the American elite was searching for practical answers to a multitude of social problems. The prospect of having a science devoted to finding solutions to these riddles was very appealing. Psychology, as Danziger (1979, 1990) has claimed, did not hesitate to volunteer its services in exchange for recognition as the "master" science of human affairs.

The turn of the century witnessed a rapid consolidation of a professional group interested in transforming speculative psychology into an applied field. Society was about to be psychologized. Judging from psychology's penetration in almost every aspect of everyday existence, that prophecy was largely fulfilled.

Several features of popular culture support the claim that psychological formulations do in fact affect the state of affairs in society. One of them is the large audience for psychological magazines such as *Psychology Today* and *Parenting*. Ann Landers, the celebrated newspaper columnist, often refers her readers to mental health workers. The popularity of how-to books dealing with emotional issues, frequently written by psychologists, also demonstrates that the community at large is exposed to what psychologists prescribe (Rosen 1987). Radio shows advising on issues of emotional well-being and sexual behavior are being broadcast all over North America.

At the governmental level, advisory committees composed of social scientists and psychologists often play a decisive role in recommending the adoption or rejection of certain policies. Desegregation, deinstitutionalization, affirmative action, child abuse, drug abuse, educational reform, aging, divorce, mental and physical handicaps, smoking, and distribution of health services are among the social problems for which legislation has been influenced, directly or indirectly, by the input of psychologists as individuals or as special-interest groups (Howitt 1991; Sarason 1986). The judicial system, schools, industries and corporations, the military, and many other agencies employ psychologists as consultants. Szasz (1984) illustrated the overwhelming intrusion of psychology and psychiatry into official matters in his recent collection of articles *The Therapeutic State*. Koch and Leary (1985) are quite correct in their view that psychology has invaded almost every single aspect of our civilized existence:

Not a few psychologists, in the first century of their "science," have been willing to serve as self-anointed prophets in relation to virtually any issue that can bear upon the human condition. If that condition be, in any context, problematic (or anxiety-ridden, or even mildly irritating), then surely a science attuned to the "lawfulness" of human function will have something to say about the remedy. Perhaps everything to say! Thus, for a century the world has been increasingly rife with scientifically based advice concerning a limitless (if untidy) dispersion of matters. . . . The fact that, at any given moment, expert advice is bewilderingly multifarious and that the central tendency or dominant technologies in any given period tend to be fads which are displaced and often reversed, on cycles of a few years, lessens society's enthusiasm not one whit. (p. 33)

The dissemination of psychological knowledge and expertise indeed make a difference in people's ideas about themselves and about society. To better understand how this process takes place, we turn now to the concept of ideology.

Chapter 4

Ideology and Psychology

Ideology is probably one of the most debated and controversial terms in the social sciences. Writers talk about its connotations as positive, neutral, and/or negative. The categorization of the term *ideology* along these lines is related not to its descriptive or explanatory values, but rather to its added meanings, which usually are associated with politics. These political connotations, in turn, elicit partisan and emotional responses that have interfered with the development of the concept of ideology as a useful research instrument (cf. Shepard and Hamlin 1987). I contend that if its controversial connotations can be neutralized, the concept of ideology has the potential to be a valuable aid in the investigation of social reproduction. An overview of the various meanings previously associated with the construct is an important step in attaining the desired neutralization. It is necessary to realize, from the outset, that an attempt to arrive at the "correct" definition of ideology would be futile. Rather than establishing *the* concept of ideology, my goal is to describe the numerous ways in which this term has been used, and to define the concept of ideology to be adopted in the present inquiry. The question to be asked is not which definition of ideology is the right one, but which one is being used.

The Concept of Ideology

The brief historical outline that follows is based primarily on the works of Geuss (1981), Giddens (1979), Larrain (1979), Mannheim (1936), Ricoeur (1978), Therborn (1980), Thompson (1984), and the *International Encyclopedia of the Social Sciences* (see H. M. Johnson 1968; Shils 1968). Destutt de Tracy is considered the first author to have used the term *ideology*, at the end of the eighteenth century. He was concerned with the development of a science of ideas, which he called "Ideology." His treatment of the concept was regarded by later scholars as highly positive, in that it provided the basis for the later connotation of *ideology* as the study and eradication of irrational beliefs about the world. A depreciative connotation was attached to it by Napoleon, who called his enemies, the intellectuals, "ideologues" for not being in touch with "reality." The negative meaning given to *ideology* by Napoleon is kept alive in *Webster's Third New International Dictionary* (1976), where ideology is defined as "an extremist sociopolitical program constructed wholly or in part on factitious or hypothetical ideational bases."

The writings of Marx generated a great deal of discussion on the issue at hand. When the notion of distortion is introduced in his metaphor of the camera obscura, according to which social circumstances appear upside down, Marx was conveying the message that people "are deluded about themselves, their position, their society, or their interests" (Geuss 1981, p. 12) by those in positions of power. At this point ideology came to be identified with either ideological delusion or false consciousness. Distortion of societal conditions in order to preserve the status quo can be regarded as the central contribution of Marx to the ideology debate.

> The ideas of the ruling class are, in every age, the ruling ideas: i.e., the class which is the dominant *material* force in society is at the same time its dominant *intellectual* force. The class which has the means of material production at its disposal, has control at the same time of mental production, so that in consequence the ideas of those who lack the means of mental production are, in general, subject to it. (Marx 1964, p. 78)

The meaning implied here gave rise to the conception of ideology as the ideas of the ruling class. When the two definitions given by Marx are linked together, as they often are, ideology represents a system of ideas espoused by the dominant segments of society to preserve their position of power by portraying a distorted image of societal conditions.

Marx's views on ideology have been a constitutive part of the Critical Theory of society developed by the Frankfurt school of sociology (Connerton 1976; Geuss 1981). This is clearly seen in one of its basic postulates: "Ideologiekritik is not just a form of 'moralizing criticism,' i.e., an ideological form of consciousness is not criticized for being nasty, immoral, unpleasant, etc. but for being false, for being a form of delusion" (Geuss 1981, p. 26).

Still in the Marxist tradition, Mannheim's *Ideology and Utopia* (1936) was an attempt to apply the concept of ideology to the realm of epistemology. His thesis was that the same sectional interests operating in the field of politics are also present in the creation of social knowledge. Mannheim went beyond criticizing the ideology of the "other" and claimed that one's own ideas must be subjected to ideological analysis. Such enterprise would be undertaken by the sociology of knowledge. His important legacy to the study of ideology was to emphasize its ubiquitous nature in the pursuit of social knowledge. Mannheim's approach is currently reflected in, for instance, the feminist sociology of knowledge advanced by D. E. Smith (1990). She contends that "*ideology* identifies the biasing of sociological statements by special interests or perspectives" (p. 32). Moreover, Smith claims that

> if the perspectives and concepts of the knower are determined, for example, by class, by gender or racial standpoints, then sociological claims to objective knowledge are invalidated; sociological knowledge is irremediably ideological, and *knowledge* a term that must be continually resolved back into *ideology*. (p. 32)

According to Ricoeur (1978), another common meaning associated with the concept of *ideology* is a set of notions that a group holds about itself, the primary function of which is to foster cohesiveness and integration. On this interpretation, ideology is group identity. When this definition is expanded to society in general, across class and sectional boundaries, it connotes "social cement" and social cohesion. This variation is usually attributed to Althusser (Abercrombie 1980; Giddens 1979; Therborn 1980).

Currently, the term *ideology* is used in the literature in two fundamentally differing ways. The first, called by Thompson (1984) the "neutral conception," refers to its use as a purely descriptive term. In this sense authors identify ideology with different systems of thoughts, values, and beliefs that generate social action or political projects. "Ideology is present in every political programme, irrespective of

whether the programme is directed towards the preservation or transformation of the social order" (Thompson 1984, p. 4).

The second meaning commonly seen in the literature "is essentially linked to the process of sustaining asymmetrical relations of
power—that is, to the process of maintaining domination. This use of
the term expresses what may be called a *critical conception* of ideology"
(Thompson 1984, p. 4; italics in the original). This interpretation has a
definite bias against the status quo. *Ideology* in this sense refers to the
study and critique of stratagems employed by "those in power to con-
ceal their real interests and advantages" (Sampson 1981, p. 731).

As can be deduced from this overview, not all interpretations are
mutually exclusive. Ideology as "social cement," for instance, does not
conflict with the definitions given by Marx, it simply adds another
dimension to them.

Among the plethora of definitions available in the ideology literature, Berger and Luckmann's "ideas serving as weapons for social
interests" (1967, p. 7) is the best-suited as a research instrument. This is
due to a number of qualities. First, the term *ideas* is comprehensive
enough to include the other two key elements usually associated with
ideology: values and beliefs. Second, it is broad enough to encompass
ideologies for and against the status quo. Most definitions are quite
restrictive in that they limit ideology to a system of ideas or beliefs in
defense of a power elite—illustrative is Reading's (1977) definition of
ideology as "a belief system which protects the interest of an elite" (cf.
H. M. Johnson 1968). Third, unlike most definitions in the Marxist tradition, it does not necessarily imply the notion of conscious deception
by the group holding these ideas.

We are now in a better position to consider the concept of ideology
advocated for the purposes of this investigation. Simply stated, ideology
as a research instrument can be defined as ideas affecting the social
order, where (a) ideas are broadly conceived to encompass moral, cultural, and sociopolitical values and beliefs; (b) no specification is made
as to the direction in which ideas influence the social order; and (c)
ideas can affect the social order in ways that people holding them were
not necessarily aware of. In my view this is a viable concept of ideology
for an inquiry into the sociopolitical implications of psychology.

IDEOLOGICAL ELEMENTS IN PSYCHOLOGY

In effect, psychology can be used to support and criticize the status
quo at the same time. And evidence could be found to support both

arguments, because psychology is not a monolithic entity; it is comprised of several schools of thought, and thousands of individual professionals who happen to differ in their appraisal of the social order. The question should be asked, however, what kind of evidence can be marshaled to support either argument. Although a case can be made to support either psychology's endorsement of, or its opposition to, the status quo, the literature seems to indicate that the predominant bias is toward the affirmation of the existing state of affairs.

Undoubtedly, there have been numerous attempts to make the discipline an instrument of social change. Some of these challenges have been undertaken by prominent figures, such as presidents of the American Psychological Association. Among them are Kenneth Clark (1974) and George Albee (1981, 1986, 1990). Other initiatives to develop a psychology at the service of social change include the Radical Therapist movement (Agel 1971; P. Brown 1973); community psychology (Heller and Monahan 1977; Levine and Perkins 1987; Mulvey 1988; Rappaport 1977, 1981, 1990; Sarason 1982b, 1984a), feminist psychology (Allen and Baber 1992; Hare-Mustin and Marecek 1990; S. Holland 1992; Kitzinger 1991b; Morawski 1990; Riger 1992; Unger and Crawford 1992; Wilkinson 1991), as well as some behavior analysts (J. G. Holland 1978; Nevin 1982, 1985). The Section for the Psychological Study of Social Issues (SPSSI) of the American Psychological Association, as well as the Section for Social Responsibility of the Canadian Psychological Association are also concerned with matters related to social change. Though eloquent and forceful, these social critiques remain marginalized within the discipline.

Psychology at the service of the status quo, on the other hand, represents a much larger and pervasive phenomenon than the sporadic efforts of psychology to promote significant social change. As it will be exemplified later in part II, some of the ideological elements supportive of the status quo in psychology are part and parcel of mainstream theories and practices in the behavioral sciences.

Beneficiaries of the present social structure regard psychological science as one of their more treasured possessions (e.g., Woolfolk and Richardson 1984). At the structural level, a pervasive dichotomy between the individual and society is observed in psychology (e.g., Sarason 1981b, 1982b; Wexler 1983; Wilkinson 1991). An immediate ideological benefit is derived from such a dichotomy—namely, the individual is studied as an asocial and ahistorical being whose life vicissitudes are artificially disconnected from the wider sociopolitical context. Following this ideological reasoning, solutions for human predicaments are to be found almost exclusively within the self, leaving the social order conveniently unaffected (Albee 1981; Chesler 1989; Cushman 1990; Fox 1985; 1993; W. Ryan 1971). In this context, Bevan argued in his 1982 presidential address to the American Psychological Association that

> one of the most powerful intellectual tides of this century is a general propensity, by psychologist and nonpsychologist alike, to think of all human issues in psychological terms. It is a temptation that often leads to *oversimplification*, but it is a temptation that is hard to resist. (pp. 1305-1306; italics added)

Further support for the reigning ideology can be found in concrete governmental policies and in the advancement of heralded cultural beliefs. Activities carried out in the name of psychological science can be, and have been, used to rationalize social policies whose purposes were not always the pure promotion of "human welfare" (Napoli 1981). The testing movement (Kamin 1974; Sedgwick 1974) and social Darwinism (W. Ryan 1971; Thielman 1985) are salient examples reflecting psychology at the service of political thought. As well, psychology has been instrumental in upholding the predominant ideology by promulgating values such as individualism (e.g., Danziger 1990; Sampson 1977; Spence 1985), male supremacy (Chesler 1989; Gilligan 1982; Hare-Mustin 1991; Kitzinger 1991b; Shields 1975; Unger and Crawford 1992), political conformity (Jacoby 1975), and a purblind faith in technology's ability to solve human predicaments (e.g., Skinner 1972; cf. Woolfolk and Richardson 1984).

Some concrete examples of the ways psychology operates as a prototype agent of socialization are now in order:

(1) Values that benefit dominant segments of society are portrayed as benefiting society as a whole (Giddens 1979; Sampson 1983). This mechanism is recognized in industrial psychology, whereby steps intended to advance managerial goals are depicted as invariably valuable for the workers as well (Baritz 1974; Ralph 1983; Wells 1987).

(2) Social problems that originate in the structure of the socioeconomic system are discussed in terms of psychological maladjustment. The essence of this ideological stratagem is best captured in the title of W. Ryan's influential book *Blaming the Victim* (1971). According to Ryan, almost all unfavorable experiences in a person's life are thought to be caused by faulty mechanisms *within* himself or herself. When this approach is applied to the analysis of "maladaptive" behavior, it often

results in what Albee (1981) has termed the "defect model." An excellent illustration is provided by Caplan and Nelson (1973). Their research indicates that 80 percent of psychological studies dealing with African Americans attributed their predicaments to some intrapersonal variable rather than to sociohistorical circumstances.

This approach results in therapeutic efforts being almost exclusively directed at changing the individual and not the socioeconomic situation (Ussher and Nicolson 1992; Wineman 1984). This model has been proposed not only by psychologists and psychiatrists, but by sociologists and social workers as well (Carniol 1990; C. W. Mills 1943; Wilding 1981; Wineman 1984). Its origins can be traced to a market system whose entrepreneurial morality promulgates the notions of self-help and equality of opportunity. One's welfare is one's responsibility. No matter how adverse the societal conditions may be, an ingenious, diligent, strong-willed individual should be able to face them with dignity and would eventually attain happiness (London 1969). Thus, remedies are rarely advocated in terms of community changes.

An extensive lexicon of person-blame terminology supports the defect model (Gergen 1990), among them *maladaptive coping mechanisms, cognitive deficiencies, weak-ego, maladjusted personality,* and *character disorder*. This language is not at all surprising considering that "American psychology has been quintessentially a psychology of the individual organism" (Sarason 1981a, p. 827).

(3) Social realities are abstracted from their sociohistorical context and regarded as unavoidable (Ingleby 1972). In Sampson's words, "The present moment is reified and so made natural and inevitable" (Sampson 1983, p. 128). This is a basic assumption upon which many psychological explanations are constructed—namely, an *acontextual* view of people, that is, the analysis of human behavior without taking into account social and historical circumstances. Hare-Mustin and Marecek (1988) have explored how some gender theories make this mistake, much to the detriment of women's causes. Claims that "human nature" or "genetic factors" account for the majority of individual differences, such as gender roles and intelligence, respectively, are only one instance of this phenomenon (e.g., Chodorow 1990; Ingleby 1981c).

In sum, "what has been mediated by sociohistorical process" Sampson (1981) argues, "is treated as though it were an 'in-itself,' a reality independent of these very origins" (p. 738).

(4) "*Dislocation* is a process whereby something new is brought into a cultural system and has the ability to mute the partial critical insight of that cultural system" (E. V. Sullivan 1984, p. 165). In other

words, changes of a minor nature are allowed into the system with the purpose of creating an image of flexibility—but significant modifications are delayed due to the preoccupation with these insignificant reforms.

Family therapy is a case of dislocation. Facing the pressure to move away from a highly individualistic model of intervention, psychology introduced new treatments. However, instead of endorsing a truly systemic and community-based approach to therapy, psychology "invented" family therapy (James and McIntyre 1983; Poster 1978). Family therapy is a case of dislocation in that it created the illusion of radical change in therapy, but ended up being a mere reform of traditional modes of helping. Another example is the expansion of forensic services. In an address to correctional psychologists, Judge Bazelon made this point in a very eloquent manner:

> In considering our motives for offering you a role, I think you would do well to consider how much less expensive it is to hire a thousand psychologists than to make even a minuscule change in the social and economic structure. (In Caplan and Nelson 1973, p. 210)

These are some of the powerful ideological messages embedded in psychological theory. As such, they will come up throughout the analysis conducted in part II. I turn now to a succinct statement of the framework employed in the analysis.

Chapter 5

FRAMEWORK OF ANALYSIS

The main propositions advanced in this section can be summarized as follows:

1. Psychological theories and practices affect, and are affected by, the social order.
2. Psychology is ascribed considerable authority in an increasing number of human affairs.
3. Social, cultural, and political values are present in the formulation and dissemination of theories and practices in psychology.
4. There is significant affinity between the values stated in proposition 3 and those typical of dominant segments of society.
5. Prominent among these values is the maintenance of the existing state of affairs in society.
6. Psychology's affirmation of the social order does not necessarily reflect intent.
7. While extrascientific values fostering macrosocial change are also present in psychology, their social impact is outweighed by that which is stated in proposition 5.

The seventh and principal proposition calls for the identification and comparison of instances where psychological theories and practices operate as (a) conformity-promoting and (b) change-promoting forces in society.

A number of problems are elicited in considering evidence. In order to argue that certain theories of human behavior and applied fields of psychology act in support of the social system, some criteria that will serve as confirming evidence must be developed. Consequently, a definition of what constitutes a conformity-promoting message or activity is needed. This definition is provided in the conception of an ideological element supportive of the status quo as *a component of a theory or applied field in psychology that contributes to the maintenance of the prevailing social order.*

The reviewed literature suggests the following such ideological elements in psychology:

1. A tendency to attribute excessive weight to individual factors, such as genetic or psychological constitution, in explaining individual and/or social behavior. This also implies a disposition to omit socioeconomic and political variables or to portray an asocial and ahistorical image of people (Albee 1981, 1986; Fine and Gordon 1991; Henriques et al. 1984; Sampson 1983; Sarason 1981b).
2. A propensity to analyze social problems that originate, at least in part, in the structure of the classist patriarchal socioeconomic system in terms of psychological maladjustment (Caplan and Nelson 1973; Chesler 1989; Lerner 1991; W. Ryan 1971).
3. The reification of behavioral phenomena. That is, the treatment of human behavior as if it were an "in-itself," an entity abstracted from the socioeconomic conditions where it developed (Ingleby 1972, 1981c; Sampson 1981).
4. A tendency to endorse technical solutions for social, economic, political, and ethical problems. Inasmuch as such technical solutions divert attention, more-fundamental changes are postponed or evaded (Anderson and Travis 1983; J. G. Holland 1978; Woolfolk and Richardson 1984).
5. Insufficient consideration of the potentially conformist prescriptive bias inherent in psychological theories or practices. This shortcoming leads the recipient of psychological knowledge or counseling to believe that these theories or practices are essentially "value-neutral," a reflection of "truth" or "objectivity," and not affected by the psychologist's set of nonepistemic values (Fairbairn and Fairbairn 1987; Howitt 1991; Jacoby 1975; Sampson 1978; Ussher 1992).

6. A propensity to portray values that benefit the dominant segments of society as benefiting society as a whole (Baritz 1974; Chesler 1989; Clark 1974; Ingleby 1974, Nahem 1981).
7. The introduction of new knowledge or services that are likely to result in the dissipation of some critical insight into the social system. Criticism is attenuated when innovative techniques purported to create significant modifications are brought into the social system. Often, however, they only deal with superficial problems and are quite inconsequential in solving systemic predicaments (Anderson and Travis 1983; E. V. Sullivan 1984).

These ideological components are likely to *reduce* the probability that the recipient of psychological knowledge and/or practice (a) would become aware of the importance of adverse social influences on his or her life conditions, or (b) would engage in activities to promote macrosocial change.

Disconfirming evidence, or instances where psychology promotes macrosocial change, is defined as *a component of a theory or applied field in psychology that contributes to the promotion of macrosocial change.*

The following are some examples whereby psychology can be considered to foster macrosocial change:

1. Consideration of the social determinants, and the need to modify the environmental conditions, conducive to psychopathology (Albee, Bond, and Cook Monsey 1992; Grusky and Pollner 1981; J. G. Holland 1978; Mirowsky and Ross 1989).
2. Promotion of prevention programs that question the capacity of the present social system to enhance the well-being of the population (e.g., Heller and Monahan 1977; Pransky 1991; Sarason 1982b).
3. Critique of socially structured inequalities and their psychological effects. Feminist psychologists, probably more than any other organized group within the discipline, struggle to denounce and expose the consequences of structural and cultural sources of oppression (Bartky 1990; Chesler 1989; Hare-Mustin 1991; Kanuha 1990; Miller and Mothner 1981; Watson and Williams 1992; Wilkinson 1991). While feminist psychologists advocate primarily on behalf of women, feminist discourse contains the analytical elements necessary to explain the conditions of powerlessness of other oppressed groups as well. Nowhere in psychology is the call for social change louder than in feminist writings. Their relative impact will be explored in more detail later.

Several potential ways have been suggested whereby psychology can be used to help in changing or reproducing the social system. Chapters 6 through 12 will attempt to show how these ideological mechanisms manifest themselves in a sample of psychological interpretations of human behavior. Psychology is not a unified science (Koch and Leary 1985). Consequently, different systems in the discipline portray the individual and society in dissimilar fashions. Little congruence is to be found among their definitions of psyche (mind) or even of their very subject matter.

The theories to be analyzed will neither bluntly and openly support the status quo, nor portray modern society as a source of innumerable opportunities for self-actualization. The conformity-promoting components of psychological conjectures are conveyed to the general public often in a very subtle way.

The presence of ideological components will be explored in seven separate fields: (a) psychoanalysis, (b) behaviorism, (c) humanism, (d) cognitivism, (e) abnormal psychology, (f) industrial psychology, and (g) school psychology. The first three are well-established schools of thought within the discipline and are usually represented in books dealing with systems of psychology (e.g., Lundin 1972; Marx and Hillix 1979; Notterman 1985) or theories of personality (e.g., Hjelle and Ziegler 1981; Sahakian 1977). The fourth area constitutes a trend whose recognition and wide acceptance are considered to have caused a "revolution" in psychology (Baars 1986; Gardner 1985). The last three are applied fields that impact upon large sectors of the population. I will emphasize the *applied* aspects of psychology that are likely to have a direct impact on the public, the more obvious being therapeutic methods derived from these theories.

PART II

THE POLITICS OF
PSYCHOLOGICAL DISCOURSE

In this part I try to discern what are the political and moral meanings of prevalent psychological discourses. By "discourses" I mean the entire range of formulations and applications that can be derived from specific theories. The sociopolitical and moral signification of dominant discourses in psychology will be discussed in light of the ideological elements defined in part I. The areas I have selected to explore are, in my opinion, the most influential ones in the world of applied psychology. Chapters 6 through 9 deal with the foundational fields of psychoanalysis, behaviorism, humanism, and cognitivism. The emphasis is placed on the applied derivations of these schools of thought. Chapters 10 through 12 cover the extensive fields of abnormal, industrial/organizational, and school psychology. While there is some overlap among them, there are sufficient distinctions to warrant separate treatment.

Some areas, simply because of their longer history and expansive reach, require more-extensive treatment than others. In the case of psychoanalysis, for instance, I attempt to be sensitive to the numerous transformations the theory has undergone. Neo-Freudian interpretations are just as prevalent, if not more prevalent, than some of the original Freudian postulates. Therefore, chapter 6 is longer than chapters 7, 8, and 9. Chapter 10 requires a somewhat more elaborate discussion than chapters 11 and 12, because I attempt to place various fields, such as family therapy, feminist psychology, and community psychology, in a framework containing four separate paradigms, ranging from paradigms deemed asocial to those with a macrosociopolitical orientation. The areas covered in chapters 11 and 12 contain more-specific professional boundaries.

This second and longest part of the book articulates the moral and political reservations I have with respect to each of these predominant discourses. Although I offer some insights as to the possible moral and political rehabilitation, wherever feasible, of these professional sectors, an explicit formulation of an alternative social and ethical framework for psychology is presented later in part III.

Chapter 6

PSYCHOANALYSIS

An elucidation of the progressive or conservative social repercussions of psychoanalysis must, of course, begin with the work of Freud. At the same time, one should bear in mind that the current implications of psychoanalysis for social change derive not only from Freud's original postulates but also from ramifications, interpretations, and elaborations of the same. Consequently, this analysis will not be limited to Freud; considerable attention will also be paid to his followers.

THE POLITICS OF FREUD

As in the cases of Skinner, C. Rogers, and Maslow, I shall concern myself not with Freud's personal motives or convictions, but rather with the social functions for which his views have been appropriated. Adaptations of Freud's ideas to justify ideologies, both for and against the status quo, have arisen within and outside of psychology and have changed from era to era. An interesting contrast between the progressive connotations of psychoanalysis outside of psychology and its conservative reverberations within the discipline will be noted.

Given Freud's voluminous writings, the evolution of his thinking, and a lack of *consistent* and *categorical* political commentary on his part, it is not at all surprising that contradictory social positions have been ascribed to Freud. Characteristic of his enigmatic position in this respect was his pronouncement: "Politically I am just nothing" (Roazen 1986, p. 243). This is in line with Roazen's assertion that "Freud was not much interested, aside from criticizing sexual mores, in the social sources of suffering and exploitation" (Roazen 1990, p. 130).

I shall present some of Freud's views that may have had, in varying degrees, lasting political significance. An analysis of the sociopolitical impact of his disciples will follow.

Freud the Conservative

Freud has been accused of generating conservative thought on many accounts (e.g., Bartlett 1939; Brooks 1973; C. I. Cohen 1986; Frosh 1987; Kovel 1988; Nahem 1981, Wortis 1945). Three representative charges deal with his (a) decontextualized view of the individual, (b) emphasis on "biologism," and (c) antifeminist implications.

The first claim has been forcefully presented by Freud's contemporary, Bartlett (1939). The phylogenetic basis of developmental stages, their relative independence from environmental circumstances, and their claimed universality are the central points of contention for Bartlett. Armed with the well-known research of Malinowski, which refuted the omnipresence of the Oedipus complex, Bartlett questioned the validity of Freud's assertions with respect to the primarily asocial character of sexual and psychological maturation (see, for example, Freud 1940/1949). Moreover, Bartlett attributed to Freud a social atomism according to which society was depicted more along the lines of a human conglomerate rather than a human gestalt. In Freud's view, Bartlett argued, "society as a *system* of active, practical relationships, evolving according to laws which are not deducible from the nature of individuals, does not exist" (p. 70). To document his claim, Bartlett quotes Freud's statement that "sociology, which deals with the behavior of man [sic] in society, can be nothing other than applied psychology" (in Bartlett 1939, p. 70). Wortis (1945) wrote that Freud "not only neglected the social situation . . . but stood everything on its head by regarding social situations as the expression of people's ideas or unconscious strivings" (p. 815). He further noted that "from this point of view war, for example, is the expression of aggressive instincts" (p. 815). A similar reading of Freud has been voiced by Brooks (1973), who argued that "Freud's individualistic concepts are not merely asocial, but define society as only a collection of atomized individuals connected by cathected libidos" (p. 361). More recently, Frosh (1987) echoed these concerns in reviewing "psychoanalysis' tendency to reduce what is social to what is individual, for example, by interpreting institutions or groups solely in terms of the psychological characteristics of their individual members" (p. 268).

These individualistic interpretations of psychoanalysis converge in their portrayal of Freud as a highly conservative thinker. When specific socioeconomic factors are not fully taken into account, the resulting theory of human behavior is not only partial in its explanatory value, but also ideologically conservative—conservative, in that problems that may have originated in the social structure are situated in the individual and call, therefore, for individual solutions.

Whereas these critics may have cast Freud's picture of human predicaments more individualistic than his writings warrant (as we shall see below), their ideological indictment of the "Freudian" way of solving problems seems to be well founded. The preferred way of treating *unconscious*, instead of environmental, factors (e.g., Freud 1940/1949) lends considerable support to that assertion. Inasmuch as the unconscious obscures *"the power relations between people by locating the dynamics and issues of intersubjective life inside the individual"* (Brooks 1973, p. 344; italics in the original), it can be argued that psychoanalysis serves to depoliticize human relations where the opposite may be what is really needed.

Closely related to the first, the second accusation made against "Freud the conservative" is the primacy attributed to the instinctual roots of human behavior (i.e., C. I. Cohen 1986; Frosh 1987; Ingleby 1981c; Nahem 1981 Wortis 1945). The political significance of such a tenet is clearly articulated by Freud himself in *Civilization and Its Discontents* (1930/1961), where, given the pervasive nature of the destructive instinct, he basically precludes the possibility of peaceful civilized coexistence.

> The existence of this inclination to aggression, which we can detect in ourselves and justly assume to be present in others, is the factor which disturbs our relations with our neighbour and which forces civilization into such a high expenditure of energy. In consequence of this primary mutual hostility of human beings, civilized society is perpetually threatened with disintegration. (p. 59)

When asked by Albert Einstein in 1932 for his participation in preserving peace, Freud replied in an open letter that war "seems quite a natural thing, no doubt it has a good biological basis and in practice it is scarcely avoidable" (quoted in Nahem 1981, p. 25).

In *Civilization and Its Discontents* (1930/1961), which can be considered one of his more explicit political commentaries, Freud derogates socialism in no uncertain terms. In his opinion, socialism fundamentally contradicts human nature. Thus, "the psychological premises on which the [socialist] system is based are an untenable illusion" (p. 60).

Instead of understanding the "psychic processes and needs of man [*sic*] as a product of a social and historical development, psychoanalysis derives them from instincts inherent in the organism, thereby giving a narrowly biological interpretation to all forms of a man's psychic activity" (C. I. Cohen 1986, p. 6). Frosh (1987) admits that this is one of the most regressive aspects of Freud's legacy, one with which feminist and Marxist sympathizers of Freud continue to struggle.

Although Freud may not have envisioned the practical ideological uses of his theories, Nahem (1981) contends that Freudianism is highly advantageous to the ruling segments of society:

> What could be more pleasing to a dominant class than to convince people that their problems are due to their unconscious conflicts? And what could pay off more handsomely than the idea that human history today, with its wars, racism and oppression, is due to unconscious, destructive and libidinous forces and not to capitalism? (p. 34)

In addition to Freud's individualistic and instinctual reductionism, his antifeminist remarks have also contributed to his being characterized as a highly conservative and patriarchal thinker (Brooks 1973; Dinnerstein 1976; Henriques et al. 1984; Hyde and Rosenberg 1980; Lerman 1986; Unger and Crawford 1992; Zaretsky 1986). Indeed, it is argued that "the most serious criticisms of Freud focus on his views on female sexuality and the patriarchal orientation of his theory" (J. C. Smith 1990, p. 43).

One of the salient features of women's psychology, according to Freud (1930/1961), is their immature superego. "The work of civilization," wrote Freud, "has become increasingly the business of men, it confronts them with ever more difficult tasks and compels them to carry out instinctual sublimations of which women are little capable" (p. 50).

Other central personality traits of women in Freudian theory are passivity and masochism. Freud maintained that young girls have a desire for a penis, hence their "penis envy." Since their desire for a penis cannot be fulfilled, that wish is transformed into an urge to be impregnated by their father. "In choosing the strategy for obtaining the desired penis by being impregnated by the father, the girl adopts a passive approach—to be impregnated, to be done to, not to do—and this passive strategy persists throughout life" (Hyde and Rosenberg 1980, p. 38). That very wish to be penetrated is also the source of masochism, for intercourse and childbirth are said to be painful (Hyde and Rosenberg 1980). These, among other Freudian observations on the female psyche, might have led Henriques et al. (1984) to the accurate conclusion that Freud's "anti-feminist implications are indisputable" (p. 206).

Feminists are divided in their critique of Freud's androcentric views. Two distinguishable orientations can be discerned. On the one hand there are theorists, such as Lerman (1986), who find the entire edifice of psychoanalytic thought inimical to feminism and devoid of any possibilities of fruitful reconstruction. This is not only on account of Freud's denigrating views of women but also due to the highly speculative nature of his reifying theories. Thus, the explanatory value of elusive intellectual constructs, the validity of which cannot be persuasively ascertained, is thrown into question. Therefore, in addition to the androcentric regressive statements uttered by Freud and his followers, feminists like Lerman denounce also the very epistemological foundations of the psychoanalytic paradigm. Lerman (1986) decries the Freudian legacy not only because "assumptions about the inherent inferiority of women are embedded in the very core of psychoanalytic theory," but also because it employs "ideas whose validity has not been demonstrated despite years of trying" (p. 6).

On the other hand, there are feminists like Chodorow (1978, 1990) and Dinnerstein (1976) who retain the main methodological assumptions of psychoanalysis and attempt to rehabilitate the theory by excising or reformulating its patriarchal elements. Their theories are founded largely on the object-relations school, according to which the infant-mother relationship is of crucial importance in the development of the child's emotional life. In essence, these feminist authors claim that the creation of gender identities under the predominant system of mothering tends to perpetuate the dominance of men over women. That is so because boys, in order to establish their sexual identity, need to accentuate their differences from the primary female caretaker— differences that are culturally defined as benefiting men and devaluing women. Because of their tenuous sense of self, and in order to develop a male identity, they need to emphasize the "me/not-me" distinction between themselves and their mothers. Girls, on the other hand, do not need to reinforce the separateness from the female caretaker, because they are of the same gender. "Girls grow up with a sense of continuity and similarity to their mother, a relational connection to the world" (Chodorow 1990, p. 431). As a result, these theorists claim, women have a facility to associate through relationality, a capacity that is deficient in males, who relate to the world primarily through separateness and competition, traits that are reinforced in patriarchal societies. Given the dominant agreement whereby mothers look after babies and male characteristics are favored, gender identities along the lines depicted above tend to reproduce themselves. Men pursue independence and power and put up boundaries, while women seek personal closeness. Chodorow (1978, 1990) and Dinnerstein (1976) argue that parenting arrangements do not change to include more paternal involvement because men, who are the powerholders of society, benefit from the current arrangements. They contend that Freud upheld patriarchy in the sense that he did not challenge the predominant parenting arrangements and treated them as a natural state of affairs that could not, or should not, be changed. Although this feminist critique advances the possibility of more egalitarian parenting obligations, its reasoning is profoundly pervaded by a rather socially decontextualized Freudian logic. I concur with Frosh (1987) in his view that "feminist object relations theory lives with the danger of collapsing back into biologistic categories forced upon it by its utter reliance on the formativeness of mother-child encounters" (p. 180).

Admittedly, a comprehensive analysis of object-relations feminist theory is beyond the scope of this chapter, and I cannot possibly do justice to all their propositions here. However, I would argue that, despite considerable efforts at refashioning psychoanalysis in a more progressive light, these authors do not provide an alternative that radically escapes the interpersonal microscopic and biological reductionism of Freudian thought criticized above. (For a lucid and well-informed critique of this feminist psychoanalytic approach, see Frosh 1987, chap. 7; see also Hare-Mustin and Marecek 1988).

Thus far we have dealt with those elements of Freud's thinking that could be used in support of the status quo. The definition and treatment of human, and particularly female, predicaments in individualistic and biological terms, which is a well-known ideological strategy to avert any grave menace to the status quo, might have gained considerable impetus from psychoanalysis. And yet there is another, more progressive aspect to Freud. To this we now turn.

Freud the Progressive

Against the charges that Freud fostered conservative thinking and cultural myths—such as women's inferior capacity for sublimation—many authors have come to Freud's defense by arguing that social factors *do* play a meaningful role in his theory. These authors have set out to "prove" that Freud was not only progressive, but in many ways a radical (e.g., Jacoby 1975; Jones 1955). Jones (1955), Freud's friend and biographer, stated, for instance, that

> Freud would have been in favor of any obvious social reforms, but on a longer view he was not sure that they would produce a really satisfactory civilization. Something more radical was needed, and he was a revolutionary rather than a reformer. (p. 414)

Counteracting the accusations made against Freud the conservative, four arguments emerge that focus on these elements: (a) Freud's powerful cultural critique; (b) the social or, at the very least, interpersonal nature of his theories on human behavior; (c) his implicit prescriptions for social ethics; and (d) his contributions to personal liberation.

As a critic of his culture, Freud astonished many contemporaries with his claims regarding sexuality, particularly infant sexuality (Freud 1940/1949). Wortis (1945) correctly noted that Freud "helped shatter the taboos against an examination of sexuality" (p. 814). At the time that Freud developed and made public his theories on sexuality, he and "his followers were regarded not only as sexual perverts but as either obsessional or paranoic psychopaths as well, and the combination was felt to be a real danger to the community" (Jones 1955, p. 109).

Not only did he shock people with his unprecedented notions about sexuality, but he also horrified them by dethroning religion in *The Future of an Illusion* (Freud 1927/1964). Freud stripped religion of its sacrosanct apparel to make it a mere psychological mechanism "born from man's [sic] need to make his helplessness tolerable and built up from the material of memories of the helplessness of his own childhood" (p. 25). As to the idea of God, Freud argued that "when man [sic] personifies the forces of nature he is following . . . an infantile model" (p. 31). In his recent account of Freud's moral and political thought, Abramson (1984) states that, for Freud, "God is our own creation, an illusion we believe in precisely because it illustrates the world according to our infantile liking" (p. 69).

Judging from the fierce response of his culture, there is little doubt that Freud was unsettling the "natural order of things" by questioning the validity of some very basic social pillars (e.g., Jones 1955). Freud's unorthodox views on sexuality and religion are exemplified in a letter sent in 1935 to an "American Mother" in regards to her son's homosexuality: "Homosexuality is assuredly no advantage, but it is nothing to be ashamed of, no vice, no degradation, it cannot be classified as an illness. . . . It is a great injustice to persecute homosexuality, and a cruelty too" (in Bayer 1981, p. 27). While Freud's opinion on homosexuality may not seem too unusual today, it certainly was in 1935 (cf. F. L. Marcuse 1980). (It is of interest to note that although homosexuality does not constitute at present a separate nosological entity in the third revised edition of the *Diagnostic and Statistical Manual of Mental Disorders* [American Psychiatric Association 1987], it does appear in the index as "homosexuality-ego dystonic." One cannot help but wonder whether the activists who fought vehemently for the complete deletion of homosexuality from the manual are aware of its inconspicuous presence.)

Another line of argument that Freud was not a conservative has been the attempt to register his noticeable awareness of social and political circumstances. Bartlett's charge that Freud concentrated on the "isolated individual" would appear to pertain more to therapy than to theory. At the therapeutic level Freud no doubt focused on the individual. At the theoretical level, however, Freud appears to have taken into account micro- and macrosocial determinants, as Badcock (1983), Caruso (1964), Englert and Suarez (1985), Jacoby (1975), Wallwork (1991), and Zaretsky (1986) have eloquently argued.

Social interpretations of Freud endeavor to show his alertness to both micro- and macrosocial factors. At the macro level, for example, in *The Future of an Illusion* Freud did nothing less than criticize class societies. Commenting on the living conditions of the "underprivileged classes" (his words), Freud wrote: "A civilization which leaves so large a number of its participants unsatisfied and drives them into revolt neither has nor deserves the prospect of a lasting existence" (Freud 1927/1964, pp. 15-16). Another blunt criticism of the social structure and its institutions is contained in a communication with Putnam. In that letter Freud stated:

> I believe that your complaint that we are not able to compensate our neurotic patients for giving up their illness is quite justified. But it seems to me that this is not the fault of therapy but rather of social institutions. What would you have us do when a woman

complains . . . that she has been deprived of the joy of living for merely conventional reasons? She is quite right, and we stand helpless before her. . . . *But the recognition of our therapeutic limitations reinforces our determination to change other social factors so that men and women shall no longer be forced into hopeless situations.* (In Zaretsky 1986, p. 138; italics added)

Badcock (1983) has argued that the portrayal of Freud as oblivious to societal complexities is "a major distortion of Freud's thinking" (p. 69). In an attempt to recover the broad scope of Freud's theories, which in his opinion neglected neither the individual nor the environment nor the social system, Badcock (1983) emphasized the social dimensions of psychoanalysis. In doing that, he hoped to counteract the common misconception of Freud as an intrapsychic thinker par excellence.

Similar arguments have been advanced by Caruso (1964). Taking issue with the decontextualized views ascribed to Freud by many critics, Caruso noted that such a reading of Freud is very simplistic. Caruso claimed that in addition to the import of intrapsychological processes, "psychoanalysis—and this goes back to Freud—is also founded on the concrete and overall *relations* of the patient with the world" (p. 265).

Freud's concerns with microsocial institutions, such as the family, can be hardly disputed. Whereas Freud might not have fully elaborated upon the impact of social power structures on the individual, he definitely contributed to an understanding of the power structure within the family and its consequences (see Caruso 1964; Jacoby 1975; Kovel 1981a; Zaretsky 1986).

Freud's moral outlook can be as puzzling as his political predilections. Hartmann (1960) maintained that Freud "never fully identified himself with any moral system" (p. 15). Moreover, Freud is quoted by Rieff (1961) as saying that psychoanalysis does not have any "concern whatsoever with judgments of value" (p. 363). This affirmation (expressive of Freud's devotion to a rational scientific project, as opposed to a moral one) notwithstanding, the rich and numerous moral implications of psychoanalytic discourse cannot be denied (Wallwork 1991).

The notion that a social ethics can be derived from Freud's writings runs against conventional wisdom. Yet this is what Wallwork (1991) set out to prove in his book *Psychoanalysis and Ethics*. His self-declared work of "excavation" was designed to retrieve and reconstruct the moral elements of Freud's thought concerned with the welfare of society as a whole. This underexplored aspect of Freud's legacy, Wallwork contends, contains perhaps some of his most progressive ideas. In order to place Wallwork's arguments in context, it is important to bring into the discussion two previous influential works dealing with the implicit or explicit moral values of psychoanalysis. These are Rieff's *Freud: The Mind of the Moralist* (1961), and Hartmann's *Psychoanalysis and Moral Values* (1960).

An ethic of honesty can be discerned from Freud's writings, Rieff (1961) argues. This Freudian underlying thrust advances the proposition that, in order for the individual to emancipate him- or herself, he or she ought to renounce the decorum imposed by oppressive social habits. This is achieved by promoting honesty and openness with respect to one's inner desires. It is only after the person has resigned him- or herself to admit the existence of, and to live with, selfish and culturally contemptuous motives, that liberation from neurotic symptoms can be attained. To be sure, Freud did not propose libidinal anarchy, but ultimately it is "self-concern that takes precedence over social concern" (Rieff 1961, p. 362). Private emancipation, not the common good, was the cardinal domain of psychoanalysis. At the expense of substantive moral rules for fostering social welfare, Rieff claims, "the Freudian ethic emphasizes freedom" (p. 352).

In contrast to Rieff, Wallwork (1991) portrays a Freud that, even if not expressly perturbed by the welfare of community members, did nonetheless provide a guide for social ethics. The author conducts a minute study of Freud's writings to bring to light his ethical stance on a number of social issues. The four pillars of Freud's reconstructed social ethic, as articulated by Wallwork, are "the rule of law and equal treatment, liberty, distributive justice, and just war theory" (p. 274). Wallwork furnishes evidence demonstrating Freud's interest in these moral questions. For example, he documents Freud's support for laws that will protect the poor and the vulnerable, for social arrangements that will ensure the fair and equitable allocation of burdens and resources in the community, and for state-operated clinics that will offer psychological services for those unable to afford them privately.

In evaluating the diverging accounts of Freudian morality emerging from Rieff's and Wallwork's studies, I am of the opinion that the latter grants Freud a more profound sense of social justice than may be warranted (cf. Roazen 1990). Yet I still believe that Freud's moral heritage could be socially useful. The possibility of a psychologically informed ethics constitutes one of his most crucial and somewhat neglected potential contributions. This is a parallel concern of both Hartmann and Wallwork. Over and above the ideals of health, happiness, freedom, justice, and autonomy (Wallwork 1991), truth stands out as Freud's most fervently espoused value, a value that both frees and heals. This is where the three scholars examined here reach consensus (Hartmann 1960; Rieff 1961; Wallwork 1991).

Revealing the "true" nature of human beings was for Freud of paramount importance, if society was to be constructed along lines that facilitate the sublimatory release of positive and negative energies. Knowing the fundamental character of humans aids in the project of social cooperation, for then satisfactory provisions can be made for the fulfillment of psychological and material needs. Furthermore, it is a requisite for imposing humane rules and customs that will both promote well-being and protect the community from the uncontrolled aggressive instincts of the few. This view differs from most other political philosophies, in that for Freud knowledge meant the exploration of the unconscious. He was not pleased with a superficial understanding of conscious needs expressed by human agents. These he suspiciously regarded as representing not "real" desires but mere intellectualizations concocted to comply with regnant cultural norms.

Freud's unrelenting search for scientific truths led him to embrace profoundly pessimistic views about civilization and its agents. His account of war and its inevitability, for example, nurtured his fatalistic outlook on life. But if there are clear limitations on the capacities of humans for peaceful coexistence, then it is better to know that than to embellish human nature for the foolish satisfaction of feeling good and avoiding unpleasant truths. His conception of liberation was founded in a rational estimation of human capacities and shortcomings, a standpoint that allows one to deal intelligently with moral dilemmas. In short, Freud embraced an ethic of truth. Indeed, he is quoted by Wallwork (1991) as saying that "the great ethical element in psychoanalytic work is truth and again truth" (p. 209).

Freud's notion of the morally possible is dictated by the psychologically feasible. Ignoring the latter would be a recipe for ethical failure. Hartmann (1960) was attentive to this point when he observed that "intellectual constructions of ethical systems which neglect the psychological forces that actually determine moral behavior are likely to impede both the stability and the power of these systems" (p. 45). This contention comes into sharp focus when Freudian morality is contrasted with Kantian ethics. Freud finds the Kantian attempt to separate reason from desire in moral life delusive. Kant prescribes a morality dictated fundamentally by intellectual stipulations and devoid of affective foundations. This proposition notwithstanding, in carrying out moral duties, the person is not solely motivated by consciously derived altruistic reasons. Self-interest, however placated, always plays a role in ethical behavior. This realization never escaped Freud. Moral judgment cannot be independent of personal considerations. Viewed from this vantage point, according to Wallwork (1991), "any attempt to sever conscience from desire is bound to fail" (p. 233), primarily because a failure to apprehend the crucial role of desire results in an inability to control it. The suppression of natural inclinations cannot be complete. These unconscious forces "find numerous ways of rebelling that defeat the very effort to be moral through rigid consciousness" (p. 235). Consequently, Wallwork argues, "the contemptuous attitude toward sensuous motivations enshrined in Kant's portrayal of the moral self is usually self-defeating because the effort to isolate reason completely from its connections with the rest of the self has a tendency to boomerang" (p. 235).

I would criticize the Freudian legacy for ascribing undue weight to instinctual structures in the psychological formation of moral character, but I consider the possibility of developing a psychologically informed moral philosophy worth pursuing. Such enterprise need not regard human behavior as overly determined by instinctual forces, as in the case of Freud, for alternative psychosocial visions could be proposed. Such a project need not devolve into relativism or moral egoism, either, as an apprehension of the limitations of human spirit and reason does not necessarily stand in opposition to precepts of justice and democracy.

This excursus began with the proposition expounded by Wallwork (1991) that Freud was informed by, as well as contributed to, an incipient social ethics framework. Regardless of how formative this social philosophy may have been for the founder of psychoanalysis, I think that as a "liberator" Freud was more of a personal rather than a social liberator—a predilection matched by his concern with therapy more than with political action (Abramson 1984; Roazen 1986, 1990). Personal liberation through therapy, even though it risks degenerating into a hedonistic preoccupation with the self, cannot be devalued. This is not only because some individuals desperately require relief from psychological suffering, but also because, as noted above, unless individuals free themselves of certain unconscious drives and inhibitions, they will lack the necessary insight and energy to engage in social transformation or moral action of any kind. Kovel (1988) suggests that personal liberation attained through critical therapy need not succumb to the temptation of enlightened conformity or epicurean self-indulgence. Therapy that refuses to endorse "the colonization of the subjective world which defines late capitalism" can widen the "scope of choices that can be made, while a certain part of locked-in subjectivity has been freed to make real demands upon the world. In sum, they are more ready for love and the politics of liberation" (p. 145).

Given such arguments for Freud's conservativism or progressivism, what kind of conclusions can be advanced? I submit that Freud's statements and theories defy categorical classification as either in favor of or against the status quo (cf. Abramson 1984; Frosh 1987; Jacoby 1975; Lichtenberg 1969). Roazen (1986) noted that "psychoanalysis is itself neither inherently liberal nor conservative but contains strands from both" (p. 251). Freud made numerous assertions indicting class society and its repressive institutions, but at the same time he helped create one of the more powerful ideological stratagems of capitalism. His work suggests the possibility of attributing personal unhappiness almost exclusively to intrapsychic conflicts.

Jacoby (1975) contends that these contradictory tendencies derive mainly from Freud's divergent interests in theory and therapy. In his view, Freudian theory contained the necessary elements to unravel the problematic human condition and to indict repressive institutions, and hence its potential to promote well-being. Therapy, on the contrary, operates within an oppressive society to alleviate personal predicaments and does not purport to have social curative effects. In Jacoby's view, to take psychoanalysis only as therapy "is to blunt psychoanalysis as a critique of civilization, turning it into an instrument of individual adjustment and resignation. The point is not to play one against the other; both theory and therapy exist within Freud in contradiction" (Jacoby 1975, p. 120).

THE POLITICS OF FREUD'S FOLLOWERS

Not all, but much, of the political ambiguity reflected in Freud's writings dissipates in the work of his followers. Three groups can be placed along the political continuum: the radical Freudian Left, the neo-Freudian Left, and the conservative Freudians. Prior to studying the various sociopolitical trends, it is necessary to appreciate the metamorphosis of psychoanalysis in its transition from Europe to North America. Fundamental transformations in the intellectual spirit of psychoanalysis have taken place since its arrival from the Old World to the United States and Canada (Burston 1991; Fuller 1986; Harris and Brock 1991; Jacoby 1983; Roazen 1990).

The major change observed by Jacoby (1983) was what he called the "repression" of psychoanalysis. By that Jacoby meant the almost complete eradication of radical political agendas from psychoanalysis. Whereas in Europe psychoanalysis could not be conceived without its cultural and social interests, in certain circles in America it can hardly be conceived with them. Although many of its precursors in Europe, like its followers in America, were medical doctors, a marked difference could be observed between them. Jacoby (1983) maintains that "European doctors have tended to be more cultured than their American counterparts; European medical education reflects, and partly causes this richer humanist vision. American physicians obtain a more specialized education" (p. 18). Furthermore, Jacoby argues that the socialization of North American physicians "filters out mavericks, humanists, and dissenters" (p. 18). Roazen (1990) is just as critical of the American tradition: "Once psychoanalysis became part of the American psychiatric establishment . . . intellectuality became a threat to the profession's trade unionism" (p. 133).

Since its incipience, European psychoanalysis has been characterized by a close association with reformist groups. In America, on the contrary, psychoanalysis became very much part of the medical establishment (Jacoby 1983; Kovel 1988; Turkle 1978). Turkle (1978) summarizes well the "assimilation" and "accommodation" of psychoanalysis into the American scene:

> Americans accepted psychoanalysis, but they shaped it to their image of what would be "helpful." American psychoanalytic ego psychology, directed toward an active adaptation of the patient to reality, toward what came to be called "coping," brought Freudianism in line with American beliefs about the virtue and necessity of an optimistic approach. . . . The optimistic revisions of Freud focused on adaptation to a reality whose justice was rarely challenged. (pp. 7-8)

In order to qualify for the optimistic revisions that Turkle talks about, psychoanalysis had to be "desexualized" and "stripped of its emphasis on irrationality" (Ingleby 1981c, p. 12), but once it was reformulated to suit the American character, psychoanalysis penetrated this culture in unprecedented ways. This is an indisputable reality, agreed upon by Freudian sympathizers and critics alike (Fuller 1986; Fuller Torrey 1992).

Next we shall see that only a small fragment of the reformist spirit of psychoanalysis survived in America; mostly outside of psychology and psychiatry. At the same time, most of its conservative features have been fortified within medical and psychological circles (Jacoby 1983).

The Radical Freudian Left

In the past there have been numerous attempts to arrive at a synthesis between Freud and Marx. Besides the pioneer work of W. Reich and the significant contributions made by the Frankfurt school (see, for example, Bocock 1983), other well-known studies have been carried out by Fromm (1955) and Schneider (1975). Similar enterprises have been undertaken by Castilla del Pino (1981) and Kovel (1988), this last one being particularly lucid and helpful. A renewed interest in the possible contributions of psychoanalysis to critical social theory in general can be seen in the last decade (Elliot 1992; J. C. Smith 1990). The political significance of these efforts, however, goes beyond the scope of this chapter. I shall delimit this section to some relevant aspects of psychoanalysis that seem to have informed and persisted in the Left.

If psychoanalysis was to be made compatible with Marxism, and especially with historical materialism, its instinctual foundations had to be reinterpreted. This situation led to a new reading of drive theory: Instincts were no longer the exclusive product of intrapsychic constitution but also, and perhaps mainly, were products of internalized cultural practices. H. Marcuse (1966) was very influential in advancing this conceptualization of the instincts. He not only claims that "Freud [was] well aware of the historical element in man's [*sic*] instinctual structure" (p. 133), but expands on that theme himself. Although H. Marcuse gives full recognition to the phylogenetic-biological level, he argues that the sociological level is the one that determines the particular historical character of the instincts. According to his thesis, the "*organization* [italics added] of the instincts in the struggle for existence would be due to *exogenous* factors—exogenous in the sense that they are not inherent in the 'nature' of the instincts but emerge from the specific historical conditions under which the instincts develop" (p. 132). The social and historical dimensions of personality have come to be known as "second nature," as opposed to the "primary nature" of instincts in the composition of the personality.

Marcuse's sociological elaboration of Freud is epitomized in his concept of *surplus-repression*. This is defined as "the restrictions necessitated by social domination. This is distinguished from basic *repression*: the 'modifications' of the instincts necessary for the perpetuation of the human race in civilization" (H. Marcuse 1966, p. 35). Departing from Freud's explanation of organized society in *Civilization and Its Discontents*, H. Marcuse contends that repression is required not only for the continuation of the human race, but also for the perpetuation of a social configuration of domination. "The specific interests of domination," he asserts, "introduce *additional* controls over and above those indispensable for civilized human association" (p. 37). The political implication of Marcuse's analysis is that society still has a long path to traverse in order to reduce or minimize surplus-repression, particularly for those who are placed at the bottom of the social hierarchy.

Albeit they were significantly influential in the Left (see, for example, Lasch 1984), Marcuse's views, as well as elaborations of them by Jacoby, were not uniformly accepted by those pursuing social change. This was in large part due to a great reluctance in many left-wing circles to endorse Freudian concepts or any variations on them (Bramel and Friend 1982; Brooks 1973; Lerman 1986; Nahem 1981).

H. Marcuse is representative of the nonclinical branch of the Freudian Left. In contrast to his vociferous indictment of capitalist society, a much more silent, almost underground, kind of social critique has been conducted by Freudian clinicians in America. Jacoby (1983) has documented at some length the radical thought of Fenichel, Jacobson, and A. Reich. As Jacoby puts it, "Fenichel or Jacobson or Annie Reich were not merely outstanding theorists and clinicians, they were also radicals devoted to a social psychoanalysis" (p. 7). While in many respects their thinking was similar to H. Marcuse's, the fate of their political convictions would be much different.

Almost all of these politically progressive Freudians came to the United States as refugees from Europe in the 1930s. As such, "they were fearful of jeopardizing their tenuous legal status" (Jacoby 1983, p. 19) by publicizing their rather unpopular views on social matters. "They generally desired social and political invisibility" (Jacoby 1983, p. 19). As a result of their hidden positions on such issues, little is left for the public to study of their critiques (for some recently found material, see Harris and Brock 1991). In fact, these analysts are well remembered for their clinical—not sociopolitical—contributions to psychoanalysis.

The political seclusion observed in the European refugees is a trademark of the medicalization of psychoanalysis in North America. As noted earlier, since its arrival at the beginning of the century this doctrine became a medical expertise deprived of whatever social connotations it might have possessed in Europe (e.g., Jacoby 1983; Kovel 1981a, 1981b; Roazen 1990; Turkle 1978, 1981). As Turkle (1978) pointed out, "in America, medical professionalization contributed to defusing much of what was most radical in [Freud's] vision" (p. 150).

Concurrent to its medical professionalization, American psychoanalysis underwent a process of political sterilization. This is not to say that psychoanalysis became apolitical, but rather it aspired and pretended to be apolitical. As Kovel (1981a) has noted, only a few have survived this process, Kovel being one of them. He is an example of an almost extinct species.

Kovel's (1981a, 1981b, 1988) Marxist orientation to psychoanalysis can be summarized along four lines of reasoning. First, he utilizes Marxism to criticize the ideological uses of psychoanalysis—that is, its diverting attention from political issues and its individualistic approach to human predicaments. Second, Kovel denotes the affinity of goals between psychoanalysts as interested parties in a class society and their functions as agents of socialization. Third, at the level of praxis, he combines psychoanalysis to help individuals deal with their psychological repressions, with a Marxist view of the whole person that does not end in the therapy room. "It is absurd to think of caring for someone in a purely psychological way, i.e., without seeing to his/her so-called material needs. Care is given to a whole person, not just the psyche" (Kovel 1981a, p. 252). Finally, he sees in therapy the dual possibility of allaying psychological pain and fostering in the person a questioning attitude toward the social world, an ability developed through the process of extricating oneself from unconscious repressive cultural mores.

Kovel's personal attempt to reconcile Freud with Marx is unique in that he does not artificially attempt to reduce one in order to make him compatible with the other. Both exist in a creative tension. While he emphasizes that both systems fight repression, he acknowledges their different targets and scope, with psychoanalysis focusing on the individual and Marxism on the community at large.

In a similar vein, Frosh (1987) constructs a vision of therapy where private emancipation is connected to the project of radical politics. Struggling in therapy with the internalization of social scripts designed to reproduce forms of domination can be an arduous but potentially liberating and socially useful task. Therapy, as critical self-examination, can unearth the patriarchal, racist, and oppressive inclinations all of us have absorbed through subtle, and not so subtle, socializing messages. It is in the understanding of the mechanisms whereby cultural hegemony conquers the individual psyche that therapy can be progressively helpful (see also chapter 14). Frosh sees in psychoanalysis an invaluable tool for the examination of how the external becomes inscribed as internal, of how "the social world enters into the experience of each individual, constructing the human 'subject' and reproducing itself through the perpetuation of particular patterns of ideology"

(p. 11). To the extent that psychoanalysis can live up to this expectation, its utilization in the project of countering hegemony deserves thoughtful consideration.

The Neo-Freudian Left

It should be made clear at the outset of this discussion that authors disagree widely in their interpretation of the sociopolitical contributions of the neo-Freudian leftists. Fromm (1955, 1965) provides a good example. According to P. Brown (1981), Fromm would belong in the radical Left fraction. This is congruent with Roazen's analysis of Fromm's legacy. Roazen (1990) wrote about him that "socially he has been the most radical of psychoanalytic thinkers. . . . No psychoanalyst tried more relentlessly to reconcile Freud and Marx" (p. 128). And Burston (1991) observed "how shortsighted it is to classify Fromm as a neo-Freudian" (pp. vii-viii). According to Jacoby (1975, 1983) and H. Marcuse (1966), Fromm's sociopolitical legacy is revisionist and far from radical. Yet Lasch (1984) places Fromm somewhere in the middle and calls him a "neo-Freudian leftist." Fromm may very well occupy a category of his own in the history of psychoanalysis. However, because of his closeness to the ideas of Horney and H. S. Sullivan, I decided to include him in the neo-Freudian category.

This section, then, will concern itself primarily with the work of Fromm, Horney, and H. S. Sullivan, all of whom have been identified, with slight variations, as belonging to the more progressive branch of neo-Freudianism (e.g., Bartlett 1945; P. Brown 1981; Fuller 1986; Roazen 1990). Fromm's *The Sane Society* (1955), Horney's *The Neurotic Personality of Our Time* (1937), and H. S. Sullivan's *The Interpersonal Theory of Psychiatry* (1953) are representative of this cultural trend of psychoanalysis. In their respective studies these thinkers deviate from Freud in the significance attributed to social and cultural factors—variables that were, in their view, underestimated by Freud. Their position is succinctly presented by Lasch (1984):

> They tried to press psychoanalysis into the service of social reform by emphasizing cultural instead of biological determinants of personality. The cultural school had set out to strip Freudian theory of its 'biological determinism,' its 'disregard of cultural factors' and 'social conditions,' its undue emphasis on sexuality at the expense of 'feelings of inferiority' and the 'hunger of appreciation or affection,' its neglect of 'interpersonal relations,' its 'patriarchal' bias, its

'hydraulic' theory of psychic energy—everything, in short, that allegedly stamped Freud's thought as a product of nineteenth-century mechanistic science and bourgeois culture. (pp. 227-28)

According to H. Marcuse (1966), the main objections of the neo-Freudians to Freud "may be summed up as follows: Freud grossly underrated the extent to which the individual and his neurosis are determined by conflicts with his environment" (p. 248). And P. Brown (1981) claimed that Fromm and Horney "emphasized the manner in which competition radiated from its economic origins to play a dominant role in personality development" (pp. 21-22).

Although their works have been regarded as very sensitive to social influences and as a result as quite progressive, the neo-Freudians' ultimate political impact is difficult to ascertain. This is so because their critique of society as pervaded by competition and injustice might have been undermined by their "optimism" regarding the individual's ability to attain happiness in such society (e.g., Ingleby 1981c; Roazen 1990). In other words, the emphasis placed on the curative effects of therapy and the potential of the individual to overcome circumstantial barriers might have drawn attention away from the need to "cure" society as well.

Ironically, the leftist neo-Freudians have been called the "cultural, social, and interpersonal school," but when it comes to improving the well-being of the population, they rely heavily on the therapy room. Such an attitude has gained them the label *idealists*—in the sense that they hope to change society by altering ideas and predispositions without effecting major modifications in material and economic conditions (Caruso 1964). Objecting to this trend, Caruso (1964) asserted: "No one wants to fall back into the error of those ready to construct a New Society by *means* of psychoanalysis" (p. 275). In order to make psychoanalysis conform with the spirit of the times, the neo-Freudians had to make it "practical." As a result, the radical opponents contend, they have advanced therapy at the expense of critical social theory (Bartlett 1945; Caruso 1964; Jacoby 1975, 1983; H. Marcuse 1966).

When the cultural and social repercussions of the neo-Freudian Left are compared to those of the radical Freudian Left, two differences are apparent. First, the neo-Freudian message appears to be by far less challenging and more conforming than that of the radicals. Second, the reformist spirit of the neo-Freudians has reached a much greater audience, not necessarily within psychology but in the general public. That is mainly, I think, due to the popularity of Fromm's books (Burston

1991). Within mainstream psychology, only the clinical contributions of
H. S. Sullivan appear to have survived the test of time. The discipline of
psychology remains vastly unappreciative of Fromm's contributions.
Burston (1991) explains the rejection of Fromm as follows:

> Apart from his emphasis on the qualitative dimensions of psy-
> chology and its emancipatory, disillusioning function, his belief in
> the possibility—indeed, in the logical necessity for—an objective
> ethics, grounded in laws of human nature, struck many psychol-
> ogists as grossly unscientific. In psychology and psychiatry, the
> prevailing orientation was predicated—as it is today—on the
> belief in the reality of objective *knowledge*, but not on the possibil-
> ity of an objective *ethics*. (p. 188)

A few tentative conclusions can be attempted from this brief
overview of the Freudian Left. If the Left is a small minority within the
political scenario of North America, then the Freudian Left is only a
minority within an already small circle. And if psychoanalysis is only a
small subspecialty of medicine and psychology, then it would not be
difficult to argue that progressive psychoanalysis is indeed rare (Jacoby
1975, 1983; Kovel 1981a; Turkle 1978, 1981). Hence, I would pose that
the impact of progressive psychoanalytic forces upon society at large are
very limited indeed. I would further say that, because of its acceptance
in therapeutic quarters of individualistic orientations, the next group we
shall discuss has had a more enduring and profound effect on our culture.

The Conservative Freudians

Although psychoanalysis can be thought to have numerous progressive implications, "there is a marked tendency for these to be sup-
pressed in favor of therapeutic techniques which in effect focus on fostering the individual's adjustment to his or her environment"
(Henriques et al. 1984, p. 207). As we have seen in this and previous
chapters, a common strategy utilized by conservatives to avert opposition to the status quo is to "blame the victim" for his or her own misery
and propose solutions based on personal changes. Therapy, Kovel
(1988) argues, "has in some respects been even more successful than
religion in deflecting energy from the need for radical social change"
(p. 121). In this section I shall provide a few examples of human suffering where psychoanalysis has been invoked to stress individual or
group "pathology" to exculpate society.

Few writers have so clearly exposed the "blaming the victim" ideology as W. Ryan (1971). His detailed documentation of instances where social and economic factors are minimized in, or omitted from, descriptions of the origins of poverty contains illustrative examples of the role played by psychoanalysis in upholding that ideology. For instance, Ryan takes issue with Kardiner, a psychoanalyst who believes that poverty will be eradicated not "merely by housing, more jobs or improved education" (p. 140), but by some kind of compensatory emotional education. Kardiner's proposed plan would be

> to organize cadres of women who, after a short training program, would go into emotionally impoverished homes where they would attempt some educating and guiding of the adults as to how they can provide some of the needed nurture. . . . Whatever the plans, we must treat the causes of the disease, not the symptoms. (In W. Ryan 1971, p. 140)

Kardiner states in no uncertain terms that for him the emotional problems are not symptoms of poverty but its very cause.

W. Ryan (1971) also quotes extensively from Chilman, an expert in poverty. All too familiar with the language of psychoanalysis, Chilman asserts that the poor have less "ego strength," are "immature," and have a marked tendency toward "impulsivity." Ryan himself acknowledges that *some* of these characteristics *may* apply to *some* poor people *some* of the time. Nevertheless, he correctly points out that under no circumstances should it be concluded that the emotional problems of some are generating poverty and that, as a result, the psychological, and not the economic, roots of poverty should be treated.

According to the psychoanalytic view, "the problems of the poor are, at bottom, manifestations of neurosis or character disorder. That is, they are *intrapsychic* problems that can only be corrected by therapeutic intervention in the psychic processes of the poor person" (W. Ryan 1971, p. 147).

Another case of psychoanalysis at the service of conservative interests can be observed in psychoanalytic explanations of the behavior of African Americans. Since the turn of the century there have been numerous psychoanalysts whose writings, benevolent as they might have been in intention, were in effect quite injurious to people of color. Thomas and Sillen (1972) provide extensive evidence of psychoanalytic conjectures concerning the almost "inevitable" differences between whites and African Americans, given the "inferior" constitution of the

"Black" psyche. Their study revealed that such views were repeatedly expressed by psychoanalysts since the first issues of the *Psychoanalytical Review* in 1913, and the *American Journal of Psychiatry* in 1921, up until the publication of their book in 1972 (Thomas and Sillen 1972).

Thomas and Sillen's incisive account of the use of psychoanalysis to justify the oppression of one race by another is replete with examples of degrading commentaries about African Americans. Although the anguish and torment experienced by the latter are seldom directly attributed to their "inferior" mental development, many psychoanalysts insinuate, in one way or another, that the "Black" is incapable of conducting an independent life. This is due to either a passive-submissive character or a chronic dependency on whites. The stigmatization of African Americans as submissive goes back to McDougall's "instinct of submission." In 1921 McDougall claimed that "in the great strength of this instinct of submission, we have the key to the history of the Negro race" (in Thomas and Sillen 1972, p. 15). Claims of both submissiveness and dependency on whites were resorted to by psychoanalysts Hunter and Black in their explanation of African Americans' alleged inability to function autonomously. They claimed that "in view of his unprepared ego, the permission to individuate, given by law to the Negro slave in 1863, was essentially a useless privilege" (in Thomas and Sillen 1972, p. 61). It may very well be that it was a privilege African Americans could not benefit from, but certainly not because of an "unprepared ego."

"Also characteristic of psychoanalytic explanations," Thomas and Sillen note, "is the misevaluation of the objective cause of black anger— the real oppression. . . . The black man's [*sic*] anger is stripped of its genuiness and validity" (p. 63). Instead, anger and protest are largely discredited as manifestations of psychological—not material—needs. Similarly, regarding improving the fate of African Americans, few talked about reshaping social institutions and attitudes. Instead, a "supernigger" was to be created (F. L. Marcuse 1983). Psychological oversimplifications of the kind presented above are a trademark of the many psychoanalytic authors reviewed by Thomas and Sillen (1972).

Homosexuality has been yet another area in which psychoanalysts have, intentionally or otherwise, upheld the status quo. Whereas Freud's view on homosexuality was one of tolerance and acceptance as an alternative way of life, many of his American followers hastened to declare that it was a pathological state (Bayer 1981). Bieber, author of *Homosexuality*, a major study of the New York Society of Medical Psychoanalysts conducted in the 1950s, is quoted by Bayer as saying that

"all psychoanalytic theories *assume* that homosexuality is psychopatho-
logic" (in Bayer 1981, p. 30). Like Bieber, Socarides was to become, two
decades ago, a major representative of the psychoanalytic position that
homosexuality constituted a severe psychopathology (Bayer 1981).
Bayer's review of Socarides' work revealed that according to Socarides
"almost half of those who engage in homosexual practices have a concomitant schizophrenia, paranoia, or latent or pseudoneurotic schizophrenia, or are 'in the throes of a manic-depressive reaction'" (Bayer 1981, p.
35). These analysts go into great detail explaining homosexuality as a
result of pathological family relationships or other psychological distortions. Although their arguments concerning the basic pathological nature
of homosexuality have been refuted numerous times (e.g., Halleck 1971;
Spiers 1973), their assertions were not easily dismissed (Bayer 1981).
Indeed, their assumptions hampered the efforts of those interested in
having homosexuality deleted from the nomenclature of psychiatric illnesses (Spiers 1973). Ultimately, the work of psychiatrists such as Halleck
and homosexual activists (Minton 1993; Spiers 1973) resulted in the deletion of homosexuality as a major entity from the *Diagnostic and Statistical
Manual of Mental Disorders* in 1973 (Bayer 1981).

Two final examples of the way in which psychoanalysis indirectly
endorses conservative policies and discredits reform are provided by
analysts Bettleheim and Hendin (Nahem 1981). Commenting on activist
student leaders, the former says that they are "emotionally fixated at the
age of the temper tantrum" (in Nahem 1981, p. 24). Similarly, Hendin
writes of students who protested against Nixon's policies:

> These young radicals have suffered in families . . . which ignored
> and frustrated their personal needs and continue to be blind to
> them as people. . . . Identification with the poor and the oppressed
> permits these radical students to react to poverty and oppression
> without having to face how personally impoverished, victimized
> and enraged they feel. (In Nahem 1981, p. 31)

In sum, two distinct psychoanalytic features with direct and indirect conservative repercussions have been reviewed. The first is the
"pathologizing" of certain segments of the population, such as the poor,
African Americans, and homosexuals, with the clear implication that
whatever problems these people may experience are largely the result of
their own pathology and not of a discriminatory and profoundly unjust
society. The second is the discreditation of protest as a manifestation of
unmet psychological needs.

CONCLUSION

Like others before me (Frosh 1987; Ingleby 1981c; Lichtenberg 1969; Roazen 1990) have done, I would point out that psychoanalysis can *potentially* be employed to either support or oppose the status quo. From a structural point of view, the theory tends to reify "human nature" and reduce it to instinctual or biological drives. Unfortunately, some progressive trends that renounce this biologism tend to confine their interpretive horizon to the microsocial environment, inadvertently expunging from their analysis much of what is socially constructed about the self. Similarly, the insightful research of Wallwork and Hartmann concerning the creation of a psychologically informed ethical framework seems to lack a critique of the very concept of "human nature" employed by Freud. Beneficial as it might be to gain awareness of the ethical limits of human behavior, one should bear in mind that human nature is as much created as discovered through the process of psychoanalysis (Sass 1992). Consequently, the very tools by which we can discern capacities for morality shape the outcome of the investigation. Though incomplete, the work of these authors has prepared the ground for further dialogue between psychology and moral philosophy. Finally, the latent possibility that psychoanalysis would be useful in exposing socially destructive myths, internalized by citizens during the socialization process, remains a tantalizing but as yet elusive and unfulfilled promise.

Against this wealth of undelivered progressive expectations we are faced with the accomplishments of conservative psychoanalysis. The psychodynamic approach contributed significantly to what was earlier called the "psychologizing of society" (Fuller 1986), that is, the pervasive tendency to frame social issues in increasingly sophisticated and creative intrapsychic terms, at the expense of a shrinking aptness to contemplate political solutions.

"The main theme of the history of psychoanalysis," Kovel (1988) is resigned to admit, "is that of the absorption of critique by the dominant culture" (p. 142). The challenge for progressive sympathizers is to overcome the political sterility that pervades much of psychoanalysis, and to resist the conservative forces that continue to employ this theory to deflect societal crises.

Why is it that psychoanalysis remains politically ineffective for progressively oriented people? It would be a mistake to blame the political inefficiency of psychoanalysis entirely on American medicine. Roazen (1990) has painful but important insights to share in this regard.

According to him, "Freud may have had emancipatory purposes, but the upshot has been academicism and pedantry" (p. 133). The public at large cannot benefit from the lessons of psychoanalysis if its discourse remains the exclusive privilege of intellectuals, medical doctors, or therapy clients. If, and this is a big if indeed, psychoanalysis has in fact important offerings to make to the process of political consciousness raising, then ways must be found to share this knowledge. If, on the other hand, this theory is imbued with regressive tendencies to the point of no repair, as Lerman (1986) has argued, then there may be no point to this dissemination exercise.

Chapter 7

Behaviorism

The influential work of B. F. Skinner has shaped our culture and institutions probably more than that of any other contemporary psychologist. Behavior analysis principles are applied in a myriad of settings. The impact of behaviorism is felt in virtually every human endeavor where behavior modification is sought, including schools, industries, hospitals, government agencies, therapy, parenting courses, and the like.

Given the controversial character of Skinner's propositions regarding human nature (e.g., Skinner 1972), it should come as no surprise that much confusion and misinterpretation surround his writings (G. R. Hughes 1991). The purpose of this chapter is not to review the extent and utility of behavior analysis methods, but rather to clarify, from a conceptual point of view, Skinner's sociopolitical legacy. In the context of examining Skinner's legacy for social improvement I will not limit myself to his contributions but will also incorporate the views of his followers, who are generally referred to as "radical behaviorists."

Skinner wrote extensively on social and political issues. He advanced very concrete notions as to how to improve society (Skinner 1948, 1953). As will be pointed out later, however, his potential contributions to macrosocial change have been almost completely undermined by an underlying conservative social philosophy and overshadowed by an occupational preoccupation with microsocial settings. Skinner's ideas concerning the possible reform of government and educational systems have atrophied in face of psychologists' narrow interest in practical molecular technologies designed to maintain, not challenge, the organizational status quo. While eager practitioners devoted endless energies to modify behavior X or Y and its proximal contingencies, they paid negligible attention to distal, yet powerful, societal structures that may have occasioned, or at the very least perpetuated, the behavior under scrutiny. Fortunately, there has been an attempt recently to bring back to radical behaviorism the *social context* (Baer, Wolf, and Risley 1987; Lamal 1989; Malagodi 1986; Nietzel and Himelein 1987; Task Force on Public Policy 1988). The resurgence of interest in larger environments holds the promise that radical behaviorism may in fact contribute to create a better society.

An examination of Skinner's views reveals an inherent contradiction between a rhetoric of social change and a philosophy of adjustment. I would argue that if one is to critically assess the social legacy of B. F. Skinner, serious attention must be paid to this problematic tension. A superficial reading of his writings would undoubtedly categorize him as a social reformer, but an analysis of the same in light of his implicit functionalist views would lead one to conclude that adjustment to society, not social change, was primordial for Skinner (Cosgrove 1982).

This chapter has two principal topics. The first is the contradiction between the rhetoric of change and the philosophy of adjustment. The second is the potential of radical behaviorism for social improvement and why this potential has not been fulfilled hitherto.

SOCIAL BETTERMENT THROUGH BEHAVIORISM

Skinner's legacy for social betterment is far from clear. Contending opinions characterize his social heritage as either highly progressive (Comunidad Los Horcones 1989; Ulman 1991) or strongly conservative (Geiser 1976; Nahem 1981). I suggest that, when viewed in the context of his underlying philosophy of adjustment, Skinner's exhortations for social improvement are rendered incapable of producing meaningful social changes. I will examine this argument in more detail now.

To understand Skinner's philosophy of adjustment, it is necessary to explore his position on values in general and social values in particular. What are the values according to which society should be constructed, or changed? For Skinner, values can be derived from naturalistic observations (B. Schwartz 1986). Essentially, he contends that an "ought" statement can be derived from an "is" statement, an error philosophers refer to as the "naturalistic fallacy" (J. A. Mills 1982; Steininger 1983).

Skinner believed that science possesses the necessary tools to answer moral questions. "If a scientific analysis can tell us how to change behavior, can it tell us what changes to make?" (Skinner 1972, p. 97). In understanding Skinner's position, as Day (1977) pointed out, "the important thing to realize is that Skinner's answer to this question is essentially yes" (p. 12). Being able to account for the values held by individuals, however, is not the same as knowing which values are intrinsically advantageous for the promotion of human welfare (cf. Eacker 1975; Steininger 1983). As Freedman (1972) put it: "The statements of the 'values or goals sought' cannot come from science, even though behavioral scientists may be able to explain why an individual holds one set of values rather than another" (p. 6). As noted earlier, Robinson (1985) referred to this mistake as the "externalization" of scientific values. If scientific knowledge does not confer any privilege whatsoever in the selection of values to be held or goals to be pursued, then radical behaviorists cannot claim authority on the choice of values based on technological expertise (Freedman 1972). C. B. Rogers (1977) put it well:

> In the same sense that nuclear physicists shouldn't determine the conditions under which an atomic bomb should be used, or doctors shouldn't determine whether patients have a right to live or die, behaviorists shouldn't determine the desired type of behavior to be sought from people in a society.... Behaviorism has much to offer, both as a science and as a technique for attaining a variety of goals. It has no more to offer than any other group when it comes to deciding what those goals should be. (pp. 361-62)

In a recent book Barry Schwartz (1986) offered an argument essentially the same as that of Rogers. Behavior therapists can "provide a set of techniques that will help people create a good society. But they decidedly cannot indicate what a good society should be" (pp. 218-19).

For Skinner, the "is" upon which values should be based is positive reinforcement. Actions and situations are "good" if they are maintained through positive reinforcement (J. A. Mills 1982; Skinner 1972), hence, his appeal to the value of survival (Skinner 1978). Reproduction, not transformation, is the value implicitly invoked by Skinner. For Skinner, a culture is "good" insofar as it *reproduces* itself. The changes proposed are only to make society run more efficiently, not to transform it. "The behavior we call ethical makes a group function more effectively" (Skinner 1978, p. 93). Inasmuch as this society appears to "survive," because it is not extinct yet, whatever will prolong this pattern of social interaction is to be regarded as desirable. Cosgrove (1982) captured this Skinnerian tenet well.

> Looking at Skinner's view that value is that which is reinforcing and aids the survival of man [*sic*], we can conclude that he believes that whatever is, is good and ought to exist. If a single behavior or an entire culture exists, then it must contain a reinforcing values system and is therefore good. If it is reinforcing it must be good. (p. 87)

In other words, what is good is based on what exists, and since whatever exists, exists because it has been positively reinforced, positive reinforcement of what exists is good.

Skinner's position on social values, then, may be summarized as follows: Since good is essentially equated with the survival of the present state of social affairs, whatever positively reinforces it is desirable. Consequently, contributions to the reproduction of the status quo are regarded as valuable.

The argument could be made, in Skinner's defense, that survival is in fact a highly desirable goal (O'Donohue, Hanley, and Krasner 1984). This may hold if the only alternative were destruction of the human species. But excluding this possibility, survival may, and does, take many different forms. Currently "surviving" societies may be classified as more or less democratic, more or less just, more or less tolerant, and so on. Given that many kinds of cultures survive, how is Skinner to decide which one is the best? If they all survive, they are, according to the Skinnerian point of view, equally good. This dead end is occasioned by the lack of external criteria as to what constitutes a good society, other than the singular value of cultural survival (cf. Bethlehem 1987; Machan 1974).

The question should now be posed, how does one reconcile, if such is at all possible, this social philosophy that upholds the status quo with Skinner's calls for social reform? It would appear, in light of the preceding discussion and Skinner's (1978) declaration that "the behavior we call ethical makes a group function more effectively"

(p. 93), that his exhortations for social change are circumscribed to making *this* society run more efficiently. Fundamental issues pertaining to the morality of a culture, such as distributive justice and power inequalities, are neglected in his social vision and not targeted for change.

Having excluded the possibility of social transformation from the main agenda of radical behaviorism, the remaining way to improve society is by adjusting the individual to the existing social arrangements, a task for which psychologists are traditionally well suited (Napoli 1981). The next section of this chapter will show that, in effect, this is primarily what behaviorism promoted, the changing of individuals to fit the environment.

The argument presented so far claims that the conceptual framework of radical behaviorism does not provide a satisfactory account of the criteria according to which the "good" society should be shaped. The Skinnerian philosophy allows only for the reproduction of the existing social system. But if its social vision is rejected, can we still make use of scientific behavioral principles in trying to create a better society, one firmly grounded in social moral philosophy? In my opinion it is worth investigating the potential uses of radical behaviorism for the advancement of the good society.

Even though Skinner's social *philosophy* was found to be inadequate, there is merit in exploring how his *techniques* might be used to change detrimental environmental conditions, and what might frustrate these attempts. This discussion is organized around three themes: (a) the gap between theory and practice; (b) the preoccupation with technology, sometimes at the expense of ethical inquiry into the social repercussions of behavior modification; and (c) the adjustments needed for radical behaviorism to fulfill its potential for macrosocial change.

SOCIAL BETTERMENT UNDERMINED: GAPS BETWEEN THEORY AND PRACTICE

Probably more forcefully than any other modern psychological theory, radical behaviorism has upheld the tenet that human behavior is determined by contingencies contained in the environment (Day 1987; Lee 1988; Michael 1984; Skinner 1953, 1972, 1974). Needless to say, Skinner's conceptions reached beyond the psychological laboratory. His vision entailed the utilization of behavior analysis to solve social problems (Skinner 1985). Malagodi (1986) states the radical behaviorist position with respect to social issues as follows: "Social problems originate in social environments, not in the minds of individuals, and solutions to them can be forthcoming only by radically changing environmental contingencies" (p. 4).

If suffering individuals are to be helped by radical behaviorism, then experimental analyses of social circumstances conducive to human suffering are to be undertaken (J. G. Holland 1978). These analyses are in contrast to futile exercises of blaming the victim, where attempts are made to change the person and not the environment (Kvale 1985). Unfortunately, the blaming-the-victim practice has dominated the behavioral field. Behaviorists have been mostly concerned with changing, not environments, "but the inner nature of individuals" (J. G. Holland 1977, p. 203). Having reviewed the literature on this very point, Stolz (1978) concluded that "in the practice of behavior modification, . . . society has controlled the definition of deviance, located the problem within the individual, and directed treatment toward changing the individual" (p. 48). Thus, disruptive children are conditioned to obey rules without questioning whether the educational environment is aversive or just uninteresting. Similarly, alcoholics are retrained to exercise more control without ever questioning the commercial and social pressure to consume more and more alcohol.

More recently, these shortcomings were unequivocally expressed by the Task Force on Behavior Analysis and Public Policy: "Despite calls for system change at both community and societal level[s], too few behavior-analytic interventions go beyond implementation with individuals or small groups" (Fawcett et al. 1988, p. 19).

The primary use of behavior modification principles has been in highly circumscribed settings, where the main target of change is usually an individual's behavior (Burchard 1987; Malagodi 1986). Change is focused at the molecular level, with an attempt to alter only the most proximal contingencies, leaving structural arrangements intact. Questions regarding the operational integrity and morality of the system as a whole are seldom posed. As a result, behavioral interventions often facilitate the maintenance of inadequate social structures that are inimical to the welfare of the population directly or indirectly affected by them (Krasner 1976).

As most interventions are almost exclusively directed at the micro level, the very institutions where behavior modification is mostly used are rarely challenged to reflect on their policies and procedures. These interventions conduct a small-scale restructuring of the contingencies. This has been the case in mental hospitals, penitentiaries, and schools. The school system, where behavior modification has had a tremendous impact, provides an illustrative example. More often than not, interventions are designed to neutralize rebellious children, pacify troublemakers, and simply make them more docile (Geiser 1976; Winett and Winkler 1972). This kind of behavioral engineering is very appealing to those who are reluctant to take another look at their educational practices (Sarason 1990). Embarrassing questions dealing with the structure of the educational system as a whole may be strategically avoided when those who do not follow the rules can be given behavioral treatment. As Geiser (1976) pointed out, "a great danger of behavior mod technology is its tendency to reinforce the status quo and to discourage the uncomfortable questions" (p. 92). On the particular issue of behavior modification in the schools, Geiser observed:

> Because the methods do work to a degree, behavior mod has strengthened the reign of law and order in poor school systems. . . . Behavior moders . . . are hired by those in power in institutional settings, and their methods serve the status quo of the establishment. . . . Their extremely narrow focus concentrates on a subject's behavior in an immediate situation. . . . [They] redesign the child to fit the existing environment. (p. 97)

The missed opportunity for social betterment dealt with in this section derives from Skinner's philosophy of adjustment and from the eagerness of practitioners to fix relatively easy and small problems. Both of these forces steered behaviorism away from complex social predicaments into a therapeutic microcosm.

This rather conspicuous discrepancy between theory and practice has not gone unnoticed in behavioral circles. Calls to regain the "lost" social context in behavioral applications are appearing in the literature with increased frequency, and in the most *behavioral* kind of publications (Baer, Wolf, and Risley 1987; Jason and Glenwick 1984; Kvale 1985; Malagodi 1986; Task Force on Public Policy 1988). If their plea is answered favorably, behaviorists may face a harder, yet more rewarding, challenge.

SOCIAL BETTERMENT MISGUIDED: A GOOD TECHNIQUE IS NOT ENOUGH

Radical behaviorism has been absorbed by, and has contributed to, the mechanical spirit of our century. This movement has promoted the view that the betterment of society depends mainly on the progress of technology in general, and of a technology of human behavior in particular (Woolfolk and Richardson 1984). Developing a sound methodology to shape behavior has been of paramount importance to Skinner and his followers. In many areas, they have been more successful than others in modifying almost intractable habits (Nietzel, Bernstein, and Milich 1991; Wilson and O'Leary 1980). The praise received for their accomplishments in the technological field, however, may have blurred their vision with regard to the broader implications of technological successes. Oppenheimer issued a powerful warning in this respect. Commenting on the development of the hydrogen bomb, he stated: "When you see something that's technologically sweet you go ahead and do it and argue about what to do about it only after you have had your technical success" (in Marcatillo and Nevin 1986, p. 63).

The eagerness to control human behavior and change it should not precede, or come at the expense of, questioning the moral implications of change for the individuals immediately affected and for society as a whole (cf. Emerson and McGill 1989; Pitt 1987). A rare and high standard of "technological restraint" was set by Krasner (1976) and his colleagues when they decided to terminate a token economy system in a mental hospital because it was serving to maintain a particular undesirable social institution.

Indeed, the *first* commitment of behaviorism should be to moral reasoning directed at improving the lot of the unfortunate. Its *second* concern should be the design of methods to attain the ethically dictated goal. Traditionally, behaviorism has shown a preference for constructing technologies first and adopting ethical safeguards for their applications later (Malagodi 1986). I am suggesting that we reverse the order: Technology should be subservient to ethical decision making. Once a social issue is selected as a target of action, behavioral technologies can be developed to address the task at hand. The coalition of social activists with behavior analysts "may produce effective means for using behavior change techniques to combat abuses of power, whether political, economic or social; helping disenfranchised groups gain access to resources; and assisting communities to realize their potential for change and improvement" (Fawcett et al. 1988, p. 19).

SOCIAL BETTERMENT POSSIBILITIES:
SEIZING POWER—THE MISSING VARIABLE IN BEHAVIORISM

Conspicuous for its absence in behavior analysis is an examination of power, which is unquestionably a prime reinforcer. Unless the distribution of power in an institution or in society in general is brought under close scrutiny, innovative reforms are bound to prove only minimally, if at all, helpful. Sarason (1990) has provided ample evidence for this assumption in the case of educational reform. Wells (1987) noted how the lack of redistribution of power in industries impedes meaningful changes. Finally, several other authors have shown how avoiding the issue of power results in the best fortification of the societal status quo (Edwards, Reich, and Weisskopf 1986; Gross 1980; W. Ryan 1981; M. Schwartz 1987).

From a conceptual point of view, it is highly surprising that power would not be brought under consideration in behavioral interventions more often than it has been; for power allows its possessors to treat people equitably, fairly, or unjustly. Further, it allows granting or withholding privileges. This is an expression of the contradiction between calls for social change and the underlying conservative philosophy detailed earlier in this chapter. Behavior analysts have endorsed a piecemeal approach to the eradication of systemwide predicaments, an approach that does not threaten existing power structures.

An experimental analysis of behavior, however, can be employed in discerning the mechanisms involved in the perpetuation of systemic inequities and exploitation, and in designing a more just distribution of resources in society.

> It takes changed contingencies to change behavior. If social equality is a goal, then all the institutional forms that maintain stratification must be replaced with forms that assure equality of power and equality of status. If exploitation is to cease, institutional forms that assure cooperation must be developed. (J. G. Holland 1978, p. 170)

The progressive seeds of radical behaviorism may come to fruition quicker if its practitioners consent to give more than cursory attention to the distribution of power. Lest the wrong impression be created, I hasten to point out that the same criticism applies to most branches of applied psychology, where the issue of power is all too often neglected (Halleck 1971; Howitt 1991; Jacoby 1975; Nahem 1981; E. V. Sullivan 1984).

CONCLUSION

B. F. Skinner purported to have a vision for a new society. However, "the outstanding feature of Skinner's 'new' society," Nahem (1981) writes, "is that it is the same system of capitalism" (p. 48).

Skinner's social philosophy—or lack of—amounts to a justification of the prevailing social order. Changes are designed to perfect it, not transform it. Consequently, behavioral principles continue to be used primarily to reinforce the status quo, a status quo that radical behaviorism is conceptually unable to challenge. This conservative stance permeated the application of behavioral principles to the point that, despite promises to change the environment to advance human welfare, practice continued to focus on changing the individual to advance the welfare of the social order. As will be recalled, the values of efficiency and survival—not social justice—were of paramount importance for Skinner.

In the absence of an overarching social philosophy, can any socially progressive use be made of principles of behavior modification? This is theoretically possible; but when all that behavior therapists are trying to change is a person's behavior and only the immediate surroundings, much of the potential use of Skinner's ideas for social change remain just that—ideas. In light of the excessively narrow focus on behaviors and the inadequate attention given to environments, we may speculate that the contribution of radical behaviorism to society would have been more meaningful had it centered more on *environmental* than on *behavioral* analysis.

Skinner's legacy for society is a story of unfulfilled promises. This is not because Skinner shied away from the social arena, but rather because he and his followers could not resolve the contradiction inherent in trying to reproduce this society and radically change it at the same time. They ultimately became preoccupied with modifying single organisms and microsocial settings. Related to this intrinsic shortcoming are the neglect of power issues and the notion that science can resolve moral dilemmas.

Nevertheless, in this era of renewed belief in intrapsychic psychologies and cognitive therapies, radical behaviorism is still a useful and potentially corrective measure to remind ourselves that to know a person's behavior is to know the person's physical, social, and affective environment.

The progressive potential for social change contained in radical behaviorism need not be remembered by historians as a missed opportunity. A behavioral and environmental examination of social arrangements conducive to inequitable distribution of resources or reinforcers may be a first step in employing Skinnerian principles for the enhancement of human welfare. The allocation of resources or reinforcers according to principles of distributive justice may follow. The tools for the task are readily available. Will the experts pick them up?

Chapter 8

Humanism

What kind of an imprint is humanistic psychology (HP) having on the present social order? How is the "third force" in psychology influencing society? Is it transforming societal regulations and institutions, or is it perhaps affirming the status quo? And what are the social and ethical implications of endorsing or challenging the status quo? This last question is of utmost importance, for if HP is inadvertently endorsing an undesirable state of social affairs, it may in fact be contradicting its own principles and undermining its mission of propagating humanistic values of respect for the individual and growth.

I contend that HP's fundamental values of compassion, justice, and morality (Goble 1970; Graham 1986; C. Rogers 1972; Tageson 1982) are totally incompatible with a societal status quo that glorifies competition, maintains inequality, and perpetuates social injustice. Yet, despite the irreconcilable differences between the values espoused by HP and those of the dominant capitalist philosophy, the former has not only failed to challenge the latter but has also supported it (e.g., Beit-Hallahmi 1977; Bell and Schniedewind 1989; Buss 1979a; Nord 1977; Shaw and Colimore 1988). The following conservative elements of HP have played a significant role in upholding a basically unjust state of social affairs.

THE PERILS OF "SALVATION" THROUGH
SELF-ACTUALIZATION

Contrary to Freudian and Skinnerian interpretations of our lives as controlled by either impulses, the unconscious, or external stimulation, HP advanced the notion that human beings are capable of making choices and being in charge of their own lives (Fuller 1986; Graham 1986; Tageson 1982). Humanistic psychologists took upon themselves the task of creating a self-generated image of the person, an organism that would rise above environmental conditioning and be able to conduct her or himself through life as a self-guided, self-governed individual. "The suggestion implicit in the humanist concept of 'psychological freedom' is the *individual ability to transcend society*" (Larsen 1986a, p. 227; italics added). Moreover, humanistic psychologists mandated themselves to rescue the self from the lack of reflection and contemplation endorsed by behaviorism and from the imposition of unconscious drives advanced by Freudian psychology (Fuller 1986).

Buss (1979a) contends that many liberal psychologists could not reconcile the pursuit of self-determination with either behaviorism or psychoanalysis, for both paradigms are highly deterministic. In this regard humanistic psychologists may have confused the messenger with the message. To the extent that psychoanalytic and behavioral principles can be found to be correct, they represent a certain situation, they do not necessarily create conditions for control or determinism. The claim would be tantamount to holding Newton responsible for the existence of the law of gravity.

The emphasis placed on personal and global liberation through self-actualization is one of the principal tenets of the humanist movement. This notion entails a number of political implications that have been succinctly presented by Buss (1979a):

> The excessive individualism contained in the doctrine of self-actualization serves to mask the larger social questions surrounding society's structures and institutions. A theory that predisposes one to focus more upon individual freedom and development rather than the larger social reality, works in favor of maintaining that social reality. (p. 47)

The importance placed on therapy and on the almost unlimited possibilities of change in the individual, along with a rather constricted social critique, might well lead to the conclusion that *nothing is wrong with society, it is "I" who has to change* (cf. Caplan and Nelson 1973; Hall 1983).

A parallel between the idolization of the self by humanistic psychologists and the reverence of individualism in modern America can be easily drawn. As Lasch (1984) noted, "Rogers's own approach to therapy . . . was 'as American as apple pie'" (p. 211). The American dream is ratified by humanistic psychologists who lead individuals to believe that it is within their power to satisfy all their aspirations, regardless of adverse material and social circumstances, thus leaving the social order unaffected. "Those who believe that self-actualization will occur in a socio-economic vacuum support the status quo" (Larsen 1986a, p. 226).

Another latent conservative facet of humanistic psychology is the phenomenon known as "retreatism." This is a form of

> system maintenance by encouraging or aiding those who experience frustrations with the system to retreat into the self or into groups embracing emotional but not political expression. The clearest case is the encounter group movement, which . . . has strong elements of sociopolitical withdrawal. (Bermant and Warwick 1978, p. 393)

Marien (1983) draws an analogy between the activities of humanistic psychologists and children playing in a sandbox. In the "sandbox syndrome," as Marien calls it, just as children play in the sandbox without disturbing the adults, humanists entertain ideas of change without considering the political complexities involved. In their sandbox, humanists nurture each other and foster the belief that a better world is *inevitably* coming, without intervening in the real world. This is a dangerous perception, for the "belief in a transformation that is happening in fact keeps it from happening" (Marien 1983, p. 7), simply by deflecting attention from structural, material, and economic concerns.

Humanistic psychologists (e.g., Ferguson 1983; Tageson 1982) point with pride to the fact that industry is gradually adopting humanistic concepts and techniques. Both Ferguson (1983) and Tageson (1982) see this as evidence that a more "humane" corporate world is in the making. The introduction of T-groups and organizational development are given as examples of measures taken by management to humanize the workplace. Completely absent from their analysis is the well-documented argument that these stratagems serve primarily to increase productivity by conveying to workers the *illusion* of control and participation (Baritz 1974; Bramel and Friend 1987; Ralph 1983; Wells 1987; see also chapter 11). Talking about teamwork, worker participation, collaboration, and so on, does not substitute for more actual control and a real redistribution of power in industry. This consequential omission led Lerner (1991) to claim, correctly, that "because Humanistic Psychology rarely discusses issues concerning class and the organization of the world of work, its prescriptions seem class-biased" (p. 183).

A rather illuminating apologetic statement of industrial capitalism is furnished by Tageson (1982) in his chapter on eco-psychology. He poses the question, "Is a humanistic capitalism possible?" (p. 231). Judging from his congratulatory coverage of HP in industry, Tageson would lead us to believe that a humanistic capitalism is indeed possible and that it can benefit greatly from heavy doses of HP.

The concepts of first- and second-order change advanced by Watzlawick, Weakland, and Fisch (1974) may help clarify the uncritical attitude of HP toward the social order. According to these authors, a first-order change is a mere change of form that does not threaten the structural configuration of the issue or situation at hand. A second-order change attempts to restructure the foundations of a problem or situation, thus leading to radical transformations, not only of form but also of essence. Humanistic psychologists appear to confuse first- and second-order change. While their activities amount basically to first-order operations, their pronouncements usually reach the level and rhetoric of second-order transformations.

GLOBAL "SALVATION" THROUGH SELF-ACTUALIZATION

A reading of works by leaders of the humanist movement (e.g., Maslow 1965, 1970b, 1971, 1979; C. Rogers 1967, 1972) reveals a concern for social and global issues such as alienation, war, the environment, and human rights. Humanistic psychology's hope is to expand the rewarding experiences of self-actualization to as many people as possible. The transition from self- to community actualization, however, may not be as simple as envisioned by humanists such as Ferguson (1983), Maslow (1971) or C. Rogers (1972).

The primary mode of addressing these issues is a highly individualistic one. The underlying assumption is that if we all become better individuals through self-actualization, constructive changes in the structure of society will necessarily follow. Societal conflicts are treated as if they were merely interpersonal or intrapsychic problems (cf. Van Hoorn 1984). As Doyle (1986) observed, "humanists and psychologists . . . are addressing change at the interpersonal level of politics rather than structural change" (p. 203). Consequently, caution is recommended when predicting the humanization of society through methods whose feasibility has been chiefly proven in artificial collectives created for the purposes of self-development (Back 1978). Such caution is doubly necessary when facing an embellished picture of the future and exaggerated claims about the ability of humanist technology to bring about an ideal state of affairs. Here is one such claim made by C. Rogers (1972):

> I believe that our American way of life will be radically altered by the growth of a new value system, a new culture in which feelings and subjectivity and openness (rather than hypocrisy) have a prominent place, alongside intelligence. We are going to have a new America, in my judgment, an America of change and flow, of people rather than objects. We have the know-how, the skills, to bring about this new America. . . . I think it is not unrealistic to believe that there will come into being a portion of the global community, residing on this North American continent, of which we will no longer be ashamed, but in which we will feel a quiet, peaceful pride. (p. 60)

Rogers's unfounded extravagant optimism is completely astonishing.

Personal accounts do tend to confirm that encounter groups and humanistic therapy in general facilitate the process of self-actualization (Lafferty 1981). Clients report considerable improvement in the way they feel about themselves and the way they get along with others. Lafferty (1981) notes that his humanistic therapy "produced profound and highly rewarding personal results" (p. 47). These satisfying personal outcomes, however, should not be confused with, or taken as, social amelioration. The individual spiritual elation that may be occasioned by humanistic therapy does not automatically translate into steps toward a better society. This is the realm of social and political action. "Without action toward social change, humanistic psychology will remain a class psychology for upper middle class families" (Larsen 1986a, p. 226). Hitherto, the beneficial effects of humanistic therapy appear to have been reserved for a small privileged community whose socioeconomic status affords them the luxury of seeking personal development (Campbell 1984).

Global "salvation" through self-actualization presupposes that social relations can be changed through individualistic means par excellence (Nord 1977). In other words, there is an unwarranted tendency to extrapolate from personal to global salvation.

PSYCHOLOGICAL VERSUS POLITICAL POWER

Political power is a largely neglected issue in HP. Attitudinal changes are given much more consideration than power redistribution. As with many other issues, political power is conceptualized in psychological terms, such as authoritarianism (Maslow 1965, 1979), and therefore it can be given psychological remedies.

There is little doubt that if a consequential redistribution of resources in society is to occur, a political rather than a psychological approach to power is called for (e.g., M. Schwartz 1987). When preoccupation with psychological transformations, however important they might be, divert attention from unprosperous socioeconomic realities based on inequality of political power, the result is the inadvertent strengthening of the status quo. If one is to seriously challenge Nord's (1977) assertion that "much of humanistic psychology may be too psychological to be effectively humanistic" (p. 83), the consolidation of a more politically mature stance in human affairs is imperative. Some encouraging indications may be observed. Witness, for instance, recent social critiques appearing in the *Journal of Humanistic Psychology* (e.g., Bell and Schniedewind 1989; Shaw and Colimore 1988). Nevertheless, if humanistic psychologists are not only to lose their political innocence but also become active agents in the advancement of human welfare, the emerging signs of political maturity must be fortified. In order to solidify the tenuous political inroads made in HP, there is a need to moderate the belief in the ability of self to transcend society. This notion may have occasioned a severe case of myopia or, to use Jacoby's expression, social amnesia (1975). There is now overwhelming evidence that adverse socioeconomic and political circumstances inflict deep physical and emotional wounds (e.g., Catalano 1991; Cereseto and Waitzkin 1986; Elder and Caspi 1988; Jahoda 1988; McDowell 1989; Mirowsky and Ross 1989; Rutter 1988; R. Taylor 1989; Weisband 1989).

As long as HP continues to focus on the self as its main facilitator of progress in face of unpropitious realities, politicians may continue to use this as an excuse to pursue psychological—as opposed to material and political—cures (cf. Chomsky 1988; Herman and Chomsky 1988).

After all, there are very few exceptional individuals like Victor Frankl who can endure the most traumatic experiences and emerge with a sense of personal dignity and integrity. Most human beings are likely to be severely affected by much-less-taxing vicissitudes.

An improved understanding of the long-term effects of noxious psychosocial environments on the individual will help humanistic psychologists realize the need to direct considerable efforts at changing society. The publication of *Politics and Innocence* (Greening 1986), a collection of essays on the politics of HP, has given the field the necessary impetus to explore the social repercussions of its endeavors. It is a consequential step in educating humanistic psychologists on the numerous social and ethical ramifications of their actions. There is a need now to capitalize on that accomplishment, and further the understanding that meaningful improvements in the lots of a great many people will necessitate political changes. Reform in the structure of economic and political power may have to precede psychological growth, if the welfare of vast sectors of the population is to improve. When helping individuals living in materially depriving and emotionally injurious environments, much more than psychological help is needed. An interdisciplinary dialogue may prove fruitful for HP in its efforts to amalgamate person-oriented with system-centered paradigms. For example, preventive and therapeutic approaches that take into account the psychological as well as the social, political, and economic needs of individuals and groups have been central in community psychology for over two decades now (Heller et al. 1984; Levine and Perkins 1987; Pransky 1991; Rappaport 1977). Currently, an effective model for integrating therapeutic and social concerns is being developed by Lerner (1991) at the Institute for Labor and Mental Health in Oakland, California.

Improved social conditions will derive neither from retreatism nor from a magical extension of the effects of self-actualization on a number of fortunate individuals. Social betterment is more likely to occur as a result of social action. This is not an easy lesson for psychologists to learn. Having been trained in intrapsychic models, highly reflective of the prevalent individualistic cultural ethos, psychologists deal with individuals as if they were asocial entities. As noted earlier, psychologists suffer from an occupational disease that interferes with their seeing human beings in social context, from both a diagnostic and a therapeutic point of view. Therefore, our remedies are prescribed almost entirely in intrapsychic terms. As Gergen (1990) recently put it, "Furnish the population with hammers of mental deficit, and the whole world needs pounding" (p. 363).

CONCLUSION

It has been argued that HP may have inadvertently contributed to the perpetuation of the status quo. To the extent that that has been the case, humanistic psychologists may have endorsed an unfavorable state of affairs. If this is to be avoided in the future, the political vision of HP will have to continue to mature at an accelerated pace.

For as long as psychologists and social scientists continue to neglect the simple truth that a multitude of handicapping human conditions derive from social factors, and not necessarily from intrapsychic or interpersonal factors, their contribution to human welfare will be remembered by historians as a great, unique, and missed opportunity.

Chapter 9

COGNITIVISM

Various currents of research and thought may be incorporated under the comprehensive umbrella of cognitive psychology. Theories referred to as "cognitive" are prevalent, inter alia, in the areas of personality (Kelly 1971; Hjelle and Ziegler 1981); clinical (Beck 1976, 1982; Freeman and Greenwood 1987; Mahoney 1977; Mahoney and Freeman 1985); developmental (Buck-Morss 1979; Gholson and Rosenthal 1984); social psychology (Furby 1979; Israel 1979); learning (Anderson and Travis 1983); and information processing, perception, and artificial intelligence (Baars 1986; Costall and Still 1987; Gardner 1985). Cognitive psychology's objects of study are the internal processes according to which the individual filters and manipulates physical and/or psychological stimulation. Its purpose is to unravel the mystery of the mind and how it affects behavior. Following Sampson (1981), I shall take cognitive psychology to be "that broad and diverse range of psychological approaches which emphasize the structures and processes within the individual's mind that are said to play the major role in behavior" (p. 730). I concur with Gardner (1985) that, even as these approaches emphasize cognition, they de-emphasize affect, context, culture, and history.

With these defining characteristics, the modern cognitive paradigm may in fact be considered the vivid legacy of Cartesianism.

As Gardner (1985) observed, "Rene Descartes is perhaps the prototypical philosophical antecedent of cognitive science" (p. 50). Descartes has largely set the parameters not only of cognitive psychology but of psychology as a whole. Capra (1982) has stated rather categorically that "the science of psychology has been shaped by the Cartesian paradigm. Psychologists, following Descartes, adopted the strict division between the *res cogitans* and the *res extensa*" (p. 164). And while behaviorism attempted to do away with mind altogether and restrict psychology to the science of the observable, we witness today in psychology a resurgence of dualism in favor of *res cogitans*. Skinner (1987) admitted, with some disdain, that psychology has remained "primarily a search for internal determiners" (p. 780). "The 'new' cognitive sciences are to some extent retracings of an older 'mentalism' that the behaviorists had attempted to bury" (Robinson 1985, pp. 18-19). Although this trend has not gone unchallenged (Gergen and Gigerenzer 1991; Shotter 1991), and some psychologists try to promote antidualism and mutualism (Still and Costall 1987), opposition has done little to undermine its supremacy (Costall and Still 1987; Sampson 1981).

The Cartesian dualism created difficulties for understanding not only how mind and body interact but also how mind and social context interact (Valsiner 1991). Reconstituting the mind as an autonomous entity relegated both organic and environmental variables to second place. To the extent that cognitive psychology has adopted the Cartesian "mind," it has propounded and affirmed an abstracted person (Sampson 1983, chap. 9; Still and Costall 1987), a person conceptualized primarily as a self-generated being:

> In this Cartesian viewpoint, the individual was presumed to be a substance or *entity* (a thinking entity as distinct from a material body) rather than a *relation*. . . . Insofar as our psychology insistently extirpates the actor from the scene, we become incapable of learning that the scene is as important in shaping the actor's performance as the actor is in shaping the scene. (Sampson 1983, pp. 96-97)

This epistemological position of cognitivism has sociopolitical repercussions that, given the place of prominence enjoyed by cognitive theories in psychology today (Baars 1986; Skinner 1987), must be subjected to scrutiny. Two important works have dealt with the sociopolitical implications of cognitive theory: Sampson's paper "Cognitive Psychology as Ideology" (1981), which focuses mainly on its research and theory construction, and Anderson and Travis's book *Psychology and the Liberal Consensus* (1983), which centers on the educational applications of cognitive theory. Neither has addressed the growing specialty of cognitive therapy. The present analysis will attempt to fill that void.

COGNITIVE THEORY AND RESEARCH

Central to understanding the social and political implications of cognitive theory and research is the concept of reification. Reification is

> the act of regarding an abstraction as a material thing. An analysis of any relationship in a complex world involves a process of simplification through a set of abstractions in which certain aspects of a given phenomenon are selected and stressed. . . . If they are taken as a complete description of the real phenomenon and the resulting abstractions endowed with a material existence of their own, the process exemplifies . . . a special case of the fallacy of reification. (Labedz 1988, p. 735)

In other words, reification is the treatment of one particular instance of a phenomenon as a discrete entity accounting for the phenomenon itself. In the case of human behavior, certain cognitions that may be involved in the overall phenomenon of behaving are regarded not only as distinct events, standing on their own, but also as causative forces of the behavior under examination. Two intimately related cognitive tendencies, obvious derivatives of Cartesianism, may be said to be conducive to reification in cognitive psychology: (a) personal cognitive causation, and (b) de-emphasis on context. These practices, as I shall point out, have significant implications for the social and political realm.

Personal Cognitive Causation

Personal cognitive causation, in the explanation of human behavior, is the primacy given to individual thought processes that have been conceptually disconnected from the sociohistorical context. In the study of personality this a is common practice, for "most researchers of personality use measures [and concepts] that are taken out of context" (Gergen, Comer-Fisher, and Hepburn 1986, p. 1261).

A popular analogy (attributed to Kelly) is that of the "person as scientist" (Hjelle and Ziegler 1981). A person acts as a scientist in that he or she selects the information available to him or her, interprets it, and functions accordingly. This process entails the elaboration of hypotheses, their confirmation or rejection, and the building of personal theories that assist the individual in his or her daily decision making and performance. Much like scientists, laypeople differ in their interpretation of the world. A number of these cognitive moments involved in decision making and acting become reified when they are "abstracted from the particular sociohistorical conditions of [their] constitution" (Sampson 1981, p. 737). As a result, cognitive abstractions are granted a "timeless, objective standing" (Sampson 1981, p. 737).

An illustrative case of the personal cognitive causation tendency is the construct *locus of control*. *Locus of control* "refers to the individual's perception of where the causal agent of an observed environmental change is located" (Furby 1979, p. 170). That individuals who attribute change to internal or personal causes behave, under certain circumstances, quite differently than do external attributors (e.g., Mikulincer 1988) is not disputed here. What is debatable is the privileging of "internalizers" in the literature.

Several authors have documented the explicit preference of psychologists for those with an internal, as opposed to external, locus of control (Anderson and Travis 1983; Furby 1979; Gergen, Comer-Fisher, and Hepburn 1986; Gurin, Gurin, and Morrison 1978). Great efforts have been directed at finding ways to both reduce external locus of control and increase internal locus of control (Furby 1979). Why, it may be asked, have psychologists idealized those with an internal locus of control? The answer does not lie in correlates of psychological well-being, for under certain conditions externalizers have been found to cope with adversity better than internalizers (e.g., Mikulincer 1988); rather, it lies in the belief that "events in any individual's environment are generally contingent on that individual's behavior" (Furby 1979, p. 173). Psychologists' long-standing love affair with this version of self-contained individualism has been eloquently presented by Sampson in his "Psychology and the American Ideal" (1977). Self-contained individualism is the belief in the supreme self—an omnipotent individual empowered to cope with misfortune. It is quite amazing that, in spite of the fact that countless events in one's environment are not controlled by one's actions, psychologists continue to foster the (illusory?) concept of internal locus of control.

At this point the sociopolitical implications of the nurturance of internal locus of control become quite clear. By praising those who attribute success and failure to internal causes, supporters of the internal model reinforce the existing Protestant ethic, a constitutive element of American society. Hard work and determination, in spite of societal obstacles, will lead to prosperity (Bellah et al. 1985). Furby (1979) summarized the political effects of the promotion of internal locus of control as follows:

> Those in positions of power and affluence have much to gain from increasing the *internality* of beliefs about locus of control, and much to lose from increasing *externality*. If one perceives the inability to find a job as the result of one's own actions, then the response is likely to be either apathy or 'self-improvement.' In contrast if one perceives unemployment to be the inevitable result of an economic system incapable of supporting full employment, then one's response might be much less pleasant for those in power. (p. 176)

Locus of control was presented as one instance of personal cognitive causation. In reinforcing the internal type, psychologists may be preventing the advent of social changes by fortifying the belief in the individual's potential to change him- or herself to cope with misfortune, keeping social structures more or less intact. Other examples of personal cognitive causation, such as motivation, may be found in Anderson and Travis (1983, chap. 4), Israel (1979), and Sampson (1981).

De-emphasis on Context, Culture, and History

Gardner (1985) contends that a constitutive element of cognitive science is the demotion of context, culture, and history. By definition, "cognitivism is the attempt to explain human . . . cognition in terms of internal representations and rules" (Costall and Still 1987, p. 15). The search for internal operations and avoidance of environmental contamination has led cognitive psychologists to rely heavily on the computer. Not only has the human being been compared to the "bright machine" (Robinson 1985), but there are mounting projects attempting to reveal something fundamental about human thought through artificial intelligence (AI) (Dreyfus and Dreyfus 1987). Although this is not the place to examine the merits of AI, I shall only say, as did Robinson (1985), that the psychological aspects of AI remain entirely with the programmer and not with the machine. At any rate, it is quite obvious that cognitive psychology has gone to great lengths to sterilize its subject matter from material pollution.

By focusing almost exclusively on internal processes, the cognitive psychologist is exposed to the risk of losing sight of sociohistorical variables that may influence our ways of thinking and operating in society. Behavior is the product not solely of thinking but also of external conditions.

What are the possible sociopolitical repercussions of this asocial position? Inasmuch as cognitive psychology may be considered the psychology of the day, and its acontextual theories and postulates extend to applied fields such as psychotherapy, education, social problem-solving, and conflict resolution, it would not be unreasonable to expect that cognitivism would stress the need to adjust the mind, and not society, in order to promote well-being. Conceptual changes would take precedence over social changes.

COGNITIVE PSYCHOLOGY AND EDUCATION

The social impact of the applications of cognitive psychology in education has been discussed at length by Anderson and Travis (1983). Therefore, I shall limit this section to discussing their main arguments and more recent developments.

According to Anderson and Travis (1983), the technocratic philosophy regnant in North America helped develop the notion that social problems will be solved by the social sciences—through education, in particular. Although this belief gained credence at the beginning of the century with people like Dewey, it was only after the Second World War that the approach flourished. This formula for social improvement proved to be particularly appealing for those in positions of power, for the basic social structures would not be threatened, or even questioned. "The social change envisaged was not institutional but conceptual" (Anderson and Travis 1983, p. 10).

If poverty could not be eradicated before, proponents of the liberal consensus argued, it was mainly because there were not educational methods, endowed with cognitive theories, to successfully teach slum children. Although no one within the "liberal consensus" would deny the detrimental effects of growing up in a ghetto, a set of priorities was established that placed educational change in front of environmental change. In the sixties and seventies, cognitive psychologist Jerome Bruner was highly instrumental in supporting a national agenda in the United States that stressed the improvement of minds over settings (Anderson and Travis 1983, chap. 3). This was based on a vacuous promise that educational "know-how" would enable children to rise above deleterious living conditions and attain upward social mobility. "The problem of the poor environment is dodged by arguing that what counts is training the child to get as much as possible out of his [sic] environment by way of acquiring problem solving skills" (Anderson and Travis 1983, p. 27).

Though Anderson and Travis's analysis pertains primarily to the sixties and seventies, there is evidence to suggest that cognitive psychology's drive and actual impact on numerous areas of daily life, including, of course, education, has not diminished. Witness, for instance, the recent establishment of the academic journal *Applied Cognitive Psychology*. In one of its issues Sternberg (1988), a leading psychologist in the area of intelligence, concludes that "cognitive psychology has given the study of intelligence a 'new lease on life', and that the testing and teaching of intelligence can and should be viewed as a primary focus of application for the principles of cognitive psychology" (p. 231). He further makes the point that "in education, the time is truly at hand for the application of cognitive theory to testing and training" (p. 250). Undoubtedly, many benefits could be derived from a refined cognitive psychology, and Sternberg (1988) does an excellent job of showing its potential. These advances, however, are undermined by the primacy attributed to the improvement of the mind by mind-techniques exclusively. While certain affluent sectors of the population may derive great enjoyment in perfecting their cognitive skills by intellectual exercise, others less fortunate worry about more fundamental needs.

When combating social ills, governments usually focus on a limited range of variables. Very rarely do governments approach a systemic problem from a systemic point of view. They are more likely to concentrate their efforts on a well-defined and narrow piece of the puzzle. It is because of this mode of functioning that explanatory preferences and priorities established by social scientists are of crucial importance. When theorizing about social mobility, a social scientist speculates about the percentage of variability accounted for by cognitive and environmental factors. Should his or her theories give more weight to the cognitive part of the equation, governments will be more than happy to quote that scientist and focus their attention on reshaping the mind and not the environment. Anderson and Travis (1983) cogently argue that this was precisely what happened with the work of Bruner, and if history has something to teach us, it is not unlikely that Sternberg's contributions will be used in a similar manner.

COGNITIVE THERAPY

In the last fifteen years the prominence of the cognitive modality in the therapeutic community has become almost indisputable. Cognitive therapy, largely shaped by the initial work of Beck with depressed patients (Beck 1976), has by now expanded significantly and is being applied in numerous settings to a variety of populations, including children, the elderly, chronic patients, and alcoholics (Emery, Hollon, and Bedrosian 1981; Freeman and Greenwood 1987).

The primary objective of cognitive therapy is to modulate and eventually eradicate irrational thoughts that are said to be conducive to emotional disorders (Beck 1976; Ellis 1985; Ellis and Harper 1961; for an updated overview, see Freeman 1987). "The therapist helps a patient to unravel his [sic] distortions in thinking and to learn alternative, more *realistic* ways to formulate his [sic] experiences" (Beck 1976, p. 3; italics added). Beck (1976) further argues that "psychological problems can be mastered by sharpening discrimination, correcting misconceptions, and learning more *adaptive* attitudes" (p. 20; italics added). Notice the similar emphasis on "reality" and "adapting" by Freeman (1987): "The goal of therapy is to help patients uncover their dysfunctional and irrational thinking, *reality-test* their thinking and behavior, and build more *adaptive* and functional techniques for responding both inter- and intrapersonally" (pp. 19-20; italics added). The "reality" alluded to by both Beck and Freeman is never questioned.

To be sure, therapists are not expected to be leaders in social change. But, also to be sure, their activities may inadvertently generate a significant degree of conformity in their clientele and, furthermore, promote individualistic—as opposed to institutional—changes. Cognitive therapists, by virtue of their focal attention on thought processes, are particularly prone to foster both of the above. A few examples will illustrate this claim.

Ellis (1985; Ellis and Harper 1961), founder of rational emotive therapy, and one of cognitive therapy's pioneers, has compiled a list of irrational thoughts said to interfere with healthy psychological functioning. Irrational idea number 9 deals with accepting reality (Ellis and Harper 1961, chap. 18). Basically, irrational idea number 9 contends that you should not feel terrible if things are not the way you would like them to be; if you do, you engage in irrational thinking. Ellis and Harper (1961) explain: "When people and events are the way you would like them not to be, there is actually relatively little pernicious effect they can have on you unless you *think* they can" (p. 163). The immediate implication is that if you change your *thinking* about people and events they will obviously stop annoying you. Once again, the implication here is modify your mind, not the material circumstances. Irrational thought No. 9 may be in fact renamed "prescription for conformity No. 1." In another source, Ellis (1982) details how one of his patients was not pleased with his working conditions and some of the demands placed on him by his employer. While there certainly might have been room for negotiation for improvement in working conditions, Ellis chose to guide his client to a quiet, peaceful, and "rational" acceptance and resignation in the workplace. These are but two examples of the numerous conformity-promoting messages implicit in Ellis's rational emotive therapy.

Other instances where cognitive therapy may inadvertently strengthen the status quo, even when environmental changes are required for immediate therapeutic purposes, come from the fields of school and child clinical psychology. Cognitive therapies for school-age children have become very popular in the last decade. An array of cognitive therapies has been suggested to treat learning as well as social and behavioral problems (Di Giuseppe 1981; Gholson and Rosenthal 1984; Kendall and Braswell 1984). The many virtues of these mechanisms can frequently be questioned because of their lack of emphasis on environmental changes required to suit the particular needs of the youngster. In the same way that governments prefer a "mind fix" over a "setting fix," many school administrators, teachers, and parents favor "mind" therapies that focus on the child and leave the adults, the classroom, and the social order of the school unaltered.

A final and recent example of the way cognitive therapy may serve the status quo has been furnished by Stoppard (1989). Her review of the literature on the cognitive-behavioral treatment of depressed women led to the conclusion that these theories fail to address the external factors conducive to that psychological state. Instead, there is a marked emphasis on internal deficits. This type of theorizing is likely to promote victim-blaming and to exculpate social norms and conditions that may in fact be pathogenic. Stoppard (1989) observed that

> because these therapies are based on deficit models of depression, the message likely to be given to clients is that they have become depressed because they are deficient in some way. Therapists risk falling into the trap of victim-blaming when they interpret the depressed person's negative cognitions as solely the product of distorted cognitive processes or dysfunctional attitudes, rather

than exploring the possibility that negative cognitions may reflect a negative reality. . . . Areas of presumed vulnerability are emphasized as targets for change, whereas the potential clinical importance of changing the person's situation receives little attention in therapy goals. (p. 46)

CONCLUSION

Though the preoccupation of cognitive psychology with individual thought processes lends itself to solving social problems by individualistic—thus conservative—means, this particular branch of psychology may play an important role in resisting indoctrination by guardians of the status quo. It is within the realm of cognitive psychology to develop techniques to help people discern whether the present social system is indeed "rational." Once cognitive psychologists start questioning the sacredness of the external world, their formula for solving human problems will likely incorporate sociopolitical elements and not only intellectual ones.

Chapter 10

ABNORMAL PSYCHOLOGY

The purpose of this chapter is to explore the moral and political tendencies of predominant models of abnormal psychology. Contained in each paradigm are powerful implications for social change or support for the status quo. These implications derive mostly from the effects attributed to societal factors in the etiology, emergence, and reproduction of problems usually referred to as "psychological." In most cases, the less concern with societal variables, the greater the likelihood that the political message will be conservative. Conversely, as the concern with societal variables increases, so does the likelihood that the political message will be progressive (e.g., Wineman 1984).

The field of abnormal psychology has had to endure a variety of severe criticisms for some time now. Yet these criticisms have failed to analyze abnormal behavior in a comprehensive socioeconomic, political, and ideological context. Undoubtedly, there have been serious attempts to place so called "abnormal behavior" in a social context, as the following review will document. But these formulations have been for the most part only social, as opposed to *sociopolitical*. Politics and economics have been largely excluded from the study of the behavior of most people affected with serious mental health problems. Although there are epidemiological studies to direct our attention to the rather important role played by economic factors in mental health (Catalano 1991; Elder and Caspi 1988; Grusky and Pollner 1981; Jahoda 1988; Mirowsky and Ross 1989), these have not entered the mainstream of psychopathology to the required degree. Politics, as the inquiry into the attainment of social power, its maintenance through ideological apparatuses, and its concomitant inequalities in wealth and resources, is a largely neglected issue in the study of abnormal psychology (for a rare exception, see Joffe and Albee 1981a, 1981b).

If one were to schematically depict the sociopolitical history of the field in the last forty years, one would notice a progression from an *asocial* approach, through an enhanced awareness of its *microsocial* elements, to an increased alertness to *macrosocial* variables. This portrayal may be somewhat more linear than what the data may suggest, but I believe it represents what has been happening in the field. As well, it provides a heuristic insight into the ideological trends in this area.

The main task of this chapter is to elucidate the direct or indirect ideological impacts of such approaches and to show how they tend to preserve society in its present form. The medical model, in either its organic or its psychodynamic version, captures the essence of the asocial stage, the political implications of which are markedly conservative. Theories with a salient interpersonal and transactional component, such as labeling and family therapy, are representative of the microsocial phase. Highly progressive *and* conservative interpretations can be derived from these models of abnormal behavior. An effort will be made to clarify their political repercussions. Community psychology, prevention, and the ecological approach are examples of the macrosocial paradigm. Inasmuch as these target the social moment of psychopathology and advocate social reform, they contain a strong progressive element. Unfortunately, at least for those interested in social change, they have not gone far enough in addressing the ideological and political context. Recommendations to rectify that situation will be advanced in our discussion of the *macrosociopolitical* paradigm, the paradigm that is most strongly advocated by feminist mental health practitioners.

None of these approaches has entirely superseded the rest. Rather, they coexist in a state of tension in which different approaches momentarily dominate the field. Currently, in terms of its derivatives for social change, the field is at a crossroads. On the conservative side, there is a growing "movement to 'remedicalize' psychiatry" (Reiser 1988, pp. 148-49) and abnormal psychology in general. Hence, there is a distinct possibility of a retreat into the original conservative apolitical stance. On the progressive side, there is an effort to enhance the understanding of macrosocial events and how they may impact on the mental health of the population. Should the former prevail, we would likely face a devolution into the era of the asocial.

ABNORMAL PSYCHOLOGY I: ASOCIAL

Albee (1981) has aptly conceptualized the asocial approach to the study of abnormal behavior as the *defect* model. The defect model, also known as "medical" (Braginsky and Braginsky 1976) or "mental medicine" (Foucault 1954/1987), analyzes "inappropriate" behavior in terms of an internal organic or psychological malfunction.

> Like organic medicine, mental medicine first tried to decipher the essence of illness in the coherent set of signs that indicate it. It constituted a *symptomatology* in which the constant, or merely frequent correlations between a particular type of illness and a particular morbid manifestation were picked out. (Foucault 1954/1987, p. 3)

Similarly, Braginsky and Braginsky (1976) explain that in the medical model

> aberrant behavior is seen as a symptom of an underlying illness. Like other medical symptoms, such as fever or vomiting, the behavior reflects some underlying disease process. . . . With respect to bizarre behavior, therefore, it is the task of the psychiatrist or psychologist to determine the cause (e.g. biochemical imbalances, weak ego boundaries), to diagnose the disorder (e.g. schizophrenia, manic-depressive, etc.), and to intervene with the appropriate treatment. (pp. 70-71)

In the medical view, then, whatever inability the person may suffer from is located *within* the individual. As a result, etiological reasoning and intervention strategies are predominantly directed at an identified isolated patient (e.g., D. Cohen 1990; Leifer 1990; Nelson, Potasznik, and Bennett 1985). Environmental factors are not entirely disregarded, but they are given only secondary priority and remain largely in the background. At best, these are variables to be thought of but not acted upon.

The defect model bifurcates into an organic branch and a psychological branch (e.g., Braginsky and Braginsky 1976; Foucault 1954/1987).

Its organic or biochemical form, mostly espoused by psychiatrists but also by many psychologists, contends that conduct deemed "irrational" is determined by biological, neural, or chemical abnormalities. It follows, then, that most mental diseases would ultimately be cured by biochemical methods. "In recent years, a multitude of psychopharmacological preparations have been advanced as *the* treatment, if not the cure, for a variety of mental diseases" (Braginsky and Braginsky 1976, p. 72).

The expression *Homo psychologicus* (Foucault 1954/1987, p. 74) represents the immense importance ascribed to the individual psyche in the psychological version of the defect model. As a supposedly autonomous entity, the person carries within him or herself the causes of his or her own malady, and is therefore to be modified and returned to the community as a well-adjusted citizen. Unprecedented impetus for this treatment modality was furnished by psychoanalysis. An entire language was created to account for the operations and malfunctions of the psyche. "According to this approach, mental illness is viewed in terms of a faulty mental apparatus caused not by biochemicals but by early life experiences, in particular, traumatic ones" (Braginsky and Braginsky 1976, p. 72). As Braginsky and Braginsky (1976) asserted, "Although seemingly disparate, both psychodynamic and biochemical approaches share the assumption that abnormal behaviors are symptoms of a mental illness which exists somewhere within the structure of the mind" (p. 73). As such, both deemphasize the role played by "out of the skin" elements in the etiology of any maladjustment.

Although the medical-defect model is still very influential, its dominance has been undermined by a variety of writings pointing to its major shortcomings. As a matter of fact, in the last three decades the field of abnormal psychology has witnessed the emergence and gradual consolidation of a body of literature characterized by a disillusionment with the classical medical model (e.g., Chesler 1989; D. Cohen 1990; Foucault 1961/1965, 1985; Ingleby 1981b, 1981d; Kovel 1981a, 1981b; Laing 1967, 1972, 1980, 1985; Magaro et al. 1978; McNamee and Gergen 1992; Sarbin and Mancuso 1980; Ussher and Nicolson 1992). Though varied in their specific orientation, these critiques converge in their view that the medical approach studies mental illness as a separate entity, as something going on within the person that needs to be repaired, in much disregard for environmental factors. Moreover, they claim that it fails to realize the connection between mental conditions and the historical, political, economic, and sociocultural contexts in which these occur. Consequently, the individual is too frequently dissociated from the wider systems of society that shape her or his behavior extensively, thus creating an ahistorical and asocial image of individuals.

The political extensions of this asocial abnormal psychology are not difficult to discern. By dichotomizing individuals as sick or healthy, the defect paradigm helped to promote the notion that maladapted persons are the sole product of a less able organism and/or a genetic handicap. In the first decades of the century, this notion was very popular not only in mental health circles but among policy makers as well (e.g., Hofstadter 1955; Rose, Lewontin, and Kamin 1984). Congruent with the theories of social Darwinism and eugenics, the organic perspective of psychopathology facilitated the formulation of restrictive and discriminatory immigration policies in the United States (Kamin 1974; Thielman 1985).

Perhaps one of the most potentially conservative repercussions of the medical model has been its utilization by power elites in developing a sophisticated stratagem according to which systemic contradictions are either denied or presented as personal problems (e.g., Gross 1980; W. Ryan 1971). Some examples are in order: "Urban unrest is attributed to the lack of impulse control among young men raised in households without strong father figures" (Sampson 1983, p. 123). Carothers, a former official of the World Health Organization, commented: "The African makes very little use of his [sic] frontal lobes. All the particularities of African psychiatry can be put down to frontal laziness" (in Nahem 1981, p. 151).

When human suffering is predominantly interpreted as the result of a deficient organism, a conforming message emerges quite clearly. From this perspective, poor nutrition, detrimental living conditions, unemployment, and poverty in general are "determined" by the inability of those people to help themselves (Addams 1902; W. Ryan 1971, 1981). "To blame the problems of those who are most severely affected by destructive conditions *primarily* on the deficits of 'character disorder' or 'pathology' of individuals is a classic case of blaming the victim" (Wineman 1984, pp. 44-45). Among the devastating effects of this person-blame theorizing is the acceptance of its premises by the victims themselves. Pervasive social injustice is distorted into cases of biological or psychological inferiority. This is a distortion that not only its precursors, but their victims as well, grew to accept.

Because the poor within the Western nations as well as the colonial peoples of the world were seen as naturally inferior, there was ample ideological justification for exploitation of industrial workers, including children and women, for colonialism, and for racist policies leading to genocide. . . . Although occasional voices of protest were heard, it is clear that women and the colonized, the lower class, and the rest largely accepted the view that they were, indeed, inferior. (Albee 1986, p. 895)

Bulhan (1985) provides ample documentation regarding the internalization of oppression experienced by colonized people—what Bartky (1990) has called the "internalization of intimations of inferiority" (p. 22). Bulhan eloquently exposed the role of psychology and psychiatry in solidifying the self-deprecating assessments of people living under conditions of domination. Many women have also assimilated self-blaming attitudes generated by patriarchal views of women as inferior. Baker Miller (1986) claimed that "tragic confusion arises because subordinates absorb a large part of the untruths created by the dominants; there are a great many blacks who feel inferior to whites, and women who still believe they are less important than men" (p. 11). Chesler (1989), writing on women's compliance, asserted that "many female patients view themselves as 'sick' or 'bad' and commit themselves, quite voluntarily, to asylums or to private psychiatrists" (p. 106).

The last conservative implication of the defect-medical-asocial model is its noticeable apathy, to say the least, toward preventive action. Such attitude, voiced not very long ago by Lamb and Zusman (1979), is highly symptomatic of the resurgence of the asocial model in abnormal psychology. Lamb and Zusman's attack on preventive programs translates into fewer efforts at understanding social factors affecting the mental health of the population, thereby averting challenges to social structures and the status quo. While Lamb and Zusman's views have been refuted on numerous accounts (Albee 1986; Nelson, Potasznik, and Bennet 1985), they have managed to influence the policies of at least one province in Canada: In the 1980s, British Columbia adopted their propositions in its mental health planning report (see Nelson, Potasznik, and Bennet 1985).

The fact that the asocial paradigm is gaining momentum, in spite of mounting evidence linking social factors and mental illness (e.g., Albee, Bond, and Cook Monsey 1992; Gesten and Jason 1987; Kessler, Price, and Wortman 1985; Mirowsky and Ross 1989), speaks in favor of the hypothesis that the mental health agenda may be heavily prescribed by the ideological atmosphere of the times (Levine and Levine 1970; Wineman 1984). As the Levines have persuasively demonstrated in their historical analysis, individualistic modes of therapy tend to thrive during conservative times (Levine and Levine 1970).

Albee (1986, 1990) has cogently argued that, for as long as psychologists, psychiatrists, and most importantly social policy legislators continue to believe that mental illness, criminal tendencies, and low intelligence derive mainly from a deficient organism, early compensatory education programs and primary prevention programs in general will never be satisfactorily implemented. To the extent that branches of psychology have contributed to the creation and perpetuation of the asocial perspective, they have equally contributed to the maintenance of the societal status quo.

ABNORMAL PSYCHOLOGY II: MICROSOCIAL

The microsocial approach comprises a series of studies and writings whose primary concern is the identification of psychopathogenic and/or iatrogenic (harmful effects caused by the healer) interpersonal processes in the context of a specific setting, such as the psychiatric hospital or the family. Although they differ in many respects, not the least of which being their political preferences, Laing (1967; Laing and Esterson 1974) and Szasz (1963, 1965, 1974) in their early contributions converged in their attention to what may be termed "microsocially induced mental disorders" via a stigmatizing process engendered by either family members or mental health professionals. Further interest in the microsociogenesis of mental illness was generated by the research of Rosenhan (1973), which provided a severe "blow" to the psychiatric establishment, of Goffman (1981), which unveiled the deleterious side-effects of prolonged hospitalization, and of Scheff (1976), which advanced the labeling theory in mental illness.

Microsocial may be said to be a misnomer, for the relevance of these postulates are potentially broad. Yet even though these theses are potentially significant for society at large, their proponents have not, for the most part, transcended the constricted physical or psychological environments of the specific settings where their work was conducted. In contrast to the progress made by community psychology and the ecological approach in addressing larger social issues, the name *microsocial* represents adequately a position midway between the asocial and the macrosocial models.

Whereas the content of the microsocial approach is well known by now, its political implications have not received as much attention.

Witness, for instance, the vast confusion surrounding Szasz's social philosophy (Vatz and Weinberg 1983). Unlike the almost uniform conservative stance of the asocial model, the political reverberations of the microsocial model will be somewhat ambiguous and less readily visible.

The microsocial approaches to abnormal psychology to be discussed here are *labeling* and *family therapy*. The former has been selected primarily due to the vast confusion surrounding the political views of Szasz. Contrary to popular perceptions, and his major contributions to the psychiatric consumer/survivor movement notwithstanding, his beliefs embody highly conservative principles (cf. Sedgwick 1982; Vatz and Weinberg 1983). Family therapy is worth examining because of its somewhat deceiving political stance. Though allegedly progressive when compared to asocial models, its preoccupation with the family unit militates against a comprehensive analysis of structural forces in the genesis of abnormal behavior.

The Politics of Labeling

By now a well-known body of literature has been devoted to examining the iatrogenic aspects of psychological and psychiatric practices in mental health settings (for reviews, see P. Brown 1985; D. Cohen 1990; Dean, Kraft, and Pepper 1976; Grusky and Pollner 1981; Morgan 1983; Nelson 1983; Walsh 1988). A common theme in these writings has been the contribution and consolidation of mental illnesses through labeling.

Regardless of the particulars that may have brought an individual into contact with a mental health agency, the agency is said to contribute to the perpetuation and possible exacerbation of the behavior deemed abnormal through negative societal reactions and microsocial oppression. Labeling theorists agree that most individuals engage, at some point in their lives, in some kind of socially "unacceptable" conduct. Whereas the majority of incidents go unnoticed, the few that are observed and reacted upon adversely by significant others are likely to be cemented in the person's behavioral repertoire. If these acts are "responded to and regarded as instances of mental illness, a self fulfilling process is initiated that culminates with the individual capitulating to pressures and rewards to accept the role of a mentally ill individual" (Grusky and Pollner 1981, p. 41). Or, as Scheff (1976) noted, when labeling occurs and the person who breaks the rule is stigmatized as deviant, "the rule breaking which would otherwise have been terminated, compensated for, or channeled may be stabilized; thus, the offender, through the agency of labeling, is launched into a career of 'chronic mental illness'" (p. 213).

Behavior deemed intolerable by relatives, teachers, co-workers, employers, friends, is drawn to the attention of clinical psychologists, psychiatrists, and the like. When diagnosis by the mental health professional results in a classificatory statement, apparent "scientific" justification is furnished to those who sought professional help in the first place. At this stage the wheels of the labeling process have been put into motion on a devastating journey that may result in transformation of transitory behaviors into permanent destructive patterns. This argument, supported by research conducted in naturalistic mental health settings (e.g., Goffman 1981; Rosenhan 1973), furnishes evidence for the "deleterious social consequences of labeling persons as mentally ill" (Nevid and Morrison 1980, p. 72). In the specific case of psychiatric hospitals, labeling is conducive, inter alia, to stigmatization, lack of independence, degradation, and humiliation (e.g., Grusky and Pollner 1981).

Two sharply contrasting political uses have been made of labeling theory and research. Left-wing interpretations indict the mental health establishment as a sophisticated means of social control. Right-wing interpretations indict the same on charges of furnishing an "excuse" for deviant individuals. According to the latter the mental health system is too liberal—it helps criminals go unpunished by classifying them as mentally ill. Both interpretations will be briefly explored.

Labeling is intimately related to social control. The proliferation of the term *disease* and the medicalization of social deviance for purposes of social control are widely documented phenomena in our culture (e.g., Conrad 1981; Glenn and Kunnes 1973; Johnstone 1989; Pearson 1975; Scheff 1976). The notion of mental illness has been strategically utilized as a nonjudicial mode of treating social deviants, political dissidents, and nonconformists not only in what used to be the communist bloc (Fireside 1979; Medvedev and Medvedev 1971) but in North America as well (Bayer 1981; Foucault 1985; Halleck 1971; Nahem 1981; Schacht 1985; Spiers 1973).

Moreover, left-wing readings contend that labeling theory has demonstrated quite convincingly that mental illnesses are the product not only of intrapsychic mechanisms but also of interpersonal transactions based on inequalities of power. Expectations placed on helpless individuals by mental health professionals, relatives, friends, and society at large help determine the behavior of the former. In exposing these transactions, labeling theory has been instrumental in undermining the hegemony exercised by the medical model and its concomitant conservatism. Simply put, "The community response is critical in shaping and organizing the nature and extent of what will come to be seen as pathology" (Grusky and Pollner 1981, p. 40).

The broad political repercussions of labeling as a means of social control have been succinctly articulated by Scheff (1976), who claimed that "to the extent that medical [and psychiatric] science lends its name to the labeling of nonconformity as mental illness, it is giving legitimacy to the social status quo" (p. 215). Or as Dean (1976) observed: "When used to support the status quo, labeling is one mechanism of *social control*—a device for restoring or maintaining the social order" (p. 193).

Conservative psychiatrists, such as Szasz (1963, 1965, 1974, 1984) and Wood (1986), oppose the use of labels because they (a) are supposedly "myths" concocted by professionals, and (b) provide an excuse for people who engage in deviant behavior or "lack moral fiber." In advancing the former proposition, these psychiatrists have at least theoretically and potentially deprived of services individuals requiring help. This is highly ironic in the case of Szasz, given his portrayal as a defender of the human rights of psychiatric survivors. While his contributions to the cause of psychiatric patients who have been wrongly labeled and hospitalized is undeniable, his stance on personal culpability contains potentially regressive elements. The risks involved in the myth argument have been cogently expressed by Coulter (1979):

> That there are economic, political, juridical, temporal and ideological pressures to which some clinicians succumb is a well-documented and socially important fact; but to conclude from a documentation of abuses to the non-discriminability of mental illness or to its 'non-existence' is to indulge in a distracting and potentially harmful metaphysics. (p. 149)

Yet, in spite of counterarguments such as Coulter's, the myth position keeps strengthening (Wood 1986). Perhaps the most conservative derivation of this notion is that if mental illness is basically a myth, then crimes or other socially deviant acts are never committed because of a mental illness. By promoting that postulate, Szasz, who has been erroneously regarded as a progressive and even a radical, has been acting as a protector of the status quo; for in avoiding the issue of mental illness he also eludes placing society on the stand for generating countless forms of human misery. By neglecting to admit that there are mental health problems not caused by biological abnormalities, Szasz does not entertain the possibility that society may lead certain people to develop psychological difficulties (cf. Chesler 1989, pp. 105-6). Vatz and Weinberg (1983) have already noted that indeed "a basic conservatism is central to Szasz's work" (p. 17). Consider, for example, his desire to abolish the insanity plea:

> Should people also be free to be a danger to others? This problem disappears once we recognize that criminals cannot be divided into two categories—that is, persons who break the law because they choose to and persons who break it because their "mental illness" compels them to do so. All criminal behavior should be controlled by means of the criminal law. (Szasz 1984, p. 31)

Szasz completely avoids the question of intention and possible environmental precipitating factors. Matza is quite right in asserting that according to Szasz, "everyone who has done something wrong should go to prison. . . . He thinks that the whole idea of mental illness isn't helpful at all and that we shouldn't get into the question of intent or the question of insanity" (in Pearson 1975, p. 43).

Much like Szasz, Wood (1986) perceives deviant behavior not as madness but rather as "badness":

> The view is taken here that such people are bad rather than mad, and should be treated as such, being far better off in prison than in a hospital if they have broken the law. . . . The deficiency in sociopathy is a moral deficiency. The individual exhibits no conscience, cannot hear, or chooses to ignore, its dictates. He chooses to be bad in exactly the same way as others choose consistently to be good. He represents the inferior end of the good-bad continuum. (p. 41)

Both Szasz and Wood oversimplify an intricate issue in terms of a hardly defensible dichotomy between good people and bad people. By vehemently espousing the politico-legal postulates of individual responsibility and individualistic solutions, they overlook the possibility that some individuals might engage in criminal behavior due to emotional instability, however caused, and/or due to societal *precipitating* factors, however distant and complex. As psychiatrist Marmor recently pointed out, it must be remembered that some criminal patterns "are due not to individual psychopathology per se, but to basic institutional factors that makes such behavior almost inevitable under certain circumstances. . . . Our society is so structured that many people are driven to destroy, impair or threaten the interests of other people" (Marmor 1988, pp. 489-90). Societal explanations make no difference for Szasz or Wood. Questions about society are not raised. In Szasz's opinion, one has "the obligation to take responsibility for the choices one has made without psychiatric or other forms of exculpation" (Vatz and Weinberg 1983, p. 17).

It would seem, then, that theorists concerned with the politics of diagnosis in the mental health setting have drawn significant attention to social determinants of abnormal behavior. In the case of self-fulfilling prophecy through labeling or in the case of discrediting nonconformists via psychiatric diagnosis, they have dislodged the field from the medical model, which claimed the psychopathologist was a neutral humanitarian scientist. These putative reforming trends are, however, attenuated by those who utilize labeling to endorse a highly conservative and individualistic social philosophy—always holding people fully responsible for any nonphysically coerced actions, in total disregard for psychological problems.

The Politics of Family Therapy

Since the late fifties, family processes have been identified as a source of major psychological disorders such as schizophrenia. Through elaborate interactions among family members, one person is subjected to a particular kind of treatment that may be referred to as "psychological oppression." As we proceed, we shall note that this insight was historically highly relevant in the evolution of the family therapy movement, a trend whose often contradictory political implications need to be spelled out.

Research conducted in the fifties and sixties by Bateson and colleagues (1956), Laing and Esterson (1974), and Bowen (1978) facilitated a clearer view of the function of the family in the course of schizophrenia. In their seminal article "Toward a Theory of Schizophrenia," Bateson and his associates (1956) proposed the double-bind theory. According to this theory, contradictory instructions or messages of love and rejection are given to a family member by the same person, without giving to the former an opportunity to comment on the perceived inconsistencies. The double bind is defined as a "situation in which no matter what a person does, he [sic] 'can't win.' It is hypothesized that a person caught in the double bind may develop schizophrenic symptoms" (Bateson et al. 1956, p. 251).

Two years after the publication of Bateson's research, Laing and Esterson (1974) launched a study of families of schizophrenics in England. Their conclusions were similar to Bateson's. Both groups of researchers concurred that the incapacity to comment on the double bind, and the necessity to invalidate one's own feelings in order to survive, may be conducive to schizophrenic patterns.

In 1960 Bowen reported his experiences and conclusions from a study in which schizophrenics, their parents, and normal siblings lived together in a psychiatric ward. Bowen asserted that schizophrenic psychosis is "a symptom manifestation of an active process that involves the entire family" (Bowen 1978, p. 45). Most recent investigations concerning the family dynamics implicated in schizophrenia, such as research on expressed emotion and communication deviance (Goldstein 1990), continue this tradition.

The findings of these pioneer investigations lent support to the development and eventual establishment of family therapy. Founded primarily on the principles of general systems theory, originally postulated by Bertalanffy (1968), family therapy became an essential tool in analyzing and modifying family dynamics. The notion of a system as a "complex of interacting elements" (Bertalanffy 1968, p. 55) was readily applicable to the family situation. The introduction of general systems theory into the field of abnormal psychology represented a shift from mechanistic, linear cause-and-effect reasoning to a more holistic, interactive, and circular mode of thinking (Goldenberg and Goldenberg 1985; Hoffman 1981; Karpel and Strauss 1983; Levant 1984; Tomm 1980). In addition, the adoption of a systemic frame of reference cultivated the aspiration to not only study the individual in the context of the family, but also to investigate the family in the larger context of society. In Busfield's words, "We cannot hope to understand what goes on inside families if we study them in isolation from the wider society. Without such a setting much of the meaning and significance of what happens in the family is lost" (Busfield 1974, p. 158). That very expectation, which contained the progressive seed of family therapy, remains unfulfilled (Jacoby 1975; Mannino and Shore 1984; McCannell 1986; Poster 1978; Wineman 1984).

What, then, has been the political legacy of the "discovery" of family-induced psychopathology and family therapy? I would respond that, following an initial progressive stage, family therapy suffered a severe atrophy that resulted in political stagnation. Consequently, much of what family therapy is all about today is an expanded, updated version of the traditional medical model. "Spurred by research into the dynamics of families with psychotic children, family therapy now justifies itself by calling the *family* the 'sick' unit" (Glenn and Kunnes 1973, p. 109).

The political legacy of family therapy may also be described as an unfulfilled promise. Given the strong influence exerted by general systems theory, a theory with a very broad scope, it would have been reasonable to predict that family therapy would not delimit its mandate to intrafamilial vicissitudes (Waldegrave 1990). Nevertheless, by and large, this is exactly what happened.

Laing's writings (Laing 1969; Laing and Esterson 1974), as well as the others reviewed above, contributed to the momentum necessary for a paradigm shift in abnormal psychology. Laing ardently denounced the medical model whereby people examined "heads, blood, urine, or . . . some pathology exclusively 'in' the 'psyche'" (Laing 1969, p. 7). His conceptualization of psychopathology as an interpersonal, rather than intrapersonal, phenomenon is clearly reflected in *Sanity, Madness, and the Family*: "We are concerned with persons, the relationship between persons, and the characteristics of the family as a system composed of a multiplicity of persons" (Laing and Esterson 1974, p. 19). Briefly stated, "Laing *has* been successful in his project of removing the 'disease' from a person to his [sic] family nexus" (Mitchell 1974, p. 256). In that sense, Laing, and for that matter all the recruits who have been joining the family therapy movement for the last three decades, has demonstrated a progressive attitude in moving abnormal psychology away from the asocial model. Away from the asocial model? Yes. How much? Not enough.

A minimalist reading of systems theory has led the field to perceive the family as the ultimate system to be concerned with, and to pay only lip service to wider societal systems. In a very candid disclosure, Hoffman (1992), herself a pioneer of systems-family therapy, wrote: "Twenty years ago, having discovered the family field, I engaged in a project to disappear the individual. Actually, I only replaced the individual unit with the family unit" (p. 10). Indeed, systems-family therapy has been operating under the working assumption that intervention is with *all* the family, and *nothing but* the family (e.g., Mannino and Shore 1984; Pearson 1974). Pearson (1974) observed that family therapy "rips *family structure* out of wider *social structure* and proceeds to lay the fault at the door of the family itself, labeling it a 'sick' family" (p. 147). Mannino and Shore (1984) have claimed that

> family therapists tend to concentrate their efforts entirely on the "family," to the neglect of . . . the environmental context of the

family's activities. . . . Thus, it appears that we may have moved (not in a sense of growth) from the boundaries of the individual personality structure unrelated to the environment, to the boundaries of the family unrelated to the environment. (pp. 76-77)

The transition effected by family therapists from an individualistic model to a systemic one has been rather myopic. As James and McIntyre (1983) pointed out, "Despite family therapy's claim to a broader perspective, it is a perspective which is itself limited by its failure to take account of powerful and pervasive social forces" (p. 123). A similar lament was voiced by Vetere (1992), who derogated the "narrow focus on the family which does not take account of wider social and cultural influences on family life" (p. 131). A considerable risk is run when the family is isolated from the nexus of macrosocial systems and is accused for the psychological suffering of the individual. This erroneous selective attribution portrays the family as the main generator of certain kinds of dysfunctions and omits the fact that the family is very much a product of social forces. Family therapy's analysis is reductionistic in that "society is shuffled out . . . a social constellation is banalized to an immediate human network. It is forgotten that the relationship between 'you and me' or 'you and the family' is not exhausted in the immediate: all of society seeps in" (Jacoby 1975, p. 136). By depicting the family as a central perpetrator in the infliction of psychological distress, attention is deflected from macrosocial conflicts that may actively shape and perpetuate the mental health of the population as well as that of the individual and his or her family (Hare-Mustin 1991; Vetere 1992).

Mediators should not be confused with origins. And given the sociohistorically conditioned characteristics of the family in its present form, it is more likely that the family would be a precipitating, rather than a causal, factor (James and McIntyre 1983; Mitchell 1974; Poster 1978; Zaretsky 1986).

Evidently the mediations are crucial, and the family is one of them. But they are mediations, not origins; the family does not exist in a no-man's-land [sic]. It is snarled in a historical dynamic; it has changed in the past, and it is changing now. It is as much victim as victimizer. (Jacoby 1975, p. 139)

It might be argued that family therapy protects the societal status quo, not only by neglecting to reflect upon its negative effects on the family, but also by directly bolstering the patriarchal nuclear family. Both Hare-Mustin (1991) and Vetere (1992) have shown how traditional marital and family therapy have contributed, and to a large extent continue to contribute, to the reproduction of power imbalances in the home in favor of men.

To recapitulate, research conducted by family theorists supported the assumption that psychopathogenic processes occurring in the family setting were conducive to psychopathology. The establishment of a strong family therapy movement followed. Whereas significant progress has been made in reconceptualizing abnormal behavior in more interpersonal terms, the promise to look for systemic causes has been limited to intrafamilial dynamics. Thus, the epistemological shift has been more quantitative than qualitative. Family therapists have advanced from a small systemic part (i.e., the individual) to a slightly bigger systemic part (i.e., the family).

The recent penetration of social constructionist views into the field of family therapy offers the possibility of questioning these unsatisfactory working presuppositions (Andersen 1992; Anderson and Goolishian 1992; Hare-Mustin 1991; Hare-Mustin and Marecek 1988; Hoffman 1992). Whether these critiques will move beyond negative appraisals of family therapy's epistemological foundations to propose political actions more in line with an ethics of care, democracy, and social justice remains to be seen.

As we have witnessed, the political dimensions of microsocial approaches to abnormal psychology are numerous. Through an exposition of human transactions in a microsocial context, an insight into the many facets of power and how it affects behavior was attained. It may be that changes ought to be made in social practices and in the structure of social power to prevent abnormal behavior. On the conservative side, some authors have used labeling theory to denounce the mental health system as too liberal. In the case of family therapy, the promise to adopt a systemic, thereby comprehensive and social, view of mental illness was not delivered. Systemic family therapy has focused too much on the family, and too little on society.

ABNORMAL PSYCHOLOGY III: MACROSOCIAL

We have witnessed the progression from individualistic to microsocial conceptualizations of abnormal psychology. Our third paradigm, the macrosocial, represents a much broader perception of the role played by society in contributing to mental health or illness. This position, furthered through community psychology (e.g., Heller and Monahan 1977; Heller et al. 1984; Levine and Perkins 1987; Rappaport 1977) and the ecological approach (O'Conner and Lubin 1984), has gathered impetus in the last twenty years. Rather than rejecting the two paradigms previously presented, community psychology endeavors to integrate their accomplishments with the firmly held view that psychological disorders can be neither understood nor treated in isolation from social factors.

I will argue that while "on paper" community psychology endorses an understanding of human behavior that incorporates personal, communal, and global forces, such as the economy and politics, in practice it has fallen short of properly addressing a key constituent in the sociogenesis of psychopathology: the unequal distribution of power in society and the concomitant fragmentation of society into opposed interest groups. That is to say, in principle community psychology promotes the politicization of abnormal behavior, a much needed emphasis. However, when community psychologists become involved in the political arena, the kind of politics advocated by them is not radical (Mulvey 1988). Their politics does not threaten the status quo.

Declarative statements about the purposes of community psychology include explicit mention of dissatisfaction with the status quo and a clear desire to alter it.

> Community psychology is interested in social change, particularly in those systems of society where psychologists are active participants. Change in society involves relationships among its component parts, encompassing those of individuals to social systems such as schools, hospitals, and courts, as well as to other individuals. *Change toward a maximally equitable distribution of psychological as well as material resources is sought.* (Rappaport 1977, p. 3; italics added)

To eliminate any doubts about the scope of its endeavor, Rappaport (1977) asserted that "community psychology is by its very nature dedicated to a challenge of the status quo" (p. 29). These words by Rappaport, author of the influential book *Community Psychology* (1977), clearly illustrate the *intent* to change societal structures. This aspiration emanates from the realization that "an ecological perspective, focusing on the match or 'fit' between persons and environments, rather than on 'fixing up' those who are seen as inferior . . . is the most sensible" (Rappaport 1977, p. 3).

Political activity, then, is an inherent part of this paradigm, simply because environments and social structures cannot otherwise be transformed to suit the needs of individuals and pursue the prescribed "fit." Community psychologists have, at least in principle, "overstepped the limits of the available psychological paradigms and are now interested in social change, social justice, politics, economics and social systems as well as individuals" (Rappaport 1977, p. 19). Here was, finally, a paradigm to address the human experience in a global and integrative, as opposed to fragmentary, fashion.

As envisioned by Rappaport in 1977, community psychology was indeed very promising. However, as evaluated by Sarason in 1984 (Sarason 1984a), the field was, at best, making its very first steps in the political scenario; at worst, it was still too attached to the comforts of the academic world to venture into the uncertainties of the political arena. Sarason's (1984a) observations gain further support from the lack of both political awareness and activity, as recently documented in the literature on ecological interventions (Jason and Glenwick 1984; O'Conner and Lubin 1984) as well as social and community interventions (Gesten and Jason 1987). Gesten and Jason (1987) conclude their review by stating that *"psychologists in the past have largely avoided participation in public policy matters. The concerns of the future may render such involvement on the part of a significant subgroup far more essential"* (p. 451).

There is, then, a noticeable discrepancy between the theory and the practice of community psychology. Whereas in principle it is conceptually designed to address the sociopolitical components inherent in mental health issues, in effect it has not been politically conscious in dealing with them (Prilleltensky 1993). This is in part due to the fact that community psychologists have taken into account the influence of systemic variables such as social classes and institutions, but by and large their analyses have stopped there. These are academic considerations that are not accompanied by a serious challenge of these very structures. *Coping*, more than *changing*, typifies community interventions. Though few, attempts at the latter are beginning to emerge. Examples of empowerment projects testify to that effect (see chapter 15). If meaningful social action is to occur, an adjustment in community psychology's priorities and vision of the political world is called for. These are presented in the next paradigm, as well as in chapter 15, where a more comprehensive analysis of the key concept of community psychology, namely, empowerment, will be more fully discussed.

ABNORMAL PSYCHOLOGY IV: MACROSOCIOPOLITICAL

The macrosociopolitical paradigm is intended not to replace the macrosocial perspective endorsed by community psychology, but rather to complete its task. This model commences where community psychology stops: in the failure to enhance critical political awareness. The following is primarily an outline for a paradigm that, though already advocated by some community and feminist psychologists (e.g., Albee 1970, 1981, 1986; Kitzinger 1991b; Mulvey 1988; Rappaport 1977, 1981, 1990; Sarason 1984a; Unger and Crawford 1992), still needs considerable strengthening.

Proposed here is a framework inspired by the most progressive branches of applied psychology, such as community and feminist psychology, the psychiatric survivors' movement, and radical politics. This combination provides the scientific and research background necessary for understanding the impact of societal structures on human experiences of oppression, and the insight required not only for scrutinizing the social system, but also for modifying it. Radical politics is differentiated from conventional politics in that it may question the effectiveness of the current political process itself for bringing about meaningful reforms, not the least of which is equality for all sectors of the population (W. Ryan 1981). This is due simply to the fact that governments are largely utilized to protect interests entrenched in the preservation of the present system. When the conventional political process, as well as most major endeavors affecting public life, are manipulated by the rich and powerful (Domhoff 1986; Gross 1980; Reich and Edwards 1986; M. Schwartz 1987), it is not at all certain that the interests of underrepresented constituencies such as the mentally ill or the poor will be meaningfully served (Wineman 1984). Radical politics seeks to empower the underprivileged to affirm their rights and interests.

Power is a key element in the preservation and change of the existing social order. Consequently, community psychologists ought to be more appreciative of its role and realize that such need may be best satisfied by the proposed unification between progressive psychologies, people who have been abused by the mental health system, and radical politics. These enterprises are highly compatible, in that all pursue social changes to better serve the needs of particularly vulnerable populations. It is hoped that this model may promote an infusion of activism that might revitalize important community psychology practices that have been dormant or unduly relegated to second place (Chavis and Wolff 1993).

The branch of psychology that has made political education an ineradicable part of its agenda is feminist psychology. Informed by the values and orientation of the women's movement, feminist psychology may very well be the current prototype for modeling the needed fusion of scientific and political purposes for the promotion of human welfare. I shall describe below some of the key values and objectives of the women's movement that inspire much of the work of feminist psychologists. This brief account should suffice to show how the work of feminists in psychology has the potential to move the macrosociopolitical model forward. Subsequently I will offer examples of organized resistance to psychiatric oppression, as practiced by the consumer/survivor's movement.

The Politics of Feminist Psychology

About three decades ago, against a background of patriarchal domination, women strongly united to assert their rights, demand equality, and expect better lives for themselves (Bartky 1990; Shreve 1989; M. Young 1991). These aspirations, which at first may have served primarily the interests of white and middle-class women only (Collins 1991; Harding 1991; Kanuha 1990), have been critically scrutinized to insure that the needs of *all* women are reflected in the feminist agenda. The inclusive program depicted in current feminist writings is testimony to the open and vigorous political process that has been undertaken by this movement.

Out of the realization that women of all social classes, abilities, races, and sexual orientations endured varying degrees of oppression, the feminist movement proceeded to denounce inequality wherever it existed. As a social movement, it espoused the dual objective of denouncing social injustice and announcing new and liberatory practices. Injustices perpetrated against women in the home, at work, at school, in the media, in the consulting room, were named and deplored. The role of expanding the realm of opportunities for women in every aspect of their lives was fulfilled by multiple means, from the creation of consciousness-raising groups to political action (Shreve 1989). Unger and Crawford (1992) state that the principal insight developed in consciousness-raising groups

> was that the problems experienced by women were social rather than individual in origin. One of the first things that women discovered in these groups was that the personal was political. They

learned that their individual experiences of shame, dependency, and anger were felt by others and that these experiences rested on shared conditions characterized by issues of dominance and power. (p. 603)

With the adoption of the aphorism *the personal is political*, the women's movement popularized and brought to focus the much-needed analytical connection between private and public lives. To overcome their historical cultural confinement, women pursue, among other things, what Baker Miller (1986, pp. 24-25) calls physical, sexual, and emotional frankness, opportunities for personal creativity and human development, the termination of objectification, and private and public equality.

Harding (1991) has discussed the influence of feminism in science, whereby the former compels the latter to face the effect of power relations in the creation and reproduction of scientific knowledge. Feminism joined with other critiques of science in emphasizing the socially situated nature of knowledge and its human creators. Poignant questions such as whose interests are being served by scientific discourse X or Y were forcefully advanced by feminist critics of positivism (Harding 1991; D. E. Smith 1990). Feminism launched a powerful offensive against all androcentric conceptions of the world. It was not too long before feminist scrutiny visited the psychological sciences.

The feminist critique of the mental health field was explicitly articulated by Chesler in the first edition of *Women and Madness* in 1972, now in print with a new introduction (Chesler 1989). Chesler exposes the functional role played by the male-dominated mental health field in perpetuating the subordination of women. This landmark book is one of the first examples since the early seventies of a number of works criticizing androcentric psychological views. Another influential contribution has been Baker Miller's *Toward a New Psychology of Women* (1986), also now in its second edition. Much like Chesler's, her analysis of women's oppression utilizes direct and powerful language, practicing what has become known as "naming" the realities of gender inequality. Chapters with very explicit titles, such as "Domination and Subordination" and "Doing Good and Feeling Bad," get right to the heart of the matter. The pervasive discontent of politically conscious women with what mainstream psychology had to offer them resulted in a counterculture. Women in psychology organized to pursue a professional agenda that would be congruent with their political convictions. Sections of Women in Psychology in the American, British, and

Canadian Psychological Associations are one of the vehicles feminist psychologists utilize to address their concerns. While many women differ in their definitions of feminism (Harding 1991; Reinharz 1992; Unger and Crawford 1992), and feminist psychology is not a monolithic entity devoid of disagreements (Hollway 1991; Kitzinger 1991a), I believe it is informative to provide some of feminists' themes in psychology. A useful summary of them is provided by Sue Wilkinson in the first editorial of the journal *Feminism and Psychology*. Commencing with a clear statement of its political objective, Wilkinson (1991) writes:

> As feminists within psychology, we share major dissatisfactions with our discipline's failure to engage with the lives of the majority of women, and the distortion and damage often produced when it does engage. We are committed to changing this and to developing a psychology which properly represents women's concerns in all their diversity. However, more importantly, we are also committed to the deployment of such a psychology to address a range of social inequalities (including, for example, race and class, as well as gender) and to improve the conditions of women's lives: i.e. to feminism. We believe that in these twin purposes—the reconstruction of psychology and the impetus for social and political change—lies the radical potential of *Feminism and Psychology*. (p. 5)

Some of the issues pertaining to the feminist agenda in psychology include the exclusion of women's experiences from psychological theories, professional practices that are oblivious to gender issues or manifestly oppressive, the polarization of politics and science, and the marginalization of women within the discipline, to mention only a few (Wilkinson 1991). Fundamentally central to feminist discourse in psychology is the issue of power (Holland 1992; Kitzinger 1991a, 1991b; Lerman and Porter 1990b; Perkins 1992; Ussher and Nicolson 1992). In order for women to effect a more permanent and profound sense of control over their lives, Baker Miller (1986) argues, "they will have to acquire economic, political, and social power and authority" (p. 115). Attention to political concerns could not be more directly drawn than by naming the problem for what it is: power and powerlessness.

The current impact of feminism can be felt in many areas of psychology (see, for example, Unger and Crawford 1992). Three prominent ones are moral development, conceptions of the self, and psychotherapy. The field of moral development has been heavily influenced by the work of Gilligan (1982, 1990). She drew attention to the way in which dominant earlier accounts of moral development relied almost exclusively on the experiences of boys and men. Gilligan reformulated the theory of moral development to include the unique and different voice of girls and women in matters of ethics, care, and justice. While the details of her research are beyond the focus of this chapter, suffice it to say that her work demonstrates how some widely held psychological theories had been constructed on the basis of andro-centric norms of psychological development and health.

Another instance of psychological male-centered concepts is the notion of self. Baker Miller (1990) has shown how definitions of the healthy self are based on ideals of autonomy and separateness, which are congruent with patriarchal and capitalist interpretations of happi-ness and individualism. She contrasts these postulates of the ideal self with the alternate view of self-in-relation, a construct that reflects more accurately women's ways of being. These are only two pieces of evi-dence concerning the penetration of patriarchal values in psychology. Feminist books and journals contain much more.

The third area of psychology in which feminism is widely repre-sented is psychotherapy. The political ramifications of feminist ther-apy, congruent with the proposed sociopolitical model of abnormal psychology, can be easily distilled from a sample of writings on the topic. Lerman and Porter (1990a) posit the following principles derived from feminist theory:

> (1) that women's conflicts, poor self-esteem, and feelings of pow-erlessness are intimately related to the roles women hold in society; (2) that self-determination, autonomy, and equal status in society are essential ingredients in promoting women's mental health; (3) that the relationship between therapist and client should promote egalitarianism between the two and foster the client's self-deter-mination and autonomy; and (4) that the feminist therapist be com-mitted to social as well as individual change. (p. 5)

Similarly, Watson and Williams (1992) suggest three principles that

> have remained central to the growth and development of feminist practice. First, the commitment to equality within therapy, to an egalitarian relationship between client and therapist. . . . Secondly, the commitment to bringing society into therapy, to working with

women's experience of sexual inequality. . . . Thirdly . . . the commitment to power re-distribution within society: to political, economic and social equality between the sexes. (p. 215)

Chesler (1989) argues for the need for a feminist institute of mental health "with a political agenda" (p. xxvi). Even if the actual practice of feminist therapy cannot always enact the rather demanding social and moral principles espoused by its adherents, there is no doubt that its political pronouncements affirm the centrality of power issues in therapy much more than any mainstream approach.

The political intentions of feminists are also manifestly expressed in their research methods, as Reinharz (1992) has amply demonstrated. One of ten main themes identified by Reinharz in feminist methods in social research is the effort to create social change. She writes that "for many feminists, research is obligated to contribute to social change through consciousness-raising or specific policy recommendations" (Reinharz 1992, p. 251). Her extremely well-documented book offers a plethora of examples where this has been the case.

This leads me to the final point I wish to make concerning feminism in psychology: that it promotes the fusion of epistemic with nonepistemic values informed by a moral philosophy of self-determination, justice, caring, and equality. My survey of the psychological scene indicates that feminists' unabashed promotion of a politics of equality has no rival in the profession. This is why feminism fits very well into the sociopolitical model for abnormal psychology.

Probably the key question to be posed now is how big an impact feminism is having on mainstream conceptions of abnormal psychology. According to Fine and Gordon (1991), "the transformation of psychology by feminism has been modest" (p. 20). Furthermore, their research led them to conclude "[that] feminist scholarship has barely pierced mainstream journals; that the mainstream journals have persistently, over time, ignored issues of gender, race, social class, sexuality and disability; and that feminist psychology, itself, tends problematically to reproduce the individualism and conservatism of the larger discipline" (p. 20). This situation is not entirely surprising. As I have been trying to demonstrate throughout the preceding chapters, the alliance of psychology to the status quo is zealous. The challenge is to utilize the momentum gathered by feminist psychology to politicize the field of abnormal psychology. In my opinion, the feminist discourse on power is stronger, or perhaps more categorical, than the one articulated by community psychologists (cf. Mulvey 1988). The reason may have to do with the professionalization and institutionalization of community psychology and its close links with the health fields. Illness prevention and health promotion, two prominent fields within community psychology, tend not to be as politically controversial as the language of oppression, exploitation, and domination frequently invoked by feminists. Thus, even though both movements pursue human welfare in a context of political justice, community psychology may have found a comfortable niche that tends to neutralize its radical roots and impulses (Prilleltensky and Gonick 1993). As Mulvey (1988) has pointed out, the two fields have much in common, and a joint program of political activism only makes sense.

In addition to the feminist perspective, another voice that can and should enrich the macrosociopolitical approach is the voice of consumers and survivors of psychiatric services. As key stakeholders of the mental health system, their knowledge and politics must be taken into account.

The Politics of Psychiatric Consumers and Survivors

A comprehensive appreciation of the power dynamics involved in the demeaning treatment of persons experiencing severe emotional problems must take into account the voices of victims themselves. These citizens, who increasingly prefer to define themselves as psychiatric consumers/survivors (Capponi 1992; Walsh-Bowers and Nelson 1993), have come together to oppose the continuation of repressive psychiatric practices designed to serve the mental health system more than its clients. As Judi Chamberlin (1990) put it, "the movement of people who call themselves variously, ex-patients, psychiatric inmates, and psychiatric survivors is an attempt to give voice to individuals who have been assumed to be irrational—to be 'out of their minds'" (p. 323). This is a "political movement comprised of people who have experienced psychiatric treatment and hospitalizations" (Chamberlin 1990, p. 323). This group has three main objectives: (a) the repudiation of medical practices that dehumanize individuals with mental health difficulties, (b) advocacy of full citizenship rights for persons regarded as "mentally ill," and (c) the development of alternative support systems, such as self-help and mutual-aid organizations, for people experiencing serious mental health problems (Burstow and Weitz 1988; Chamberlin 1990; "Declaration of Principles" 1985; Shimrat 1992).

Chamberlin (1990), a pioneer of the movement, which started in the 1970s, provides a useful account of its history. Two key guiding principles were the exclusion of "nonpatients" from the newly formed network, and, as in the case of the feminist movement, consciousness raising. Concerning the former, it was found that when professionals were involved in the groups, the agenda quickly turned from one of liberation to one of reform. As for the second principle, increased awareness of the extrapersonal, societal foundations of their state of misery proved to be both therapeutic and politically effective.

The earliest groups were founded in Vancouver, Portland (Oregon), New York City, Boston, and San Francisco between 1970 and 1972, followed by the creation of the annual Conference on Human Rights and Psychiatric Oppression, first held in Detroit in 1973. A San Francisco-area newsletter, *Madness Network News*, began publishing in 1972 and soon became the printed organ of the movement, with circulation across all of North America.

Through the operation of drop-in centers, residences, and advocacy groups, the movement has enacted the ideals of self-help and empowerment. Although their successes are numerous, the survivor groups have experienced many setbacks. Among them, the ill effects of—however well-intentioned—professional intervention. Most recently, the National Association of Psychiatric Survivors, founded in 1985, "was formed specifically to counter the trend toward reformist 'consumerism', which developed as the psychiatric establishment began to fund ex-patient self-help" (Chamberlin 1990, p. 333). The association fights for the elimination of forced confinement and procedures such as electroshock, psychosurgery, forced drugging, and seclusion. In Ontario, Canada, a new organization, the Ontario Psychiatric Survivors' Alliance (OPSA), was recently formed. Their philosophy, goals, and objectives are very similar to the ones espoused by the National Alliance of Psychiatric Survivors in the United States (Shimrat 1992).

There is abundant evidence from academic researchers (Walsh-Bowers and Nelson 1993) as well as consumer sources (Capponi 1992) that most psychiatric survivors "are forced to cope with such socially constructed obstacles as substandard income, housing, clothing, and health, while many must struggle with the side effects of psychotropic medications and perhaps ECT" (Walsh-Bowers and Nelson 1993, p. 9). In addition to the human costs associated with these deplorable conditions, many psychiatric patients continue to endure dehumanizing forms of treatment that rob them of their dignity. From the survivors' perspective, Walsh-Bowers and Nelson (1993) argue, "mental health workers can embody the worst features of parentalism, namely, intrusive and invasive domination" (p. 14). Against this flagrant background, survivors united to reclaim their dignity.

The language utilized by the survivors' movement is not any less poignant than the speech employed by feminists in denouncing patriarchy. As an illustration, consider a few of the principles the Conference on Human Rights and Psychiatric Oppression adopted at its tenth annual meeting in Toronto in 1983. Principle 5 reads: "We oppose forced psychiatric procedures because they humiliate, debilitate, injure, incapacitate and kill people." Number 10 states: "We oppose the psychiatric system because it uses the trappings of medicine and science to mask the social-control function it serves." Principle 17 stipulates: "We oppose the medical model of 'mental illness' because it dupes the public into seeking or accepting 'voluntary' treatment by fostering the notion that fundamental human problems, whether personal or social, can be solved by psychiatric/medical means." Finally, the last two principles of the declaration read, respectively, "We demand individual liberty and social justice for everyone" and "We intend to make these words real and will not rest until we do" ("Declaration of Principles" 1985).

Professionals may wish to discredit the survivors' movement. This would not be surprising. In fact, there are indications of great reluctance on the part of mental health professionals to acknowledge the iatrogenic consequences of many of their learned habits and procedures (Breggin 1990; Cohen and McCubbin 1990; Morgan 1983; Penfold 1992; Walsh 1988). As in the case of feminism, resistance to the survivors' movement is to be expected (Burstow and Weitz 1988). Their voice, however, cannot be neglected by those wishing to understand mental health problems from a sociopolitical point of view. Speaking as consumers and victims, they offer perhaps the most important perspective needed to educate the public as to the potential dangers involved in endorsing a medical model devoid of sociopolitical consciousness. Their agony should serve as a reminder to all providers of psychological and psychiatric services that it is all too easy to abuse power when the client is labeled "mentally ill." Undoubtedly, there will be readers inclined to dismiss this indictment of psychiatric practices as based on abuses of power that are "aberrances" of an otherwise ethically acceptable enterprise. Instances of intentional perpetration of harm may indeed be few and far between, but the unreflective reproduction of established practices that are benevolently dehumanizing may be regarded as a more insidious moral lapse (cf. Johnstone 1989).

The main contribution of the survivors' movement to a model of abnormal psychology that wishes to place sociopolitical considerations at the center of its concerns is the forceful presentation of power issues. The radical politics advanced by this coalition of grassroots organizations is a worthy antidote to the academic complacency of community psychology. Chamberlin (1990) acknowledges that the survivors' movement has not yet had a powerful impact on the community of ex-psychiatric-consumers, much like how feminist and community psychology values do not yet resonate in mainstream psychology. The challenge of disseminating alternative worldviews lies ahead.

In order to further the advocated amalgamation of forces among community psychologists, feminist psychologists, and psychiatric survivors, a few directions are outlined below. They represent an effort to form linkages among these groups and establish new priorities in practices that either are already in existence, or that have been waiting to be articulated. In either case, I believe the suggestions made below are entirely congruent with the paradigm feminism, community psychology, and the survivors' movement have been promoting. Recommendations, as will be seen, are offered in the form "From . . . to . . ." to emphasize the shift in priorities from current practices to a more desirable state of affairs.

1. From Public Policy to Political Public. Currently, whenever community psychologists become involved in politics, it is mostly through the legislative process. This is a process whereby decisions are made by individuals who are too removed from the vicissitudes of mental and psychiatric patients, visible minorities, women, the poor. Public-policy makers are not necessarily in touch with these people's plight unless the latter loudly voice their concerns. This should be accomplished by politicizing the public (Freire 1971, 1975).

Individuals should be educated to present their cases in front of legislators, instead of having professionals do that for them (cf. Capponi 1992). Professionals are too often quite removed from the suffering of their clients. Rather than going up to the legislators to advocate for the people, community psychologists should hold hands with the people to help them organize to affirm their interests. There is ample opportunity for progressively minded psychologists to contribute to the survivors' or feminist movements, among many others grassroot groups.

W. Ryan (1981) has claimed that the main task in promoting the long-term well-being of the large and silent suffering masses is to assist them in understanding the basic inequality inherent in the system. It is highly unlikely that equality will be advanced by policy makers whose interests are maintained by inequality. Public policy may at present be the most important catalyst for change, but a political community may be even more important, in that it may set the tone for the policies to be legislated (cf. Prilleltensky and Gonick 1993; Wineman 1984).

2. *From Interdisciplinary to Interclass Thinking and Action.* The need to engage professionals from other disciplines in the solution of community problems (e.g., Bechtel 1984) is heard about far more often than the equally, if not more important, need to involve community members. This suggestion may entail a shift from more expert advice to more interclass dialogue. The professional helper, who usually belongs to the middle class, needs to be educated about the plight of community members, who in many cases belong to the lower class. This interclass communication may be more fruitful than interdisciplinary communication. This is not to devalue expert opinions but rather to convey a change in priorities and to suggest supplementary procedures.

3. *From a Single Issue to Systemic Political Thinking and Action.* While concentration of energies on a single issue, such as deinstitutionalization, is useful in that it helps gather momentum for much-needed changes or at least palliatives, it is also dangerous in that it promotes a very fragmentary view of systemic complexities. A few examples should suffice to illustrate this point. In a typical primary prevention example, "efforts to reduce the incidence and management of diarrhea in infants through parent education in simple health care practices were constrained by the fact that many families had limited access to uncontaminated water" (Halpern 1988, p. 257).

In the case of poverty, it is becoming increasingly obvious that it will be eradicated not by the occasional increase in jobs or the acquisition of a few more skills by the individual but by the elimination of a system that perpetuates inequality (W. Ryan 1981).

Large numbers of discharged ex-psychiatric-consumers are exploited by landlords, live in subhuman conditions, lack shelter, and have limited access to psychiatric services (Bassuk and Gerson 1985; Capponi 1985, 1992; Levine 1981). These are not unpreventable natural disasters; they are primarily the consequences of a tradition of solving social problems without seeing through the full sociopolitical ramifications. In reviewing the implementation of the 1963 American Community Mental Health Centers Act (PL 88-164), Levine (1981) concludes:

The problem of caring for mental patients is part of the larger problem of welfare in a capitalistic and individualistic society, and funds to implement programs for assistance to the elderly and the handicapped depend upon welfare economics and health care economics and politics. . . . Everything is connected to everything else, ideas to politics, politics to economics, economics to bureaucratic organizational dynamics. One cannot understand one without looking at all the others. (p. 77)

It should not be concluded that local changes are irrelevant or futile until all of society changes. What should be concluded is that local changes should be considered only initial steps in an effort to reform larger societal structures that interfere with the solution of the specific problem at hand.

4. *From Psychological to Environmental Prevention.* Because community psychology is an offspring of clinical psychology (Sarason 1984b), it may be only natural that many of its most successful preventive efforts be psychological. Witness the progress made in the areas of social support and competence building (Gesten and Jason 1987; Nelson, Potasznik, and Bennet 1985; Saulnier 1985). While the psychoeducational focus of prevention projects is vital, it may not be as essential as environmental prevention (Pransky 1991). Environment "in this context is interpreted in its broadest sense, and includes not only our physical surroundings, both natural and artificial, but also the social, cultural, regulatory and economic conditions and influences that impinge on our everyday lives" (Health and Welfare Canada 1988, pp. 4-5).

Recently, an important proposition has been eloquently argued in *Mental Health for Canadians: Striking a Balance* (Health and Welfare Canada 1988), which incisively pinpoints structural deficits conducive to psychological vulnerability in general, and mental illness in particular. Based on the assumption that "whatever makes it difficult for the individual, the group and the environment to interact effectively and justly (for example, poverty, prejudice or poor coordination of resources) is a threat or barrier to mental health" (Health and Welfare Canada 1988, p. 8), the document addresses the imperative needs to reduce social inequality and discriminatory social attitudes and to enhance social justice. Though somewhat lacking in specific recommendations, and only time will tell whether the government is seriously committed to changing these societal adversities, the document does a much better job than recent scholarly reviews (e.g., Kessler, Price, and Wortman 1985; Strauss 1979) in stating that the "distribution of power among individuals, groups and their environments is a crucial determinant of mental health" (Health and Welfare Canada 1988, p. 10).

As Halpern (1988) has recently observed, the factors a primary prevention program such as early intervention "can influence directly (parent child-rearing behavior, knowledge, and attitudes) are themselves strongly influenced by other factors much more difficult to alter in a discrete social program (e.g., economic insecurity, limited access to services, dilapidated housing)" (p. 253). Consequently, it is necessary to establish priorities and determine how much effort should be invested in remodeling each portion of the communal puzzle.

Attitudes, coping strategies, education, and interpersonal support are indeed unquestionably important parts of prevention projects. Yet efforts to reshape the psychological world of citizens may be wasted if the environmental world, as broadly defined above, is not reshaped first. The urgent obligation to recapture this foundational premise of community psychology was recently voiced at a symposium entitled "Understanding and Overcoming Oppression: The Political Sphere of Primary Prevention" (Prilleltensky 1993). The politicization of mental health is a notion that may be foreign to many psychologists, but it certainly should not be to community psychologists; for they are committed to promoting the best *fit* between individuals and environments.

5. From Scientific to Political Activities. By advocating that we move from scientific to political activities, I do not mean to detract from the scientific base of community psychology, but rather to convey my opinion that, at this juncture, political awareness may be restricted by an approach that is too scientific and academic.

"Politics is not wrong or bad. It is bad or wrong only if we blind ourselves to those inevitabilities" (Levine 1981, p. 9). According to Levine (1981), professional helpers are blind to the political context where their endeavors take place. Unfortunately, it would seem that this situation has been at least partially created by the unbalanced priority given to more "credible" enterprises such as science.

Levine (1981) has documented at length the political innocence of mental health workers in the United States for the most part of this century. His indictment is followed by this conclusion:

> The field of mental health by no means belongs exclusively to the professional mental health workers no matter how fervently we wish it. . . . It may be that it is our task as professionals, and as teachers of the next generation of professionals, to engage in consciousness raising so that political science, law, and economics

become as much parts of the mental health curriculum . . . as abnormal psychology or psychotherapy. (Levine 1981, p. 206)

As noted above, the feminist and survivors' movements provide the discourse and the leadership required to fuse analytical and moral philosophical passions. The victimization of women and psychiatric patients has made them painfully cognizant of the prominent role of power and politics in mental health. Science and health care do not exist in a political vacuum. Their coronation in the age of instrumental rationality obfuscated the simple fact that the production of science and the provision of care are always embedded in contexts of personal and social power and powerlessness. The ascendance of social constructionist and postmodernist views has stimulated the restoration of political language in discourses of knowledge and help (Kvale 1992; McNamee and Gergen 1992; Parker 1992). The ultimate point is not to privilege epistemology at the expense of moral philosophy, or vice versa, but to advance both for the promotion of human welfare and social justice. Hitherto, scientism has reigned in the field of abnormal psychology. A renewed appreciation for the place of politics should tip the scale in the direction of action for social change and justice.

CONCLUSION

The purpose of this chapter has been to review the political repercussions of different models of abnormal psychology. Four paradigms have been presented and discussed. Whereas the first three are widely practiced, the fourth, the macrosociopolitical, constitutes more a desideratum than an existing model. The fourth paradigm was outlined with the clear intent of activating dormant tenets of community psychology, one of the branches of psychology with the most potential to reshape the environment in order to make it more suitable for the promotion of well-being. Unless community psychology enacts a new set of priorities to vivify its seeds of political activism, it will likely regress to the stage where preoccupation with psychological dimensions only enables the social order to proceed unchallenged. Much can be learned from the feminist and psychiatric survivors' movements. It is high time for academic community psychologists to forge alliances with these groups in order to retrieve the radical sentiments espoused by the founders of the discipline.

Countless obstacles will be encountered by those willing to invigorate the field of abnormal psychology by entering the turbulent political scene of community life. Psychologists prepared to give up some of the comfort afforded by the scientist-professional model to question existing social structures are likely to risk severe opposition from their employing institutions. In addition, by revoking their membership in the "politically neutral" academic club, they will face isolation from colleagues who may perceive their activities as derogating their hard-won reputation of so-called scientific objectivity. This embroilment is occasioned by a model whose chief goal is the promotion of human welfare, as opposed to paradigms designed to dissect the human experience in the hope of finding replicable laws of behavior. The latter may be conducted without disrupting the social order. The former is bound to perturb it.

Chapter 11

INDUSTRIAL/ORGANIZATIONAL
PSYCHOLOGY

As an applied field, industrial/organizational (I/O) psychology impacts upon the lives of thousands, if not millions, of workers around the world (see, for example, Bass and Drenth 1987; Catano and Tivendell 1988; Wells 1987). Thus it plays an important role in the promotion or containment of change, not only in business but in society as a whole.

The main argument to be advanced in this chapter is that the social sciences in general and psychology in particular have been typically used *by* and *for* those interested in preserving the industrial status quo (Baritz 1974; Ralph 1983; Shore 1982; Wells 1987). Interestingly enough, it was not until very recently that psychologists began to question the moral and ideological implications of this state of affairs (Bramel and Friend 1981, 1987; Huszczo, Wiggins, and Currie 1984; Warwick 1978).

Historically, social scientists were brought into businesses for the purpose of increasing productivity. Baritz (1974) stated it rather bluntly when he wrote that "managers, as managers, are in business to make money. [And] only to the extent that social scientists can help in the realization of this goal will management make use of them" (p. 196). Cognizant of that situation, organized labor has traditionally been apprehensive of psychological "services" (Huszczo et al. 1984). In this regard Huszczo and colleagues (1984) commented that "unions have perceived the contributions of psychologists, at best, to be unrelated to their needs and, at worst, to be antithetical to their interests" (p. 432). In their review of the literature describing the relationship between psychology and unions, they concluded that, inter alia, labor distrusts psychologists

> A. because of their association with management.
> B. because of their association with F. W. Taylor's Scientific Management (i.e., emphasis on efficiency, time and motion studies). . . .
> C. because unions are ignored in textbooks and journals of I/O psychology.
> D. because methods (e.g., attitude surveys) have been used to avoid or bust union organizing attempts or lower pay demands. . . .
> E. because methods of psychological testing emphasize differentiation among workers (thus antisolidarity and antiseniority principles). . . .
> F. because "talking cure" methods probe the past and emphasize internal rather than external sources of mental stress and relief. (p. 434)

Despite the pseudoneutral language of "organizational development," and the humanistic flavor of numerous "human relations" courses, "quality of working life" projects, "quality circles," and "industrial democracy" programs, the fact remains that these innovations were merely instrumental in improving business and as such had a clear pro-management bias (Alvesson 1985; Bramel and Friend 1987; Hollway 1984; Warwick 1978; Wells 1987). This point was made very clear by J. A. C. Brown (1954). Commenting on the promanagement bias of Mayo's research, Brown correctly argued that "no industrial psychologist has ever shown anything else, and . . . under the circumstances in which all industrial research is carried out, such bias is inevitable" (J. A. C. Brown 1954, pp. 92-93).

The purpose of this chapter is to examine in more detail the argument outlined above—namely, that I/O psychology is highly instrumental in preserving the status quo. Simply put, this section will ask why and how I/O psychology helps in the maintenance of the present conditions in industry and in society. In order to do that, I will (a) briefly review the history of I/O psychology, (b) present its basic premises, (c) analyze the techniques used in I/O psychology to affirm the existing state of affairs, (d) consider some ethical conflicts and, finally, (e) elaborate on how I/O psychology can be used to challenge, rather than ratify, the status quo.

ORIGINS OF INDUSTRIAL/ORGANIZATIONAL PSYCHOLOGY

Broadly defined, I/O is "a branch of applied psychology covering applications of psychology in the industrial field" (Babington Smith 1988, p. 418). Traditionally, the primary goal of mainstream I/O psychology has been to increase efficiency, productivity, and profitability (e.g., Jewell 1985; Landy 1989; Maier 1946; Munsterberg 1913). The achievement of these objectives necessitated the application of psychology in a wide range of industrial areas, including, among others, personnel selection, performance appraisal, motivation, mental health of workers, interpersonal relations in the workplace, and environmental variables. The variety of these tasks called for a variety of professionals specializing in the different aspects of workers' behavior. Given their prominent role in what may be called the "politics of I/O psychology," the following discussion will focus primarily on the contributions made by experts in human relations, occupational mental health, and psychological testing.

Mayo, regarded by Whyte (1957) as the father of the "human relations" school in industry, was undoubtedly one of the pioneers in the field of I/O psychology (see also Bramel and Friend 1981). In the late 1920s, Mayo, a professor of industrial research at Harvard, became involved in the Hawthorne experiments being conducted at the Chicago Western Electric plant (Bramel and Friend 1981). This study, which was initially concerned with the effects of illumination on workers' output, evolved into a monumental industrial research project that included interviews with twenty thousand employees (J. A. C. Brown 1954).

Early in the study, specifically in the illumination experiments, researchers were surprised to find an increase in output in the experimental as well as in the control group. The investigators arrived at the conclusion that "output shot up in both groups because in both groups the workers' participation had been solicited and this involvement, clearly, was more important than physical perquisites" (Whyte 1957, p. 38). In other words, the productivity of workers went up not as a result of better illumination but rather as a result of the attention paid to them by supervisors and managers. Presently, *Hawthorne effect* is the name usually associated with the "observation that the output of the workers seemed to be responding to the transformed interpersonal relationship to the 'boss' . . . rather than to the explicitly introduced variations in physical conditions of work" (Bramel and Friend 1981, p. 870).

The Hawthorne experiments were said to have confirmed Mayo's convictions that cooperative human relations between labor and management is the key for both industrial productivity and tranquility. Following this principle of cooperation, Mayo promoted a technique according to which managers would be able to gain workers' trust and avert industrial unrest. This technique, referred to as the "nondirective interview," was premised on the assumption that any problems employees may have can be "talked out." Thus, counselors were trained to conduct nondirective interviews to provide workers with an opportunity to express their feelings about whatever problems they might have. Whyte described the philosophy of that technique as follows:

> He [*sic*] [the worker] is to adjust to the group rather than vice versa; and the alternative of actually changing reality is hardly considered. If a worker is sore at his foreman the chances are good that he is not really sore at his foreman because of some rational gripe but is merely venting on the foreman certain repressed feelings. By listening patiently, like a psychiatrist, the counselors help such persons understand that what they are really sore about flows from inner, subjective conflict. (Whyte 1957, p. 41)

The implication of this technique for industrial or social change is rather obvious: If workers have problems, they should change something within themselves, not in the working conditions—an implication that is entirely congruent with the well-known "blame the victim" ideology (W. Ryan 1971). Based on the high regard acquired by the Hawthorne experiments and the work of Mayo on human relations, it would be safe to argue that they have shaped the field of I/O psychology to a large extent (Bramel and Friend 1981; Jewell 1985; Ralph 1983). Moreover, they may have provided the basis for the relatively recent emergence of the subspecialty called "organizational development" (Hollway 1984). This branch of I/O psychology is concerned with "training managers in interpersonal skills such as expressing feelings honestly and learning how to listen and empathize. Such managerial styles would produce . . . less conflictual relations with subordinates who would thus experience commitment to the organization and become more highly motivated" (Hollway 1984, p. 32; see also de Alberdi 1990).

Another important point of departure for I/O psychology was occupational mental health. The origins of the field of occupational mental health in North America can be traced roughly to the 1920s, the same decade the Hawthorne experiments were to commence (McLean 1985). In 1919, Southard, once a director of the Boston Psychopathic Hospital and professor of neuropathology at Harvard, was invited to conduct a study on the possible psychiatric problems of discharged workers. In 1920 he reported that "60 percent of more than 4000 cases reached discharge status through traits of social incompetence rather than occupational incompetence" (in McLean 1985, p. 32). The same year he stated that "industrial psychiatry ought to exist. . . . I think that we will have a place in the routine of industrial management, not as permanent staff, . . . but as consultants. The function of this occasional consultant would be preventive rather than curative of the general conditions of unrest" (in McLean 1985, p. 33). McLean noted that the first full-time psychiatrist in an American company was hired in 1922. This was Dr. Lydia Giberson, who worked for Metropolitan Life Insurance most of her life. Macy's department store also introduced, in 1924, a team of mental health workers that included a psychiatrist, a social worker, and a psychologist. McLean's (1985) review of the field attests to the steady expansion and ramification since the early 1920s of occupational mental health. At present, many companies offer their employees mental health help in the form of employee assistance programs. These programs are becoming increasingly popular in large corporations. This is largely because "the most conservative figures indicate that comprehensive employee assistance programs return $2.00 or $3.00 in increased productivity for every $1.00 spent" (Wells 1987, p. 7).

The field of psychological testing also furnished considerable impetus to I/O psychology. Said Maier (1946): "That psychological testing has an obvious application to employee selection has been recognized by many large industries, which have not only welcomed the application of existing tests, but have co-operated in the development of new ones" (p. 151). An early precursor of the testing movement in I/O psychology was Munsterberg, who documented in his classic *Psychology and Industrial Efficiency* (1913) instances where he evaluated psychological abilities of persons working in diverse settings such as factories, telephone companies, and railway services. More recently, Hollway (1984), Shackleton and Anderson (1987), and Kavanagh and colleagues (1987) have demonstrated the vitality and utility of testing, not only in personnel selection, but also in job performance, training, and vocational guidance.

Though different in their focus, the fields of human relations, occupational mental health, and psychological testing converge in their ultimate objective: increased profitability for management (Baritz 1974; Ralph 1983; Wells 1987). This is not to say that I/O psychology cannot offer concrete help to workers, but that it has typically shown a distinct preference for working with management rather than with unions (Bramel and Friend 1987; Huszczo et al. 1984). Such bias has been attributed mainly to psychologists' class interests and financial considerations (Baritz 1974; Bramel and Friend 1981; Husczco et al. 1984). In my view, another set of factors should be emphasized, namely, the social and cultural presuppositions upon which I/O psychology is based. These assumptions simply elude the conflictual nature of labor-management relations and operate under the premise that what is good for business is necessarily good for workers.

Two Basic Premises of Industrial/Organizational Psychology

The promanagement bias of I/O psychology derives, in large part, from two intimately related basic premises. These can be summarized as follows: (a) Industry is basically a class-conflict-free enterprise, and (b) I/O psychology is social science, science is good for society; therefore I/O psychology is good for society. If one takes both assumptions for granted, one is likely to arrive at the conclusion that I/O psychology is equally good for both parties concerned, employers and employees. A completely different conclusion is drawn when these fundamental premises are challenged.

Premise #1: Industry As a Class-Conflict-Free Enterprise

Premise #1 is a recurring theme in I/O psychology. Critical organizational theory (Alvesson 1985) suggests that management can obtain tangible benefits by advancing the tacit assumption that they and the employees are all working toward the same goals. Such a view is intended to eliminate notions of fundamental contradictions between the interests of employers or their representatives and employees. Yet, to the extent that employers' profits are increased by controlling wages, serious differences do, and will continue to, exist. As Ralph (1983) argues, an increase in profit is frequently accompanied by a reduction of wages or deterioration in working conditions. This situation "creates an implicit and irreconcilable conflict between management and labor.... This conflict of interests between employers and employees is an inherent characteristic of capitalism" (Ralph 1983, pp. 60-61). Wages and the conditions of labor are also sometimes adversely affected simply because businesses are having a hard time surviving. Wells explains:

> The adversarial relationship between labor and management does not derive from some historical accident or from a colossal misunderstanding that "better communications" or a "more mature approach" can resolve. It stems from the fact that businesses survive by beating their competitors and, other things being equal, this means squeezing as much as possible out of workers. Unions did not cause this conflict; they arose as a response to it. (Wells 1987, p. 13)

Despite these arguments, which point to the conflictual nature of labor-management relationships, I/O psychology has nonetheless operated as though business were a cooperative enterprise whereby all parties benefit equally and conflicts are the result of either mismanagement or misunderstandings.

Bramel and Friend (1981) contend that Mayo and his associates were instrumental in promoting a portrayal of "the capitalist factory as nonexploitative and free of class conflict. This view, which is clearly identified with the defense of the capitalist mode of production, persists to the present time in discussions of the psychology of industry" (p. 867). Two examples of this classic attitude in I/O psychology are provided by Stagner and Rosen (1965) and by Maier (1946).

Stagner and Rosen's *Psychology of Union-Management Relations* (1965) is quite oblivious to the fundamental political and economic differences between both parties. When they speak of conflict, they do so in a psychological, as opposed to a class, language. Conflict is viewed as the result of psychological misunderstandings, not as a result of unequally distributed power.

The following quote is an illustrative example of their general approach: "In the long run ... every manager and union leader who *honestly* wants to reduce the frequency of conflict in industry must take account of the perceptions, goals, frustrations, and aggressions of *workers* (Stagner and Rosen 1965, p. 117; italics added). Three points are of interest here. First, if disputes are to be averted, psychological—as opposed to material—variables are to be taken into account. Second, though they are careful to state in the introduction that their treatment is "neutral toward the values of managers and unionists" (Stagner and Rosen 1965, p. 7), one has to question the neutrality of their treatment when they selectively talk about the aggression of workers and fail to mention the aggression of managers. Third, another significant implication is that disputes are undesirable. Disputes affect workers as well as employers. Stagner and Rosen fail to recognize that, although their short-term effects are painful, strikes and conflict are some of the few tools labor has to advance their long-term interests. In my opinion, their book is a good illustration of how a new, "class-free" interpretation of conflict is introduced into business by I/O psychology with the purpose of keeping fundamental structures unchallenged, for they clearly wrote: "Power need not be taken away from management" (Stagner and Rosen 1965, p. 131).

Similarly, Maier's (1946) *Psychology in Industry* also reduces conflicts between labor and management to inter- or intrapsychological variables. Workers' frustrations are almost always accounted for as deriving from personal problems. The class dimension is noticeable in its absence. Needless to say, by presenting employees' frustrations as the manifestation of "psychological maladjustment," Maier helps vindicate current practices of management and the distribution of power.

The last chapter of Maier's book serves as a brief guide for supervisors, counselors, and managers on how to increase productivity. In that chapter he differentiates between two types of union, one that goes along with management and another that challenges it. He condones the former and condemns the latter because of its political aspirations. Thus, Maier approves of those unions that see conflict only as "classless." In that context, Maier warns management against the risks of frustration. It is important to appreciate, Maier wrote, "the role which frustration plays in labor and political movements. Frustrated individuals are readily organized and led, and their activities are militant in nature. . . . Poorly adjusted individuals are inclined to be militant and seek the union which suits their inclinations" (Maier 1946, p. 419). Maier's dislike of militant unions derives mainly from his basic assumption that industry is a cooperative enterprise between owners and workers. In this view, whatever problems there may be can always be solved by constructive dialogue. Militant workers are not perceived as politically conscious but rather are discredited as misguided and maladjusted individuals. Such a stand has been quite common in I/O psychology (Bramel and Friend 1981).

The failure of I/O psychology to deal with power differentials in industry has recently been brought into sharp focus by Barling (1988). In an empirical investigation of the teaching, research, and practice of I/O psychology, Barling arrived at the conclusion that "industrial relations" is the "blind spot" of the field. Barling studied the extent to which I/O psychology pays attention to unions. A review of all the articles on the subject from the 1980-86 issues of the *Journal of Applied Psychology*, the *Journal of Occupational Psychology*, *Organizational Behavior and Human Performance*, and the *Academy of Management Journal* led him to conclude that "union membership is ignored almost invariably" (Barling 1988, p. 105). Addressing the question "how much coverage is devoted to industrial relations issues in frequently-used I/O textbooks" (Barling 1988, p. 105), he reviewed thirty-nine such introductory texts as well as three advanced texts. Results showed that "15 of these texts make no mention of unions . . . [and] 29 suggest that less than 1% of their contents consider union issues" (Barling 1988, p. 105). He also asked a sample of Canadian I/O psychology teachers to what extent their courses dealt with industrial relations issues. Responses were received for twenty-two courses: "Ten of the 18 undergraduate courses, and three of the four graduate courses did not deal with industrial relations at all" (Barling 1988, p. 106). Furthermore, seven of the fifteen texts used in these courses make no reference to union issues whatsoever.

One cannot help but wonder just what leads I/O psychologists to ignore the topic of industrial relations. Two plausible explanations may be considered. The first is that it is in their economic and political interests not to disturb the industrial status quo. Social scientists employed by management realize that treatment of issues such as industrial relations is an open invitation to include politics in a field that they would prefer to keep "neutral." As long as industrial unrest can be prevented or minimized by the presence of "objective scientists," both management and scientists alike are said to benefit: the former by keeping politics out of industry, the latter by lucrative contracts.

An alternative explanation to account for the omission of class and power issues in I/O psychology is simply that social scientists believe in technical, as opposed to political, solutions. Consequently, unions—identified as political forces—are not even considered to be part of their occupational endeavor. This argument cannot be easily discarded, for the pervasive character of the *technical rationality* of our times has hardly left an area of social inquiry without its imprint (Alvesson 1985; Benson 1977).

Whether because of a partisan interest in preserving things the way they are, or because of a sincere belief in the solubility of all social problems by technical means, the situation remains that I/O psychology has paid negligible attention to the class and political nature of labor-management conflicts. And inasmuch as politics is a potent tool for the transformation of power arrangements in society, the clear beneficiaries of that situation are those who would like to see things in the future stay the way they are in the present.

If I/O psychologists are interested in serving all sectors of industry, it is imperative that the working assumption that industry is a class-conflict-free enterprise be challenged. I would concur with Barling (1988) that "I/O psychologists must accept the inevitability . . . of union-management conflict in its many manifestations in organizations, and discard their attitudinal indifference toward, or ideological bias against labour unions" (p. 108).

Premise #2: I/O Psychology Is Science, and Science Is Good for Society

"Social science is science; science contributes to human welfare; therefore social science contributes to human welfare" (Warwick 1980, p. 31). This syllogism, premised on a great deal of naiveté, protected the moral conscience of many social scientists for a long time. I/O psychologists, as social scientists, found in it an elegant way to amalgamate their pursuit of scientific knowledge with what they termed a "contribution to society as a whole."

It is not my intent here to challenge the scientific status of I/O psychology; rather, my intent is to challenge its supposed contribution to "human welfare." As Steininger, Newell, and Garcia (1984) succinctly put it: "Psychology can be used to serve the interests of the powerful or the interests of the powerless" (p. 196). I/O psychologists may have intended to serve all classes, but the actual results of their efforts have benefited, almost exclusively, the powerful (Baritz 1974; Huszczo et al. 1984; Ralph 1983; Shore 1982; Wells 1987).

I/O psychologists, like with many other social science practitioners, endorse a technical rationality according to which social problems will, eventually, be solved by scientific and technical means to the exclusion of political solutions. This approach to human dilemmas has been termed by Anderson and Travis (1983) the "liberal consensus." It consists in the belief that society will be bettered by "neutral" scientists and professionals. The spirit and political implications of this technocratic philosophy, which is so much a part of I/O psychology, are well summarized by Alvesson (1985):

In the technological-capitalist society, there is a general tendency to re-define problems concerning purposes, aims, and values so as either to make them appear to be technical issues, or to make them seem irrelevant. Questions involving such matters as alienation, and the content and value of work, are defined as problems which socio-technical and other organizational principles should solve within the framework of prevailing conditions. . . . In this way, a world picture which supports the predominant rationality is transmitted. (p. 127)

This technocratic doctrine treats all human problems as technical ones. Inequality, power, discrimination, and the like are the result not of injustice but of lack of scientific progress. Thus, I/O psychology, which embraced this *Weltanschauung* since its inception, became oblivious to the politics of production. Mayo was absolutely convinced that "scientific management," equipped with the newest techniques of human relations, would advance the welfare of employers and employees alike. "Mayo argued with passion that social and clinical psychological approaches could be incorporated into an enlightened management in such a way that the social-emotional needs of workers would be met" (Bramel and Friend 1981, p. 868). This would in effect prevent workers from organizing to protest unfavorable working conditions or low wages.

Indisputable faith in the assumption that science is good for human welfare might have precluded posing the simple question: Good for whom in society? If I/O psychologists had asked that question, the sociopolitical repercussions of the field might have been radically different. As it turned out, however,

in seeming disregard for [the] American Psychological Association's vision of psychology "as a means of promoting human welfare," the mainstream of industrial psychology has traditionally labored to promote employer welfare as its principal goal. While the single-minded quest for efficiency/productivity/profitability inevitably encounters the obstruction of unions, it also results in a regard for workers—all workers, not just union members—as little more than instrumentalities for achieving management objectives. (Shore 1982, p. 334)

Thus far I have examined the basic premises that have led I/O practitioners to side with management and thereby support the status quo. The actual ways these premises are translated into actions will now be discussed.

How Industrial/Organizational Psychology Upholds the Industrial Status Quo

I/O psychology contributes to the maintenance of the industrial status quo through three different yet related mechanisms: (a) the personalization of conflict, (b) the cooperative approach, and (c) the professionalization of managerial decisions.

The Personalization of Conflict

The attribution of workers' problems to internal causes was pioneered by Mayo in the interview phase of the Hawthorne research (Bramel and Friend 1981; J. A. C. Brown 1954) and is exemplified in the books by Maier (1946) and Stagner and Rosen (1965). In essence, employees are guided to view their lack of satisfaction in life as a product of their own personal inadequacies. While managers—as the administrators of capital—are doing "all they can to help" by providing counselors, the internal nature of the workers' predicaments demand corrections of an intrapersonal character. Quoting Whyte (1957) again: "The alternative of actually changing reality is hardly considered" (p. 41).

This method of counseling not only leads to a self-blame attitude in its clients, but also exculpates management for whatever role it might have played in the workers' difficulties in the first place. An additional bonus that the personalization of conflict furnishes to owners is that they come across as caring and personally interested in the welfare of the employees, thus strengthening loyalty and commitment to the firm. As Wells (1987) recently put it, counseling programs

> are aimed at helping workers deal with their [productivity-reducing] problems of anxiety, alcohol use, depression, drug dependency, and so on. Workers are persuaded that these problems are 'personal' problems not related to the workplace, but problems that management nevertheless cares enough about to lend a hand. (p. 6)

It should be remembered that counseling services are part of comprehensive employee assistance programs that result in increased productivity for every dollar invested in them by management (Wells 1987). But increased productivity is not the only benefit for managers. In addition, psychological expertise has been able to pacify troublemakers and diffuse resentment against owners and supervisors (Baritz 1974; Ralph 1983).

With time, unions began to realize that counseling provided by employers had an undesirable side effect: It was conducive to workers' passivity and conformity. It "helped" "workers and their dependents adjust to increasingly alienated, degraded, and pressured conditions, in order to prevent labour unrest" (Ralph 1983, p. 47). Haverman (1957) wrote that unionists started referring to this kind of psychological help as "cow psychology." They saw it as "an attempt to get more production out of the worker by keeping him [sic] placid and uncomplaining . . . on the grounds that any advice paid for by the company is almost bound to favor the company's desires over the worker's psychological needs" (p. 52). The increased awareness of these side effects led unions to oppose such "benefits." Although "employers often have been able to slip mental health 'services' into a broad occupational health package . . . many unions have managed to see through this stratagem" (Ralph 1983, p. 141). This situation forced the introduction of innovative methods to gain workers' compliance and prevent industrial unrest. It might be suitable to call this new technology of human relations the "cooperative" approach.

The "Co-operative" Approach

The argument has been made that the most efficacious method of social control is that which does not elicit resistance (Skinner 1974; Zimbardo 1984). Schacht (1985) has called this type of controlling influence "softened power":

> Softened power decreases individuals' experience of political impact on their lives and thought, promoting uncritical internalization of prevailing ideologies and anesthetizing persons to the ways in which they are being led, influenced, or controlled. Softened power circumscribes their consciousness, allowing illusions of free choice to persist while available choices are curtailed through a subtle foreshortening of their imagination. (p. 513)

Fully aware that "softened power" was required, industrialists enlisted the assistance of social scientists in designing programs of worker control that would not elicit the latter's resistance. In response to that demand, two innovative approaches to human relations have been introduced. These are organizational development (OD), and quality of working life (QWL).

The concept of OD refers to interventions based on behavioral science intended to increase the effectiveness of an organization (Hollway

1984; Walton 1978). "Specifically," Walton (1978) wrote, "OD attends to the use and development of human capacities and social integration in the work place" (p. 124). Sensitivity training programs designed to enhance interpersonal understanding, team building, and reward systems for employees are key features of its methodology.

Despite its apparent humanistic aspirations of improved cooperation and quality of working life for everybody concerned (Hollway 1984; Walton 1978), OD faces criticisms similar to those leveled against employee counseling, namely, it may not be as benevolent and neutral as it purports to be. Its very name—organizational *development*—is somewhat misleading, for the word *development* usually has a positive connotation and implies unfolding toward a desired goal, a state of maturity. Yet, as Warwick (1978) has argued, development and health for "the manager or owner may well be disease for the worker" (p. 148). Pseudoneutral terms such as *team building, problem solving*, and *effectiveness* are very common in OD. To the extent that this vocabulary ignores the power structure of companies and promotes a so-called conflict-free language, one has to question the purity of the motives behind OD interventions.

"Effective OD intervention," Warwick (1978) noted, "will almost always change or reinforce the balance of power, influence and authority in a system. Some individuals and groups will gain in the ability to pursue their interests and intentions, while others will lose" (p. 149). If that is indeed the case, and OD practitioners "most often enter the system as management consultants" (Warwick 1978, p. 149), it would not be unreasonable to conclude that in the majority of instances OD lends its "scientific support" to keeping the prevailing distribution of power in industry. It could probably be argued that if that were not the case, managers would think twice before hiring OD experts. For, after all, experts are brought into business with the purpose of increasing output.

Probably the single most important feature of OD is its impartial and humanistic facade. These specialists are portrayed as neutral third parties merely interested in "improving the effectiveness of organizations that produce useful goods and services and in enhancing the quality of human experience in the workplace" (Walton 1978, p. 124). Their "impartial" and "caring" approach is reinforced by the emphasis placed on the "collaborative" model. If you want to increase productivity, you don't fight with your workers, you collaborate with them; you don't force them, you talk them into doing it. Owners and workers dialogue "as if" they were equal, thus gaining workers' cooperation and subtly dissuading them from organizing politically to fulfill their aspirations.

Similar allegations have been made against quality-of-working-life projects. These programs, which are typically carried out by "someone who is well versed in the social psychology of small groups" (Wells 1987, p. 3), are intended to bring labor and management together in an effort to make use of workers' full physical and mental abilities in a more creative and productive fashion. In addition to the job redesign involved, "QWL programs are always characterized by their focus on greater participation by workers, usually through labor-management committees" (Wells 1987, p. 2). The main thrust of these committees is to foster a purely psychological orientation to conflict in the workplace. When conflict is defined along these lines, cooperation is much easier to attain than when it is conceptualized in political terms. "The cooperation between workers and managers in these meetings is supposed to foster a more general cooperation outside the meetings: the whole point of QWL is to create a new kind of cooperation on the job" (Wells 1987, pp. 3-4). Wells (1987) concluded that, in effect, the principal objective of management in implementing QWL is to "undermine the main form of power that workers and their unions normally resort to—the negative power of resistance or refusal to obey" (p. 69).

Promises made to workers by QWL advocates depict these programs as very attractive. They offer "opportunities to fulfill one's potential," "pride," "enjoyment," "decision-making power," and so on; but over and above these pronouncements, the elemental question for unions remains: Do these projects ultimately benefit workers? Wells's (1987) response is a categorical no. His study of such enterprises revealed that the cooperation advertised by QWL exponents is a highly selective, management-biased kind of cooperation that, in the final analysis, "*reduces* the quality of working life" (p. 5).

Wells's (1987) investigation of two large QWL projects in North America led him to claim that, contrary to the expectations created by QWL proponents, "the programs were clearly designed to adjust workers to jobs, not jobs to workers. More broadly, they were designed to adjust workers to their own continuing subordination in the workplace" (Wells 1987, p. 68).

As for the decision-making power promised to employees, "the only participation that either workers or union leaders were involved in was strictly consultative, involving them, at best, in minor modifications to decisions that had already been made by management" (p. 69).

In the end, QWL is simply a softer, subtler management-control strategy, yet one that is more ambitious and all-embracing than anything seen before. Management is no longer satisfied with making workers obey: it now wants them to *want* to obey. (pp. 5-6)

Wells's research confirmed general apprehensions concerning various forms of worker participation and industrial democracy initiatives voiced by other authors (Andriessen and Coetsier 1984; Bramel and Friend 1987; J. R. Wilson 1991).

In sum, both OD and QWL interventions have promoted an approach whereby control over workers is gained through cooperation. These techniques are refined versions of human manipulation, congruous with the spirit of our age.

The Professionalization of Managerial Decisions

The professionalization of managerial decisions can be of assistance to those with a vested interest in upholding the industrial status quo. As in the cases of "the personalization of problems" and the "cooperative approach," in professionalizing its decision-making process, management benefits by diverting attention from the political arena. When, for example, detrimental working conditions, delayed promotions, and layoffs of workers can be at least partially based on "expert advice," the owners do not have to take all the responsibility for worker discontent. Ascribing these decisions to organizational and psychological science helps management deal with the frustrations elicited by some of these measures, not only because it wasn't strictly their own doing, but also because science is supposed to be removed, impartial, and fair.

The belief that "psychology is a science and that psychological assessment is therefore objective" (Hollway 1984, p. 35) is being continuously promoted in organizations, both by I/O psychologists and by management (Hollway 1984). Occupational assessment is rarely perceived as a tool that can be used to rationalize decisions whose impact on workers is negative. For the most part, psychological testing in industry is viewed as "fair" (see Hollway 1984, pp. 35-36). "The role of the assessor is seen . . . as neutral and external, and as one of fact gathering" (Hollway 1984, p. 54). Similar sentiments were expressed by Munsterberg (1913) in *Psychology and Industrial Efficiency*. The "psychotechnician" was to render "neutral" services.

A similar role may be performed by OD specialists. Changes in organizations with unfavorable consequences for part of the staff can always be justified on the basis of professional, scientific expertise. Warwick (1978), who has carefully analyzed the ethical and political implications of OD, contends that these may be obscured when OD is cloaked in the garb of science. The introduction of the OD practitioner as "Dr. Smith, a social scientist who is an expert on organizations" may create an image of impartiality and scientific neutrality that is not justified by the circumstances. Union leaders and employees in the organization would be well advised to look beyond such professional camouflage to the gritty realities of sponsorship and latent agendas. (pp. 151-52)

ETHICS IN THE PRACTICE OF INDUSTRIAL/ORGANIZATIONAL PSYCHOLOGY

Human manipulation has been a constitutive part of I/O psychology. Its ability to overcome workers' resistance, prevent industrial unrest, discredit discontented employees as maladjusted, and subtly control labor are some of the features that made the field indispensable for some companies. In the past, attempts to control workers were more in the open. Each party knew, more or less, where the other stood. But with the advent of psychology, control strategies became much more refined and covert.

> Time was when a man [sic] knew that his freedoms were being curtailed. Social scientists, however, are too sophisticated for that. The fires of pressure and control on a man are now kindled in his own thinking. Control need no longer to be imposed. It can be encouraged from within. . . . A major characteristic of the twentieth century has been the fact that it blinds the victim to the fact of manipulation. (Baritz 1974, pp. 209-10)

The witting or unwitting use of I/O psychology to manipulate workers, as described in the previous section and summarized by Baritz in the above quotation, raises an important ethical dilemma. It follows from the basic premises of the field that I/O practitioners should remain neutral (e.g., Stagner and Rosen 1965). Interestingly enough, when I/O psychologists have expressed values, these have been typically humanistic—the kind that are supposed to benefit everyone involved (Alvesson 1985; Hollway 1984; Walton 1978). Yet the assumption that the practice of I/O psychology is neutral or equally advantageous to all sides has been refuted numerous times and rather persuasively (Baritz 1974; Ralph 1983; Warwick 1978; Wells 1987). These authors have eloquently argued that I/O interventions have significant political repercussions and that, as a rule, owners gain and workers lose.

I/O psychologists face a difficult decision. On the one hand, they may feel pressured to acknowledge the political implications of their work in order to avoid the ethical dilemma of duplicity (i.e., creating expectations that cannot be fulfilled). On the other hand, acknowledgment of their promanagement bias will considerably decrease their attractiveness. For, as you will remember, it is the very "neutral" facade of social science that business finds so appealing. Thus, an admission of partisanship on the part of I/O professionals would be a somewhat self-defeating move, at least financially.

Personal distress and financial loss notwithstanding, the ethical issue will not be resolved until I/O psychologists fully realize and articulate the political reverberations of their occupation. Instead of trying to be "more" impartial, they ought to come to grips with the political nature of industrial relations and accept the responsibility implied in siding with one party. In doing so they would, at the very least, take care of the duplicity involved in promising to be apolitical and serving power at the same time.

The political and ethical responsibility ascribed to psychologists working for management also applies to those willing to collaborate with labor. The idea is simply to overcome the naiveté implicit in aspiring to be apolitical, and to disclose the inevitable presence of a sociopolitical bias.

CONCLUSION

The purpose of this chapter has been to identify some of the sociopolitical implications in the practice of I/O psychology. The evolution of the field, I have claimed, has been characterized by an unreflective stance on the political nature of industrial relations (Babington Smith 1988; Barling 1988). Operating under the assumption that they are merely offering an apolitical service that will impact favorably on owners and workers alike, I/O practitioners have often acted as "servants of power" (Baritz 1974). A remarkable disregard for the political repercussions of their occupation has placed I/O psychologists in a difficult situation whereby their promise of neutrality is simply untenable.

A number of recent developments in the literature, however, lead one to believe that I/O psychologists may have begun to face some of the criticisms that have been advanced. Huszczo and his associates (1984), for instance, made a strong case for psychologists to admit and express their attitudinal bias in working for management. At the same time, they urged those psychologists with a prolabor bias to identify themselves to, and make themselves available to, unions, thereby counteracting the long-standing pro-owner bias in psychology and discarding the neutrality myth.

The historical predilection favoring management and upholding the basic status quo does not preclude the prospect of I/O psychologists challenging it. Though few in number, some psychologists have already started collaborating with labor in advancing workers' interests (Huszczo et al. 1984). Several roles can be envisioned for a psychology devoted to helping unions, including training in bargaining techniques, assistance in establishing educational programs for workers, and teaching skills to counteract manipulation methods employed by managers. Psychologists willing to contribute their expertise to labor will be well advised not to commit the same error as those who have typically served employers, that is, to pretend to be apolitical in a field where the distribution of power is as salient an issue as can be.

Chapter 12

SCHOOL PSYCHOLOGY

It is obvious that without an improvement in the social conditions in which they live, many children will continue to experience a myriad of emotional disorders (Albee, Bond, and Cook Monsey 1992; Honig 1986a, 1986b; Mirowsky and Ross 1989; Commission on Prevention of Mental-Emotional Disabilities 1987; Joint Commission on Mental Health of Children 1973). The United Nations Convention on the Rights of the Child, recently adopted by its General Assembly, "refers many times to the maintenance of the child's mental health, as well as to the preconditions for achieving these ends (e.g., adequate shelter, nutrition, health care, education)" (Cohen and Naimark 1991, p. 63). Hence, school psychologists have a moral responsibility to promote the well-being not only of their clients but also of the environments where their clients function and develop. In spite of the fact that very few school psychologists will likely dispute these assertions, the profession has devoted a disproportionate amount of resources to treating single individuals or small groups at the expense of proactive interventions on a large scale (cf. Kovaleski 1988). This has contributed to the solidification of the educational status quo.

In this chapter I will argue that the ethical commitments of school psychologists toward society in general and children in particular demand a more active involvement in the solution of social and structural educational problems. For this development to occur, school psychology needs to widen its horizon and incorporate community and political interventions into its array of services. Although there is considerable potential for an advocacy role in school psychology (Conoley 1981; Hart 1987; Melton 1987; Svec 1990), this function remains largely unfulfilled (Trachtman 1990).

THE CURRENT SITUATION

Efforts to shift or at least balance the emphasis from the single case to the community as a whole will undoubtedly encounter numerous obstacles. The main barrier to be faced will be the individualistic philosophical orientation regnant in society, psychology, and the schools. This philosophy has shaped not only the way we think about social problems but naturally also the means by which those are to be solved (Berman 1981; Capra 1982). Consequently, there will be conceptual and philosophical obstacles as well as practical and bureaucratic ones.

School Psychology Blames the Child

With the exception of community psychology, school psychology is not any more or less biased toward individualism than any other branch of psychology. This explains why in school psychology, as in clinical and abnormal psychology, much-needed primary prevention projects have been slow in developing. The primary prevention role of the school psychologist, Alpert (1985) argues, "occurs only in our discussion of roles and in our values system, not in the real world" (p. 1118). Similarly, Zins and Forman (1988) contend that "despite the growing interest in prevention and mental health promotion, most school psychologists spend minimal time in such activities on a day-to-day basis" (p. 539).

It is quite remarkable that in spite of overwhelming evidence pointing to the social causes of psychological distress, as documented in previous chapters, most diagnostic and therapeutic efforts are still directed toward the individual child. According to present practices, not only is there a tendency to wait until the problem reaches major proportions, but once the problem is identified there is a similar inclination to treat the single child and neglect, practically and conceptually, equally important changes required in the environmental conditions (Johnston 1990; Witt and Martens 1988) and socioeconomic conditions

(Pianta 1990). Given that state of affairs, it is hardly surprising that Zins and Forman (1988) entitled their opening article in the *School Psychology Review* series on prevention "Primary Prevention in the Schools: What Are We Waiting For."

Much like most other areas of applied psychology, school psychology adopted the defect model. Kovaleski (1988) observed that "this model holds that children with school problems have discrete disorders that are internal to the child" (p. 479). As Kaplan and Kaplan (1985) have accurately asserted, school psychologists greatly ignore "the social context and . . . proceed to locate emotional disturbance . . . and learning problems *within* the child. . . . The impact of environmental conditions, other people, and societal values remain in the background" (p. 323). Similar reasoning is present in case-centered consultation, where "the position is still taken . . . that the problem lies in the child or with the child's behavior" (Witt and Martens 1988, p. 213), and in special education, where most models assume that "the problem of not learning is within the student" (Heshusius 1989, p. 406).

This is the mentality reflected in many of the traditional refer-test-place/remediate cases (Johnston 1990; Witt and Martens 1988). Referrals often come to the school clinician with three implicit assumptions: (a) that there *is* something "wrong" with the child, (b) that the psychologist can find whatever is "wrong" with the child, and (c) that the clinician can recommend either special education placement or treatment. Conspicuously absent from many referrals is the expectation to modify certain aspects of the child's human or educational environment. Simply put, the referral reads: "Change the child or place him or her elsewhere; don't change us." As assessment continues to be the predominant and most time-consuming activity of school psychologists (Lacayo, Sherwood, and Morris 1981; Levinson 1990), most practitioners should be very familiar with referrals of this nature. Although the involvement of school psychologists in consultation dealing with microsocial variables has been steadily increasing in the last decade and a half, activities of this kind are still significantly outnumbered by the more traditional role of testing (Johnston 1990). As a result, it will be very difficult to promote in the profession an orientation that fosters changes in the social and classroom environment as a viable means of meeting the needs of children.

Equally dangerous as the practice of ascribing fault to some entity within the child, is the proclivity to assume that there is something necessarily wrong within the teacher. It is highly likely that consultees (i.e., teachers) perceive the consultation process as one in which their weak-nesses will be exposed. As a result, teachers may opt for requesting more direct services as opposed to consultation. The prospect of opening the classroom to strangers and being scrutinized can be very intimidating for teachers. This is further complicated by the repercussions the consultative process may have for the evaluation of the teacher by the principal. This organizational inconvenience and its concomitant personal risks may be avoided by the teacher by expecting more traditional services such as testing and pullout remediation. Several authors have analyzed teachers' resistance to the use of classroom interventions (Johnston 1990; Tingstrom, Stewart, and Little 1990; Witt 1986; Witt and Martens 1988), but not enough attention has been paid to the *human factor*, that is, the feelings of insecurity generated by the consultative process. For consultation to work in a more efficient fashion, teachers should be empowered and not inadvertently blamed for their pupils' emotional, behavioral, or learning difficulties (cf. Witt and Martens 1988). This improvement, however, cannot take place merely at the interpersonal level. It is not enough for the psychologist to provide an accepting climate when teachers might fear negative annual evaluations by the administrator for having "shared" information about problems they have with their classes. In a school where green slips were used to refer students to the principal for disciplinary action (an action encouraged by the principal), a teacher told me that "all those slips are good for is to get *you* [i.e., the teacher] a bad report." Unless teachers feel fully supported by administrators and colleagues in the process of dealing with students, and are not afraid of negative personal repercussions, chances are high that resistance will prevail. There is a definite possibility that if consultation does not prove as successful as it might be, this will be because of a lack of sensitivity of consultants to the culture of the school. According to Sarason (1982a, 1983), this would be one more instance where program innovations are implanted in the educational system without knowledge of the human dynamics and organization of the school.

School Psychology Vindicates the System

Schools, to be sure, cannot be expected to be more receptive of a socially sensitive agenda than psychology or other social institutions (Sarason 1982a, 1990). The school, as a pillar of modern society, does not just merely accept but actively reproduces the ideology of meritocracy. That is, the achievement attained by children in schools is seen primarily as a reflection of their personal talent and dedication, and not necessarily as a product of complex social forces impinging upon their education (Apple 1982; Apple and Weis 1983; Ginsburg 1972; Sennet and Cobb 1972). Although schools are becoming more aware of the potential negative outcomes of risk factors such as poverty, racism, abuse, and family dysfunction, a recent examination of ways in which schools in the United States deal with children with behavioral and emotional problems shows that they are still very far from embracing a socially sensitive approach (Knitzer 1990). The same study also found that their interventions fell primarily within the asocial paradigm. This phenomenon may have a political explanation. Much like governments, which prefer a mind fix over a setting fix, school personnel and parents alike may favor mind therapies that focus on the individual child and leave the adults and the social order of the school unaltered. The school's drive to modify minds and intrapersonal factors at the expense of changes required in the educational environment may have been inadvertently strengthened by the many cognitive therapies for school-age children made available in the last decade (Braswell and Kendall 1988; Di Giuseppe 1981; Gholson and Rosenthal 1984).

In pursuing an expanded role for the school psychologist, bureaucratic and administrative obstacles cannot be omitted. Special education laws, and administrators in charge of their implementation, demand that a great deal of time be devoted to the classification of students. This restrictive role presents a strong barrier to making a transition from *asocial* to *macrosocial* paradigms of operation (Sigmon 1987). Strategies to facilitate this transition will have to take into account these structural obstacles.

THE POSSIBILITIES

School psychology is uniquely qualified to make a meaningful contribution to the welfare of the population. It is publicly funded, it reaches a vast number of children and families, and its services are provided in the community itself. As such, it has the potential to enhance the well-being of its clientele in numerous ways. To maximize its beneficial effects, school psychology must move toward more socially sensitive approaches, however. In practical terms this means a transition from the predominant asocial and microsocial paradigms to the macrosocial paradigm discussed in chapter 10. I advocate a shift analogous to the one from clinical to community psychology. It may be argued that contemporary school psychology resembles more the former than the latter. Community psychology has much to offer to the field, its conceptual framework being a salient possible contribution (Rappaport 1977, 1981, 1987).

The amalgamation of community and school psychology may give birth to the concept of *community-school psychology* (cf. Sarason 1983). This branch of school psychology would foster socially sensitive analyses and interventions. Two kinds of socially sensitive approaches would be advanced: proactive and reactive. The former would attempt to prevent the development of psychosocial problems by addressing socioeconomic, political, and epidemiological issues; the latter would contend with difficult situations already facing children in the schools.

Proactive Socially Sensitive Interventions

The material and affective environment where children grow is of paramount importance in their physical and psychological development (Commission on the Prevention of Mental-Emotional Disabilities 1987). The well-documented pernicious effects of life stressors such as poverty (Albee, Bond, and Cook Monsey 1992; Honig 1986a; T. Ryan 1972), malnutrition (Lozoff 1989), parental disorder (Weintraub, Winters, and Neale 1986), and family dysfunction (Patterson, DeBarsyshe, and Ramsey 1989) in the lives of children provide the fundamental rationale for promoting proactive socially sensitive interventions. Although there have been attempts to integrate community (i.e., socially sensitive) interventions with school interventions (e.g., Cowen et al. 1975; Jason 1982; Plas 1986), school psychologists have neither taken full advantage of the paradigm shift made by community psychologists nor advanced those practices to the forefront of their priorities. Three illustrative examples of future-oriented, socially sensitive interventions are (a) prevention programs, (b) the promotion of resilience, and (c) changes in social and educational policy.

As the literature on primary prevention in the schools has been reviewed recently and is well known (Alpert 1985; Bond and Compas 1989; Durlak 1985; Pianta 1990; Pransky 1991; Reinherz 1982; Zins, Conyne, and Ponti 1988), I shall elaborate only on the last two examples.

Promoting Resilience in Schools. Next to primary prevention projects, the promotion of resilience may be considered a prototype of proactive socially sensitive interventions. It is socially sensitive in that it is based on epidemiological analyses that recognize the psychological injuries sustained by children growing up in disadvantaged social conditions (Werner 1985, 1986). It is proactive in that, on the basis of identified mitigating factors, it launches interventions designed to prevent or reduce the sequel of major life stressors (Cowen et al. 1990).

Longitudinal research with high-risk children published within the last decade (e.g., Nicol 1985; Rutter 1988) furnishes support for the advancement of social interventions in school psychology. Specifically, the search for protective factors has revealed that school personnel and clinicians have an important role to play in fostering resilience in children at risk for psychopathology (Berrueta-Clement et al. 1987; Maughan 1988).

Studies have repeatedly shown that there are a number of children, a minority, who when faced with adversity will overcome adverse circumstances and develop in a psychologically healthy way (e.g., Anthony and Cohler 1987; Garmezy 1984; Masten and Garmezy 1985; Rutter 1985b, 1987; Werner 1985). These youngsters are often referred to as "resilient children." The literature points to three sets of protective factors said to enhance the level of resilience of children at risk. The first set is composed of individual attributes of the child such as positive self-esteem, autonomy, high IQ, and the like. The second category has to do with the family; family cohesion and absence of discord have been identified as protective factors. The third set of protective factors associated with resilience are the availability of, and access to, external sources of support. The presence of a caring adult, not necessarily from the family, with whom the child could develop a trusting relationship was found to have most beneficial effects (Garmezy 1984; Masten and Garmezy 1985; Werner 1985).

This last finding may be regarded as encouraging empirical evidence that school personnel, teachers, counselors, and psychologists, *can* have a positive enduring impact on the lives of children at risk, through the healing and strengthening effects of a solid relationship. Although this of course makes intuitive sense, large efforts to provide children at risk with lasting relationships within the school setting have yet to be implemented. The pioneer work of Cowen and his associates in the use of volunteers and paraprofessionals in schools can be emulated and upgraded in light of the findings described above (Cowen et al. 1975; McManus 1986). It would be important, for instance, to bear in mind the need for continuity in those relationships. Children lacking supports within their families could benefit from having an adult who will accompany them for a number of years. Recurrent experiences of attachment and separation from significant others may lead to reluctance on the part of the child to allow him- or herself to bond with new figures in his or her life (Bowlby 1988; Field 1987). The school psychologist can mobilize paraprofessionals and/or community volunteers, train them, and help schools contract with them for two or three years of committed work with a particular needy child (McManus 1986).

In addition, the educational setting can contribute to the development of resilience through rewarding academic experiences (Maughan 1988). The sense of mastery derived from participation in meaningful school activities (i.e., activities that pertain directly and concretely to the child's life) enhances the child's perception of self-efficacy (Rutter 1985a, 1987). In looking at risk and protective factors for becoming an offender later in life, the longitudinal research of Kolvin and his associates showed that for children from high-risk backgrounds a respectable school career blunted the propensity to crime. They conclude that a "sense of stability and esteem derived from meritorious school performance persists as a protective factor into later life" (Kolvin et al. 1988, p. 93). For this positive outcome to take place, however, schools must ensure that the curriculum "makes sense" to the child at risk and is relevant to his or her life events. Monotonous paper-and-pencil academics are often not the preferred way to engage those children. Alternative methods ought to be proposed, and the school psychologist can play a decisive role in generating more-adequate educational options for those youngsters.

Based on their own and related research on resilience, Cowen and his associates (Cowen et al. 1990; Cowen, Work, and Wyman 1992) have recently launched an intervention designed to provide profoundly stressed urban children with adjustment-enhancing skills (e.g., social problem solving, sense of efficacy, empathy, realistic control attributions). The intervention, conducted in small groups over a period of twenty weeks, focuses on enabling children to identify and develop support resources. As can be seen, although this is basically a socially sensitive approach, the target of treatment is primarily the child, and in that lies its major limitation. This shortcoming is clearly spelled out by Cowen, Work, and Wyman (1992):

> Even though the notion of a preventive intervention with these youngsters is intrinsically appealing, an intervention that focuses exclusively on children—even one that provides optimal conditions and imparts essential skills and competencies effectively— may have major limitations. . . . Beyond that, remains the menacing specter of limitations on human development imposed by a

social macrostructure that short-changes major segments of society in terms of such critical factors as justice, empowerment and life opportunity. (pp. 165-66)

According to the taxonomy of social interventions presented in chapter 10, Cowen and associates' approach falls within the macrosocial paradigm, and by their own admission there is a pressing need to operate from a macrosociopolitical framework as well. The next logical step should be to address the societal structures currently inhibiting the development of mental health in children.

Changes in Social and Educational Policies. Although the National Association of School Psychologists and some professionals in the field are involved in advocacy and child welfare issues (e.g., Conoley 1981; Hart 1987, 1989; Svec 1990), most individual school psychologists continue to be disturbingly silent when it comes to voicing social and political discontent (Trachtman 1990). Chances are they fall prey to an occupational myopia that excludes political activism from the realm of their professional endeavors. If that is the case, it is time we realize that the nature of social problems dictates that constructive action be taken not only at the psychological level, but at the societal level as well. At a point in the development of the social sciences where it is obvious that only systemic reasoning (e.g., Bateson 1972; Capra 1982) will help us address human problems, social action may no longer be a matter of choice but a matter of necessity. School psychologists need not apologize for becoming involved in the political arena.

A major task envisioned for the profession would be to influence policy makers' views of children's problems. To illustrate the change in direction desired, Albee's formula for the incidence of psychopathology is useful (Commission on the Prevention of Mental-Emotional Disabilities 1987, p. 199):

$$\text{Incidence of Psychopathology} = \frac{\text{Organic Factors} + \text{Stress} + \text{Exploitation}}{\text{Coping Skills} + \text{Self-Esteem} + \text{Supports}}$$

Social problem-solvers, psychologists among them, have sought to reduce the incidence of disorders primarily by increasing the denominator. This tendency has resulted in a one-sided view of a multifaceted phenomenon (Rappaport 1981, 1987). It is within the purview of school psychology to counteract this imbalance through the promotion of legislation and policies designed to decrease the numerator, particularly as it pertains to stressful environments for children, the adverse effects of which are well documented (Honig 1986a, 1986b). Specific needs vary from community to community, but the overall thrust should be to assign to environmental factors their proper weight, as they are presently severely underestimated. Coping strategies, social support, education, and attitudes are indeed unquestionably important elements in the reduction of psychological disorders. Yet efforts to reshape the psychological world of children may be wasted if the environmental world is not concurrently improved (Albee, Bond, and Cook Monsey 1992; Pransky 1991).

In pursuing a specific agenda, determined by regional priorities and designed to improve the environment where children grow, school psychologists will engage in proactive socially sensitive interventions. Useful guidelines to follow in political activism, with particular reference to school psychology, have been presented by Conoley (1981) and Trachtman (1990). Specific suggestions to pursue the changes hereby recommended will be outlined below.

Reactive Socially Sensitive Interventions

Reactive socially sensitive interventions are directed at those conditions that were either not the subject of, or could not be successfully dealt with by, proactive measures. These are problems that require immediate attention, such as behavioral and learning difficulties. Clinicians encounter those on a daily basis. Given the pervasive individualistic bias present in education and psychology, school personnel tend to neglect the social dimension of learning and conduct disorders.

A case in point is the treatment of children who exhibit aggressive behavior. In spite of the fact that research shows that demographic and family variables are crucial in both the genesis and the perpetuation of antisocial behavior in children (Patterson, DeBaryshe, and Ramsey 1989), most therapeutic efforts are directed at modifying the actions of the single child (Geiser 1976; Stolz 1978; Winett and Winkler 1972). The literature reviewed by Patterson and his colleagues (1989) clearly indicates that children who come from families with a history of antisocial behavior in other family members, whose families are economically disadvantaged and experience significant stressors such as unemployment, marital discord, or domestic violence, are at very high risk for developing patterns of antisocial behavior themselves. Those factors warrant a systemic intervention capable of addressing the ecological (e.g., familial and societal) dimensions feeding the dysfunctional behavior. As opposed to fragmentary techniques focused on the child, reactive socially sensitive approaches call for the empowerment of all the parties involved—primarily the teacher, the child, and the parents. This means a collaborative effort to regain control in some aspects of their lives without doing it at the expense of others. Knowledge of the precarious backgrounds those children come from should serve to increase the sense of urgency and collaboration needed with the family, not to inadvertently engage in a futile blame-the-victim exercise. School psychologists, by virtue of their central role in the treatment of antisocial behavior, can be instrumental in promoting the desired changes by sensitizing school personnel as to the families' plight and by organizing school-home networks to provide support to parents in need.

Through a community-school psychology approach, gains can be made not only in behavior, but in the learning area as well. Parental involvement plays a major role in the education of children (Rutter 1985a). Unfortunately, due to personal experiences of failure in the educational system many parents from disadvantaged backgrounds avoid coming to school, or feel incapable of assisting in the education of their children. They are easily intimidated by school personnel and do not get involved in school or community activities (Deutsch 1964; Heber 1984). Through a concerted effort to involve those parents in the education of their youngsters and make them feel part of the school and local community, the school psychologist could be improving the self-concept of many parents directly and helping many more children indirectly (Heber 1984).

Just as teachers' insecurities need to be considered in the consultation process, parents' feelings of inadequacy and perceived fears should be carefully monitored. Parental involvement is almost always crucial, but too often parents are reluctant participants in the plan of action. School personnel and psychologists would do well to examine the ways in which they may be inadvertently alienating parents. Some suggestions as to how to foster parental involvement and the previously discussed ideals are presented next.

THE STRATEGY

Neither portrayals of the realm of contemporary school psychology (e.g., Reynolds et al. 1984) nor visions of the future for the profession (Fagan 1989; Hart 1989) make the advent of a social ethics mentality a clear priority. If school psychologists are to become active players in the alleviation of the many social deficiencies in children's environments, then a case must be made for the advent of social ethics. To facilitate the promotion of this mentality, I propose a shift in orientation in three areas:

1. Etiological reasoning and treatment: From asocial to macrosocial and macrosociopolitical paradigms
2. Timing of intervention: From reactive to proactive interventions
3. The human factor: From alienation and reluctant participation to meaningful engagement of the people involved in the delivery of services

These three goals summarize the main thrust of the changes advocated in this chapter. In order to attain them, or at least work toward their attainment, I propose to develop two separate agendas: local and national/international. I will first describe the means by which these goals can be approximated at the local level.

Local Action

1. Education and Organization of School Psychologists. Two rules of paramount importance in social action are to have clear goals and to organize people to pursue those objectives (Alinsky 1971). The literature cited in this chapter provides several points of entry for the psychologist interested in learning more about the benefits of (a) approaching childhood disorders from a macrosocial perspective, (b) intervening early, and (c) involving all the people affected in a meaningful, nonthreatening, and constructive manner. A first step an individual psychologist may take in organizing colleagues could be to initiate regular discussion-group meetings. Clinicians working in the same school district or agency could explore means by which the goals stated above may be incorporated in their operations. In-service training and professional development days could be used for this purpose. Once frontline workers develop a coherent proposal for the initial implementation of some macrosocial or preventive activities, for example, administrative approval is to be sought. Given that this phase is most complicated at the best of times, it is very important that the proposal be endorsed by as many professionals as possible. Salient sources of power in the process of interpersonal influence are information and expertise. (For a detailed analysis of the political applications of the psychology of interpersonal influence and social power, see Raven 1990.) School psychologists ought to capitalize on those attributes in their attempt to persuade administrators to alter their philosophy of service delivery. Although administrators' approval may be difficult to obtain, it is worth trying. Otherwise, changes would have to be pursued from outside the system, thereby decreasing the chances that the recommendations will be assimilated into the operations of the school. On the other hand, when innovations are sought from within the system, and are accepted by its administrators, the process of change is much more expeditious (Alinsky 1971; Chin and Benne 1985). Having arrived at some tentative conclusions regarding the changes desired to foster a social ethics mentality, school psychologists, individually or collectively, need to disseminate their views.

2. *Dialogue with Schools.* In order to promote a specific objective in a school (e.g., the implementation of an early-identification and prevention program or the establishment of a parent-teacher support group), action can be taken at the level of the single building or across the entire school district or regional authority, depending on the scope of the program, resistance to innovations, and local needs. To develop a mental health program in a particular school, the identification of a sympathetic principal may be crucial. The idea may be introduced at the beginning of the year, a time when the psychologist may meet with school personnel to establish annual goals and priorities. An individual teacher can be very instrumental in creating support within the school for the suggested program or change. At the school district level, the goals stated above may be disseminated in ad hoc committees studying issues such as behaviorally disruptive students, or in professional development activities with teachers.

Inviting input from the school is absolutely essential. Schools have to be active participants in the development of the program. Without that, the envisioned change may be just one more in a series of unrealized good ideas (Chin and Benne 1985; Klein 1985).

3. *Dialogue with Parents.* Collaboration with parents is as crucial as collaboration with schools. It is not uncommon to work with parents who tend to define their children's problems in a completely *asocial* fashion, blaming the child for his or her difficulties. Alternatively, some parents accuse the teacher. In addition, many families tend to wait until the difficulties are extremely severe before they reach out for assistance, which is a good reason to promote the concept of prevention and early intervention in the community. Finally, like teachers, parents need to be empowered. They have to be able to have a dialogue with school offi-

cials without being intimidated or fearful. There are many things the school psychologist can do to meet these needs either at the case level or addressing parents as a group—including giving talks at PTA meetings, serving on school committees, and promoting nonthreatening communications between school and parents.

Ideally, parents could elect a few representatives to help school personnel and psychologists design socially sensitive interventions. A case in point may be the recruitment of volunteer parents to serve as mentors for children in a resilience promotion program.

4. Establishment of a Psychologist-Home-School Network. The establishment of an advisory council composed of the school psychologist, a teacher representative, an administrator, and a parent representative can serve as a catalyst for many of the desired changes outlined above. Meeting on a regular basis, the council may be instrumental in promoting community and early interventions. In addition, the council may serve as a screening committee for referrals for special psychological or educational services. Having parent representatives and teachers on the council may facilitate the sense of empowerment so much needed in these two constituencies. Although confidentiality may present a problem, consideration may be given to having a student representative on the council as well.

Another three important roles may be envisioned for this body: (a) It may serve as a forum to resolve disputes between school and parents, (b) it may organize parent-teacher support groups around specific issues such as behavioral problems or particular handicaps, and (c) it may lobby for policy changes at the local, state, provincial, or national level.

National/International Action

1. Facilitating Change through Professional Organizations. National and international organizations of school and other applied areas of psychology can play a vital role in disseminating a social ethics mentality. Symposia on the benefits of prevention and empowerment in school psychology can be organized at annual conventions. Furthermore, fruitful collaboration might take place between school psychology associations and the newly formed American Association of Applied and Preventive Psychology (AAAPP). In addition to organizing workshops and seminars at the conventions, long-term committees to explore ways for furthering the social ethics mentality can be formed. The committees might, for instance, look at means to effectively propagate the findings gathered by the Commission on the Prevention of Mental-Emotional Disorders (1987) and the American Psychological Association Task Force on Promotion, Prevention, and Intervention Alternatives (Price et al. 1988, 1989).

2. *Training Programs.* Philosophically, there is a need to comprehend the pervasive infiltration of the Cartesian paradigm in our *Weltanschauung.* This mode of thinking translates into the practice of separating the individual from his or her ecological context. In spite of much talk about systems in the social sciences, the fact remains that atomism is still largely prevalent in both psychology (Capra 1982; Sarason 1981b) and education (Heshusius 1989). Once the deficits of the dominant Cartesian paradigm are fully understood, it will become apparent that a truly systemic mode of thinking requires more than the numerical inclusion of more participants in the process of intervention. There is presently an attempt to include more people, and more professions, in the process of treatment (cf. Bechtel 1984). But those approaches remain predominantly focused on the "sick" child and/or family. What is required is a qualitative rather than a mere quantitative change. A more systemically sensitive view would question not only the child's actions but also the behavior of societal institutions impacting on the child's life. Explanation and remediation would neither begin nor end with the particular client but rather would involve a *dialectical* examination of individuals *and* their social contexts.

Information gathered by Johnston (1990) indicates that the focus of most school psychology training programs continues to be traditional assessment. In light of literature reviewed in this chapter, it would be justified to balance that state of affairs with more emphasis on systemic, ecological evaluations and interventions. Professional organizations might take a leadership role in encouraging training centers to adopt a wider approach to school psychology, much like the APA encourages programs to promote cultural diversity.

3. *Lobbying for Better Educational and Social Policies.* Professional organizations can be powerful generators of change at the legislative level. With thousands of members, these structures might identify a specific issue and use the full force of their memberships to create macrosocial conditions conducive to the healthy physical and psychological development of children. In the United States, for example, pressure might be exerted to have the president ratify the United Nations Convention on the Rights of the Child. This move would guarantee better services for poor children and families (Cohen and Naimark 1991; Melton 1991).

CONCLUSION

Change in school psychology cannot occur without a critique of present practices, their philosophical roots, and, most importantly, their social consequences. The critique should encompass, as was intended here, the global and abstract as well as the specific and concrete aspects of school psychology that impede the implementation of a socially sensitive agenda. Following a detailed analysis of the various forces perpetuating the regnant individualistic philosophy and its consequences, the need will be seen, I hope, for the emergence of a social ethics in school psychology.

Once the profession, nationally and/or locally, reaches a consensus as to the specific changes needed to foster the mentality I have described, a great deal of eloquence will be required to convince consumers (e.g., school boards, families, and community) that a shift in orientation is required. Having the conviction that an enhanced social ethics in school psychology *is not a luxury but a necessity* may greatly refine the will for persuasion.

PART III

PSYCHOLOGY AND SOCIAL ETHICS

Part II of this volume was devoted to a moral and political critique of dominant theories and practices in psychology. Part III articulates a framework for the promotion of social ethics in the discipline. *Social* ethics differ from *individual* ethics in that, while the latter is primarily concerned with the welfare of the individual citizen, client, student, or research participant, the former endeavors to enhance the well-being of all members of society, particularly of its vulnerable ones (cf. Addams 1902; Chambers 1992). As I have noted, psychology has devoted most of its ethical efforts in the direction of individual ethics. Consistent with the main thrust of this book, I wish to delineate some parameters for the emergence of a social ethics in psychology. This is done in three parts. Chapter 13 presents some tentative criteria for the definition of the "good society" that are used both as a measure against which the current social order is evaluated, and as an ideal to guide efforts toward social change. Chapter 14 utilizes the Gramscian notion of hegemony to explain why people come to believe that the present social order is the best possible one. Potential roles for psychologists as counterhegemonic agents of social change are explored. The last chapter examines in detail the possibility of employing the emancipatory language and practice of empowerment, not only in the most socially conscious branches of psychology, but in mainstream psychology as well. Building on the criteria for the good society advanced in chapter 13, I argue that an empowerment agenda of social change should be informed by an approach that balances three moral values:

(a) self-determination, (b) distributive justice, and (c) collaboration and democratic participation in public affairs. I conclude by drawing attention to the risk of favoring self-determination at the expense of distributive justice and communal cooperation. When that happens, self-determination devolves into a new fashion of individualism that is capable of nullifying the emancipatory and social justice principles of empowerment.

Chapter 13

HUMAN WELFARE AND THE STATUS QUO

It has been argued in part II that several psychological formulations and practices seem to be instrumental in upholding the societal status quo. This state of affairs has far-reaching social and ethical implications. Given that both the American and the Canadian codes of ethics for psychologists clearly state the promotion of human welfare as one of their primary aims, it would be pertinent to elaborate on the repercussions of psychology's endorsement of the present social order. Before we arrive at any tentative conclusion in this regard, a number of questions need to be addressed: (a) What is human welfare? (b) What is the good society that is likely to enhance the well-being of its members? and (c) Is human welfare being promoted in the present social system?

THE GOOD LIFE

The question of what is human welfare is posed here in the language usually used by philosophers—that is, what is the good life?—simply because human "welfare" might be perceived in a rather limited way. Whereas human welfare may be associated mainly with subsistence, the good life goes much beyond that. At the same time, the good life should not be treated as identical with pleasure, for, as we shall see below, it is conceivably more than a life of happiness.

What constitutes and how to achieve the good life are fundamental concerns in ethics. Sidgwick (1922) defines ethics as "the science
or study of what is right or what ought to be, so far as this depends
upon the voluntary action of individuals" (p. 4). *Right*, according to
philosophers Frankena (1963), Sidgwick (1922), Singer (1993), and
Williams (1972), can be interpreted as actions that will enhance personal and communal well-being. Such reasoning is implied in
Frankena's (1963) assertion that "morality is not to be a minister merely
to one's own good life but to that of others as well" (p. 77). This segment will focus primarily on personal well-being. More will be said
about duty and the well-being of others when we consider the good
society.

Consensus cannot be easily reached as to what is the good life.
Nevertheless, Olson (1978) contends that there is some agreement
among contemporary philosophers that the good life cannot be attained
by a single good-making characteristic. Among the constitutive elements of the good life Olson mentions pleasure, purposeful activity,
satisfying human relationships, a sense of personal worth, and physical
well-being. Interestingly enough, physical well-being is placed last, for
Olson (1978) himself points out that it "is a condition of the successful
experience of any of the four intrinsic goods thus far mentioned" (p. 25).
This short list bears great resemblance to the human needs presented by
Maslow in his theory of self-actualization, which is the model to be
advocated for the purposes of this discussion.

Maslow's theory of self-actualization (also referred to as "self-fulfillment") accords with a well-respected tradition in philosophy, from
Aristotle to the contemporary Blanshard (1961). Aristotle conceived of
happiness in terms of self-fulfillment. Norman (1983) correctly asserts
that the first postulate in Aristotle's theory of self-fulfillment is that
"the ultimate end of human action is happiness" (p. 38). In Aristotle's
words:

> We always desire happiness for its own sake and never as a means
> to something else, whereas we desire honor, pleasure, intellect,
> and every virtue, partly for their own sakes (for we should desire
> them independently of what might result from them) but partly
> also as being means to happiness, because we suppose they will
> prove the instruments of happiness. Happiness, on the other hand,
> nobody desires for the sake of these things, nor indeed as a means
> to anything at all. (Aristotle 1978, p. 158)

The word *happiness* contains only some of the connotations of the original *eudaimonia*. In Greek, *eudaimonia* refers to well-being, flourishing (Norman 1983), and also prosperity, the good or best life, and good fortune (Harsthouse 1986). Clearly, *eudaimonia* encompasses more than pleasure. According to Aristotle it is "an activity of soul in accordance with complete or perfect virtue. . . . Virtue or excellence being twofold, partly intellectual and partly moral" (Aristotle 1978, p. 159). The way to attain intellectual virtue is by teaching. Moral virtue can be achieved by habit (Aristotle 1978). The emphasis placed by Aristotle on fulfillment as a spiritual enterprise does not detract from his awareness that certain material conditions need to be present in order to reach such a desired state. "Aristotle recognizes as a constraint on his account of *eudaimonia* that the flourishing life should contain the real advantages of (some) material wealth and pleasure to which the vicious attach such importance" (Harsthouse 1986, p. 53).

One of the difficulties with the Aristotelian doctrine is that, instead of providing a descriptive account of what are the human needs that will account for *eudaimonia*, it appeals to the idea of human nature or human function. The argument is as follows: If individuals behave according to "human nature" or perform their "human function," this activity will foster the good life (Norman 1983). Philosophers have interpreted these concepts in various forms: (a) as an activity characteristic of human beings, (b) as a distinctive quality that differentiates humans from the animal kingdom, usually rationality, and (c) as the fulfillment of some divine purpose (Norman 1983; Olson 1978). Authors agree that the meaning given by Aristotle to human nature and/or human function remains obscure and problematic; and inasmuch as these are central concepts of the doctrine, his account of fulfillment is not entirely satisfactory. As Norman (1983) puts it, "Something more is needed than the bald Aristotelian argument that because a certain activity is distinctively human, it is therefore constitutive of a good human life; nor does the concept of function render the argument any more valid" (p. 48). As we shall see later, Maslow's model is more helpful in that it defines fulfillment in terms of specific needs to be satisfied.

The notion of needs plays an important role in Blanshard's (1961) model of fulfillment: "Man [*sic*] is a creature of impulses, needs, and faculties; what he seems to be bent on is the fulfillment of those impulses, the satisfaction of those needs, the realization of those faculties" (p. 292). This is an important addition to the Aristotelian conception of the good life, because needs are easier to define and identify than the elusive term *human nature*. Blanshard describes the good life as consisting of experiences that are "directly or immediately good. When they are good intrinsically, they perform a double function: they fulfill an impulse, drive or need, and in so doing they give satisfaction or pleasure. Both components, fulfillment and satisfaction, are necessary" (p. 293). To be more precise, Blanshard defines fulfillment as "achieving the end that our impulse is seeking" and satisfaction as "the feeling that attends this fulfillment" (p. 309).

While Blanshard is certain about the role of needs in fulfillment, he falls short of articulating specifically what these needs are. This is one of Maslow's most valuable contributions to understanding what the good life consists of.

Maslow's exposition of the good life is guided by the central concept of the hierarchy of needs. Self-actualization or personal fulfillment, the highest of human needs according to Maslow (1970a), may ordinarily be attained only after more basic needs have been at least partially satisfied. Human needs (also called "desires" or "motives") are arranged in ascending order of priority. The satisfaction of each category may be conceived as an intrinsic good in itself, and as an extrinsic good in that it facilitates the advent of the next-higher need.

The basic needs require little explanation, for they are the most obvious of all. Included here are such indispensable things as water, food, shelter, air, sleep, and sex. Without them subsistence becomes unbearable and the person cannot be expected to aspire to higher needs, for all of her or his energy is directed toward achieving these basic elements. Once the physical needs are reasonably satisfied, safety needs emerge. These are characterized by the search for predictability, security, order, certainty, and structure in one's environment.

Growth needs or metaneeds are associated with the human tendency to realize the potential inherent in the individual. These *cannot* be developed unless the basic needs are satisfactorily fulfilled. Belongingness and love needs express the desire to be part of a reference group, and to establish affectionate relationships. The gratification of these enables the emergence of self-esteem needs. Two types of esteem needs are identified: (a) self-respect, and (b) esteem from others. The former is embodied in the notion of personal confidence; the latter in recognition, acceptance, and appreciation by others. Finally, when all of the above-mentioned needs have been sufficiently gratified, the person reaches the highest stage of human desire and becomes concerned with the attainment of self-actualization. Essentially, this process entails the realization of one's potentials, and the desire for self-improvement. At this stage the individuality and uniqueness of the person express themselves fully. As Maslow (1968) points out, "Self actualization is idiosyncratic since every person is different" (p. 33). An appreciation of beauty, order, justice, and goodness characterizes the self-actualized individual.

Goble (1970) and Hjelle and Ziegler (1981) report empirical data that substantiate Maslow's claim that human desires are hierarchically ordered. Another important empirical finding was that self-actualized people indeed exist and enjoy life fully, which again would confirm Maslow's ideas about fulfillment (Maslow 1968).

Maslow (1970a) emphasized the minimal environmental requirements conducive to the satisfaction of the basic needs. He enumerates justice, fairness, freedom, and order as some of the preconditions for the fulfillment of the most fundamental needs.

It appears then that the self-actualization theory advanced by Maslow represents a viable model for the understanding of the constitutive elements of the good life. Its most helpful features are the arrangement of needs in hierarchical manner, a descriptive account of what these needs are, the empirical validation of these tenets, and the consideration of social preconditions for the gratification of essential needs. Now it is necessary to examine the society that is likely to be conducive to this good life.

THE GOOD SOCIETY

The purpose of this section is to delineate some of the essential attributes a society should have in order to facilitate the individual well-being of its members. In an *ideal* state of affairs the good society should comprise the majority of these features. While an outline of the social qualities to be cultivated cannot do justice to the intricacies involved, the aim here is to introduce some criteria of the desired features of the good society that will (a) enable us to conduct an initial moral appraisal of capitalism, and (b) provide preliminary desiderata for social change.

A comprehensive and sensible exposition of indispensable social ideals is provided by Olson (1978). His elucidation of the good society consists of six prerequisites: stability, harmony, social cohesion, justice, freedom, and material prosperity. (Inasmuch as harmony and social cohesion deal mainly with the same issue, they will be treated as one under the heading "Social Harmony.") These *ideals*, which resemble the preconditions for well-being previously attributed to Maslow, can only be partially attained. It is quite illusory to think that any one society would be able to reach these ideals fully. Yet there is merit in portraying them as facilitators of well-being as well as desiderata.

Stability

The maintenance of some degree of order and predictability in major institutions of society, such as the economy and the legal system, is a minimal requirement for the satisfaction of basic needs. The anxiety created by the lack of economic stability, for instance, consumes considerable mental energy, which becomes aimed at procuring vital necessities. A social system that does not guarantee secure employment is bound to generate fear and justified preoccupation with money, leaving little time or consideration for self-fulfillment.

When the rules of society are unpredictable, as in anarchy and many military dictatorships, people do not feel safe enough to engage in self-improvement. They are justifiably preoccupied with trying to anticipate unpredictable rules and, hence, with survival.

The emphasis on stability does not detract from the importance of social change. At times, a period of instability is necessary in order to bring about greater stability. That may be the case when social justice is advanced at the expense of temporary social instability. The promotion of greater social justice is likely to create the conditions for a more stable socioeconomic order. "Instability follows not from change itself but from unpredictable change. Predictable change is wholly compatible with stability" (Olson 1978, p. 30).

Social Harmony

According to Olson (1978) there are four kinds of dangers that beset any animal species: "(1) the weakness of the body, disease, and physical pain, (2) natural catastrophes such as floods, earthquakes, and tornadoes, (3) the aggression of other animal species, and (4) the aggression or noncooperation of other members of one's own species" (p. 32). Whereas the first three are prominent among the lower animals, the fourth predominates among humans. Social harmony can be achieved when the fourth danger listed above can be at least partially neutralized.

The main question that Olson poses here is "how does society manage to reconcile different individual interests so as to produce social harmony" (p. 33). He indicates that there are two main means of achieving social harmony. The first is the institution of external sanctions, both negative and positive; and the second is the process of socialization, whereby human beings are trained to live harmoniously with each other. His answer would appear to be rather superficial, in that he does not address the origins of the differing interests, and furthermore does not distinguish among various types of interests. Are differing interests bound to emerge as part of human nature? Are differing interests always conflicting interests? Are interests not shaped to a large degree by the socioeconomic order? Unfortunately, Olson does not elaborate on these questions. Nevertheless, it would seem reasonable to follow Olson in his view that social harmony constitutes a necessary condition for the furtherance of self-fulfillment. As in the case of stability, it would appear that Maslow would view social harmony as a precondition for the satisfaction of basic needs.

Social Justice

Whereas the problem of precise definition is always present in discussing moral issues, Sidgwick (1922) points out that "there is no case where the difficulty is greater, or the result more disputed, than when we try to define justice" (p. 264). Having stated the arduousness of this enterprise, I will try all the same to clarify what is meant by social justice and how it impacts upon personal welfare.

An illuminating introduction to the concept of justice is found in D. Miller's book *Social Justice* (1978). Miller commences his essay by asserting that "the most valuable general definition of justice is that which brings out its distributive character most plainly: justice is *suum cuique*, to each his [*sic*] due" (p. 20). Following this broad conception of justice, Miller specifically notes that social justice

> concerns the distribution of benefits and burdens throughout a society, as it results from the major social institutions—property systems, public organizations, etc. It deals with such matters as the regulation of wages and (where they exist) profits, the protection of persons' rights through the legal system, the allocation of housing, medicine, welfare benefits, etc. (p. 22)

As can be seen from the definitions given, the *distributive* character of justice is fundamental. Distributive principles are to be distinguished from aggregative principles. An aggregative principle is concerned with the total amount of good enjoyed by a particular group of people. A distributive principle, on the other hand, is concerned with how that good is shared among the individual members of the group (D. Miller 1978).

Much of the present discontent with traditional utilitarianism, according to which a just act is that which produces the greatest amount of happiness for the greatest number of people, is that it is perceived to be in essence an aggregative notion of justice (D. Miller 1978; Mullaly 1980; Olson 1978; Rawls 1972). As such, it holds that there are situations in which the rights of an individual can be violated for the benefit of the public at large. An example frequently given to illustrate this point is that of a sheriff who has in custody a person accused of a murder (e.g., Olson 1978). The sheriff knows that the individual is innocent, but the angry mob outside the jail is convinced that the prisoner is guilty, and they are determined to lynch the prisoner. If the sheriff does not go along with the mob, there will be a riot and many people will die. The utilitarian view would sacrifice one innocent person to prevent many other deaths.

Irrespective of the particular school of thought embraced, the cardinal question of justice according to Sidgwick (a utilitarian) seems to be: "Are there any clear principles from which we may work out an ideally just *distribution* of rights and privileges, burdens and pains, among human beings as such" (Sidgwick 1922, p. 274; italics added). Contemporary writers have tried to identify specific criteria for fair distribution.

D. Miller (1978) gives three possible answers to the question of how to allocate *to each his or her due*. To each, he says, according to their (a) rights, and/or (b) deserts, and/or (c) needs. The problem is to determine which one of these possibilities takes priority, for at times they are bound to conflict. That is the case when an individual inherits wealth. While that person may have the *right* to inherit the wealth, it can be argued that he or she does not *deserve* the money unless she or he has performed some services to the benefactor prior to his or her death. Similarly, it may be said that the person does not need the money or possessions inherited. While D. Miller outlines the contending criteria, he does not provide clear guidelines on how to prioritize them. Olson adds to Miller's list the notions of social utility and contribution. But he, too, fails to provide a "differential diagnosis" as to when to apply which criterion in cases of conflict.

A viable method of selecting and prioritizing criteria for social justice, in my view, is furnished by Facione, Scherer, and Attig (1978). They introduce the notion of *social circumstances* to assist in the resolution of conflicts between competing alternatives. According to them, there are two main criteria in determining the distribution of burdens and benefits: (a) work and (b) need. According to the first criterion, differential treatment may be considered justified in cases where there are noticeable differences in terms of ability, productivity, or effort. Concerning the need criterion, the authors claim that it is "reasonable to suggest that persons are strictly equal as persons. This means they all have some very basic human needs. . . . On this criterion people are equally deserving of having these needs met" (p. 186). A similar position has been advanced by Singer (1993). The applicability of one criterion or the other would be influenced by the reigning social circumstances. Consider the following social conditions described by Facione, Scherer, and Attig (1978):

> (a) there is sufficient work so that there are jobs for all who need them, (b) the jobs available to each person include jobs that the person has the abilities to perform, and (c) the jobs pay well enough so that whenever a person takes one, it will enable him or her to earn enough so that his or her needs are met. (p. 190)

The authors point out that in circumstances such as these, preference will be given to the criterion of work.

Consider now the following scenario:

> (a) It may be that there are fewer jobs than there are people who need them. (b) Persons may be unable to perform the jobs that are available owing to simple lack of ability. . . . The lack of ability may be socially dependent in the sense that skills that people do have can become outmoded and no longer needed in a rapidly changing and technologically progressive society. Or it may be that in a nation as a whole there are sufficient jobs to match the abilities of the people, but the people with the abilities are not located where the jobs are. . . . It could also be that some are denied opportunities to do the work for which they are qualified owing to various forms of job discrimination. (c) It may be that the jobs for which some people qualify, or that they are able to handle given their other responsibilities, simply do not pay well enough to meet their needs. The wages may be extremely low, or the work may be part-time or seasonal. (Facione, Scherer, and Attig 1978, pp. 190-91)

If any of the circumstances just depicted occurs, preference will likely be given to the criterion of need. For if we accept the proposition that there are some needs that human beings, as human beings, are entitled to have met, then they deserve to have these needs gratified.

The notion of social justice is indispensable in the construction of the ideal good society. As we saw in the preceding discussion, there are times when the just distribution of resources becomes imperative in order to fulfill basic needs, without which we can hardly expect self-actualization.

Social Freedom

Basically, social freedom can be thought of in two different ways: as (a) positive freedom or freedom of choice, and (b) negative freedom or freedom from restraint (Facione, Scherer, and Attig 1978; Olson 1978).

Freedom from restraint has to do with the ability to pursue one's goals without undue or excessive frustration. In this respect, a free society is that which facilitates the attainment of objectives set by its members. Obviously this is only an ideal state. Nevertheless, it would not be erroneous to evaluate societies comparatively in terms of the different degrees of freedom from restraint to which their members are subjected. Complete negative freedom may be not only impossible to achieve but also undesirable; for then individuals will be subjected to the will of other, less-moral persons who may infringe upon their capacity to seek the goals they set for themselves. It is precisely for that reason that societies may justifiably limit their constituents. Facione, Scherer, and Attig (1978) argue that restrictions may be rightly imposed for the purposes of

> (a) treating people equally under the law, (b) giving all people a fair chance in society, (c) preventing anyone's doing bodily harm to others, to their property, or to himself or herself, (d) promoting further development of each person's positive freedom, and (e) restricting socially offensive or morally distasteful behavior. (p. 115)

These social restraints are imperative if conflicts of interests are to be resolved fairly. The importance of limiting freedom from restraint can be conveyed by paraphrasing the old saying "One person's negative freedom ends where another person's positive freedom begins."

Freedom of choice refers to "the number of options, or possible courses of action, society makes available to its members and the extent to which individual choices are informed and rational" (Olson 1978, p. 45). According to those terms, society can increase freedom of choice by

(a) enhancing the range of options from which people can choose, and (b) informing people about the existing options and educating them how to arrive at a rational choice that will benefit them.

A delicate balance ought to be maintained between negative and positive freedom, if everyone is to benefit from them. The intricacies involved in such delicate balance is beyond the scope of this discussion. It should be clear, however, that freedom is an indispensable ingredient in the making of the good society—and, as Maslow asserted, an essential one in the good life.

Material Prosperity

The last condition cited by Olson (1978) as a prerequisite for the good society is the presence of material prosperity. In many respects this is an obvious expectation. An impressive list of desirable goods is associated with economic progress—among them, improvements in health care, transportation, production technology, and communication systems.

The question that is less self-explanatory is how these goods ought to be distributed, which brings us back to the above discussion on social justice (cf. Singer 1993, chap. 8). For the purpose of this section it would suffice to say that material prosperity—when achieved without violating the principles of distributive justice—is a desirable attribute of the good society and, much in the same way as basic needs are elementary for the attainment of self-fulfillment, so are material goods.

Thus far we have considered criteria for the good life and the good society. However tentative and incomplete those criteria may be, it is a first step in the portrayal of an ideal state of affairs against which the present social system may be evaluated.

THE GOOD LIFE IN THE PRESENT SOCIAL ORDER

Is the present social order conducive to the good life? In order to answer that question, it will be necessary to explore (a) to what extent criteria for the good society are met in the North American social order, and, subsequently, (b) what degree of good life is attainable under these social conditions. Task (a) will be carried out by examining the presence (or absence) of the social ideals already described. It should be appreciated from the outset of the discussion that the existing social structure precludes the treatment of society as a uniform conglomerate. Not only the relevance but also the prevalence of some social ideals are highly dependent on the division of classes. Material prosperity and positive freedom, for instance, are more prominent in upper classes. Socioeconomic status, then, will be a source of variability when considering the fulfillment of criteria for the good society.

Another point to bear in mind is that the analysis will endeavor to compare the dominant social order with an ideal or desired state of affairs and not with other forms of social structures or political arrangements. Mention of other systems will be limited to illustrative examples.

Finally, scrutiny of the criteria will reveal that most social ideals may be regarded as subordinate to social justice. Hence, special attention will be given to that criterion. While I am painfully aware that no definite answers can be given, it seems instrumental to approach the issue in the form of leading questions.

Is There Stability?

As we saw in the preceding discussion, the criterion of stability refers to some degree of order and predictability in major institutions of society. According to Edwards, Reich, and Weisskopf (1986), observation of two such institutions, the political system and the economy, suggests that whereas the former enjoys considerable stability in North America, the latter is continuously affected by fluctuations:

> The reality of an "economic crisis" forced itself upon most Americans in the 1970s. Soaring rates of unemployment and inflation, declining levels of consumption, and widespread economic difficulties unmatched since the Great Depression of the 1930s shattered the prevailing myth that economic prosperity and stability could be taken for granted in a modern capitalist society. (p. 359)

Undoubtedly, crises affect the population overall, but the disadvantaged are likely to be hit the hardest. The unemployed, obviously the most vulnerable segment of all, constitute a significant percentage of the population in times of recession. Rates of unemployment in the United States, for instance, reached 18.3 percent in the 1929-37 depression, and 6.9 percent in the 1973-81 crisis (Bowles, Gordon, and Weisskopf 1986). In Canada, statistics for 1986 show that, with an average unemployment rate of 9.6 percent, some provinces had rates as high as 14.4 percent (New Brunswick) and even 20 percent (Newfoundland) (Statistics Canada 1987).

The cyclical character of crises and the different degrees of resilience with which people confront them lead to the notion of distributive justice. Whether crises in capitalist systems are the result of unplanned economy and socially irresponsible policies, or an inevitable result of unknown dynamics or of natural disasters, the cardinal question remains: How is the burden shared in the present social order?

Is There Social Harmony?

The ideal of social harmony is accomplished when "aggression or noncooperation of other members of one's own species" (Olson 1978, p. 32) is eradicated. A society aspiring to meet this goal would strive to keep aggression or noncooperation to a minimum. Aggression or noncooperation can be interpreted in numerous ways. For our purposes, aggression of one nation against another and violent acts performed in crimes will be excluded. The former can be rationalized as acts of self-defense, and the latter as deviant behavior of sick individuals. It would seem congruent with this analysis to outline forms of noncooperation that are constitutive of the social system. Following Edwards, Reich, and Weisskopf (1986), it can be argued that at a structural level there are at least three prominent sources of social tensions: (a) socioeconomic inequality, (b) male dominance, and (c) racism. The pervasive divisive effects of these phenomena would seem to be an integral part of our social order (see Brittan and Maynard 1984; Edwards et al. 1986, particularly chaps. 6, 7, and 8).

Illustrative of economic inequality is a comparison between the poorest and the richest 20 percent of the families in the United States since World War II. According to Ackerman and Zimbalist (1986), while the former "have consistently received less than 6 percent of total family income, . . . [the latter] have gotten more than 40 percent" (p. 218). The authors also note that "in 1983 the top 5 percent of all families received nearly 16 percent of total family income, more than three times as much as the entire bottom twenty percent" (p. 218). As for individuals who do not live in families, that income is even "more unequally distributed than that of families" (p. 218). Finally, it should be pointed out that inequality of economic welfare is further exacerbated by the uneven distribution of wealth.

Despite the recognition that women do not enjoy the same economic opportunities as men, that they still have the primary responsibility of looking after the children and doing housework, whether or not they work outside the house, and that they are stereotyped by much advertising, and "despite the undermining of patriarchy and advances in women's rights, male dominance has survived in contemporary capitalism" (Edwards et al. 1986, p. 251; see also Bartky 1990; Brittan and Maynard 1984; Hartman 1976; Miller and Mothner 1981).

On the question of racism, M. Reich (1986) writes that in the "early 1960s it seemed to many that the elimination of racism in the U.S. was proceeding without requiring a radical restructuring of the entire society" (p. 305). However, Reich notes that the optimism of the sixties had vanished in the eighties. "Despite new civil rights laws, elaborate White House conferences, special government employment and training programs, the War on Poverty, and affirmative action in hiring, racism and the economic exploitation of blacks remain with us" (p. 305). Reich's final assessment of racism in the present social order is that "instead of disappearing, [it] seems to be permanent" (p. 305).

As the reviewed literature would appear to confirm, much of the tensions created by the conflicting interests of the different parties involved (management and labor; men and women; visible minorities and dominant majority groups) have to do with the way burdens and benefits are distributed in society.

Is There Freedom?

We have distinguished between negative freedom, or freedom from constraints, and positive freedom, or freedom of choice. Rand (1967) regards freedom as the pillar of the capitalist system. In comparison to other social arrangements, such as those in some former communist countries, people in the present social order enjoy a great deal of negative freedom. And while Benne (1981) is correct in asserting that "those who have wealth and power have access to legal defenses that gives them a huge advantage over ordinary citizens" (p. 215), and this could therefore expand their potential negative freedoms, all citizens remain in principle equal before the law.

In principle, all people have the freedom to choose what they want to do with their lives. However, economic factors and the individual's cultural conditioning will likely limit the range of both perceived and feasible options (Sennett and Cobb 1972). Since positive freedom depends on the range of options available to the individual, it would then seem reasonable to infer that it would vary with one's socioeconomic status. For it is unquestionable that the rich have much more alternatives to choose from than the poor. Once again, we are drawn to the conclusion that the way benefits and opportunities are shared in society will affect the degree to which a certain social ideal is experienced and enjoyed by a person.

Is There Material Prosperity?

Is there material prosperity? The initial response to this question is yes: "American capitalism has produced the most stupendous wealth any society has ever known" (Edwards et al. 1986, p. 2). This statement, however, has to be qualified. As was the case with the social ideals previously considered, this desirable social feature does not benefit the population as a whole, but benefits, rather, those who can afford to purchase the material, technological, and scientific advances that financial prosperity has fostered.

Although Canadians may wish to think that the situation in their country is much better than in the United States, the statistics on poverty in Canada are also quite devastating (see R. Taylor 1989).

The mixed response hereby presented is only consistent with the main thread of this discussion, namely, that the relevance and prevalence of a criterion for the good society varies according to socioeconomic status.

Is There Social Justice?

Social justice seems to emerge as the principal criterion for a good society. Given that desired social qualities are unevenly distributed in the population, it is incumbent upon us to examine just how the distribution is determined; for the overall appraisal of the social order would invariably be affected by the rule followed in making such distributive decisions.

In the study of social justice, a number of criteria for the distribution of what can be summarized as pains and pleasures can be identified. D. Miller (1978) named rights, deserts, and needs. Facione, Scherer, and Attig (1978) limited the criteria to work and needs. Deserts, as used by the former, and work, as used by the latter, are basically equivalent and will therefore be treated as one. It is likely that Facione, Scherer, and Attig do not include rights because this particular criterion has often been classified as conservative justice, that is, enforcement of the law (e.g., Sidgwick 1922), whereas distributive justice deals mainly with ideal justice, that is, a desired state of social justice.

Serious difficulties arise when trying to prioritize between desert and needs in cases of conflict. Facione, Scherer, and Attig (1978) suggest what appears to be a viable solution for this dilemma. In their view the decision-making process is greatly facilitated when social circumstances are taken into account. As stated earlier, when social conditions are such that there are jobs for everyone and these jobs have adequate pay, it would probably be justifiable to adopt work as the standard for distributive justice. On the other hand, when jobs are scarce and people are unemployed, not because of choice but due to socioeconomic factors, it would then be appropriate to adopt needs as the ruling criterion. Given that the present socioeconomic circumstances largely resemble the second scenario, it would be reasonable to expect that the dominant principle of distributive justice would be to each according to his or her needs; yet the market system greatly favors "the conception of justice as the requital of desert" (D. Miller 1978, p. 291). Such interpretation of justice is a natural extension of the reigning individualistic social philosophy that characterizes market societies, in both their early (laissez-faire) and their advanced (welfare state) stages. This philosophy is individualistic particularly in the sense that a person's will and determination can outweigh the effects of socioeconomic circumstances. D. Miller (1978) captures the essence of this doctrine: "No barriers of a legal, social, or economic type would prevent the man [sic] with determination to succeed from gaining his rewards" (p. 291). In sum, Miller argues that

> this interpretation of justice as the requital of desert was bolstered by the view that a man's [sic] character was made by him, not for him, so that the various abilities, skills, and efforts which formed the basis of desert were seen as being within a person's own control. Conversely, incapacity and failure of will were seen as the results, not of external circumstances, but rather of inner weakness. (p. 292)

Undoubtedly, the needs criterion has become more prominent in "welfare state" capitalism than it was in its earlier periods (e.g., Mishra 1977; Wolfe 1989). Nevertheless, an implementation of the need rule of distributive justice to the extent required by the social circumstances is very unlikely in free-enterprise societies such as the United States, Canada, or other Western industrial nations. This is mainly due to the conflicting values underlying the competing conceptions of justice. Inasmuch as individualism, competition, and achievement are the prominent values in the capitalist system, it is hardly surprising that welfare policies have failed to reduce social inequalities (Mishra 1977). If a public welfare system, attuned to the needs of society's members is to flourish, the stress on the virtue of self-help must be replaced by stress on the need to help others. Individualism must be replaced by a concern for the community at large; competition by co-opera-tion; achievement must be defined in social and communal rather than individual terms. (George and Wilding 1976, p. 118)

In sum, whereas current social circumstances would seem to jus-tify a conception of social justice based on the criterion of needs, the present system largely favors the criterion of desert. As a result, it might be claimed that this social order is very far from meeting what has emerged as probably the most important criterion for the good soci-ety: social justice.

Is the Current Social Order Conducive to the Good Life?

Needless to say, in comparison to people in many other countries, peo-ple in North America can be thought of as having a substantially better lot. However, my goal was to draw comparisons not with other existent social systems, but with an ideal one.

Based on the documented economic instability, social tensions, unequal distribution of material prosperity, positive freedom, and, most importantly, a dominant conception of justice that is incongruent with the social circumstances, it would appear that the present social order does not satisfactorily meet the preconditions for the good life and self-fulfillment.

This conclusion is reaffirmed by the massive inability of some people to realize their own basic or growth needs and the same needs of those they care for. Homeless and hungry children growing up in poverty (their number is estimated to be in the millions in North America) are dramatic reminders of this state of affairs (Bassuk and Rubin 1987; Hamilton 1989; McDowell 1989). As far as growth needs are concerned, numerous publications in the last forty years have reported on the large-scale incapacity to gratify Maslow's first growth need, belonging. Titles such as *Man Alone: Alienation in Modern Society* (Josephson and Josephson 1962) and *The Quest for Community* (Nisbet 1969) capture the essence of that literature (see also Geyer and Schweitzer 1981, part 1; and Pappenheim 1959). Lasch (1984) contends that, far from seeking self-actualization, people in contemporary North America merely care about the survival of the self; unstable social and economic conditions have led, perhaps justifiably so, to a preoccupation with survival as opposed to growth:

Everyday life has begun to pattern itself on the survival strategies forced on those exposed to extreme adversity. Selective apathy, emotional disengagement from others, renunciation of the past and the future, a determination to live one day at a time—these techniques of emotional self-management, necessarily carried to extremes under extreme conditions, in more moderate form have come to shape the lives of ordinary people. (pp. 57-58)

CONCLUSION

Part II advanced the proposition that psychology supports, at least partly, the status quo. The first section of part III has evaluated the status quo in comparison to the society that is likely to be conducive to the good life. The negative appraisal of our social order that emerged from this inquiry, based primarily on a concept of social justice that neglects to consider pertinent social circumstances, has direct ethical implications for psychology. By reason of its endorsement of a social system that is not as conducive to a good life as it might be, neither American nor Canadian psychologists are living up to one of their chief self-imposed mandates, namely, the promotion of human welfare. It is therefore imperative to reflect upon the social ethics of the discipline. To this we now turn.

Chapter 14

PSYCHOLOGY AND SOCIAL CHANGE

I have just argued that the regnant social system does not satisfactorily meet some of the essential requirements for the existence of the good society. What is psychology to do vis-à-vis this adverse state of affairs? Hitherto, it has mostly contributed not to the promotion of social change but rather to the preservation of the status quo (Anderson and Travis 1983; Prilleltensky 1989). Although it would be reasonable to expect that a psychology determined to promote human welfare would engage in activities to bring about an improvement in the social preconditions for well-being, that expectation has largely remained just that—an expectation.

This situation is largely due to the rather narrow concept of ethics that psychologists have adopted as their working moral code. Such a model focuses primarily on obligations toward the individual client at the expense of proactive moral behavior toward society at large. This bias is reflected, though in differing degrees, in both the American and the Canadian ethical principles for psychologists. In the former there is very little explicit mention of duties toward society (American Psychological Association 1990). And while the latter devotes an entire section (principle 4) to "responsibility to society," this obligation is considered the least important in value when in conflict with other principles (Canadian Psychological Association 1991). The Canadian code falls short of properly addressing the social dimension of our ethical duties, for if we continue to regard social change as the least important of our moral values, our clients may continue to face less than optimal conditions without our active support. Serious consideration should be given as to how best to advance principle 4 to the forefront of our priorities.

The plea to engage in community action as a way of fulfilling their moral obligations with respect to society goes as far back as Dewey (1900), but psychologists have only recently begun to revive that plea. Albee, one of the most eloquent contemporary psychologists dedicated to the eradication of social injustice, used his 1970 presidential address to the American Psychological Association to ask that "psychology throw its resources into the efforts" to eliminate social ills such as war and racism (Albee 1970, p. 1077). Hillerbrand (1987) claimed recently that "community discourse . . . [is] vital to ethical behavior" (p. 117). In a similar vein, Steininger, Newell, and Garcia (1984) suggested that "psychologists should increasingly question the values base of their activities and openly discuss questions of fairness and justice" (p. 217). Sarason (1982b), who has been a very vocal and ardent supporter of a community-oriented psychology, has been extremely influential in resurrecting what could be called the "social ethics" of the discipline. A renewed appreciation for the moral obligations of psychologists toward society at large is also manifested in the writings of many feminist therapists (Lerman and Porter 1990b) and in "Ethical Guidelines for Feminist Therapists" (Feminist Therapy Institute 1990). Rosewater (1990), for instance, contends that

> advocacy is one way to create a meaningful change in societal structure. The need to create such change, for feminist therapists, is an ethical imperative. Feminist therapy differs from all other therapies in its insistence that advocacy is an essential part of its ethic. (pp. 229-30)

In spite of these recent calls for a more community-attuned psychological ethics, these pleas do not seem to have been followed by programmatic action. This chapter is intended to contribute toward bridging the gap between the vast literature dealing with moral duties toward the individual and the relatively underdeveloped area of social ethics in psychology. Two noticeable exceptions to the latter are Bermant, Kelman, and Warwick's *The Ethics of Social Intervention* (1978) and Steininger, Newell, and Garcia's *Ethical Issues in Psychology* (1984).

Both books are helpful in discerning the moral dilemmas to be confronted in community interventions. Yet both seem to fall short of recommending a proactive plan of action to remedy some of the problematic situations that they so aptly describe.

CONSCIENTIZATION

Conscientization is a general term for a preliminary proposal for furthering the social ethics of psychology; it entails the concurrent implementation of two tasks: (a) denunciation and (b) annunciation. The former endeavors to deconstruct ideological messages that distort people's awareness of sociopolitical circumstances that shape their lives; the latter seeks to elaborate means of advancing the social ideals conducive to the good life. Both concepts, borrowed from the Brazilian educator Paulo Freire, have received considerable attention in educational circles (Bruss and Macedo 1985; Giroux 1985; Martin 1986) but very little in psychology (e.g., Alschuler 1986).

An approximation to the social ideals thought to be conducive to the good life must be preceded by a lucid perception of the political and economic forces regulating current society. Unless individuals become reasonably aware of the ideological deception of which they are victims, it is unlikely that they will be able to engage in any process of social change. And while consciousness does not, in and of itself, guarantee constructive action, in making explicit the mechanisms of the dominant ideology, psychology can assist in the course of social change.

The function hereby advocated for psychology is best captured in Freire's use of the concept *conscientization* (Freire 1971, 1975). According to him, *conscientization* refers to the process whereby people attain an insightful awareness of the socioeconomic, political, and cultural circumstances that affect their lives, as well as of their potential capacity to transform that social reality.

Women's groups have been operating under the propositions of conscientization for over two decades now, with encouraging results.

> Consciousness-raising (CR) groups have evolved as a way for women to understand the intricate relationship between public, systemic conditions and the individual aspects of their experiences. Through CR "the personal becomes political." In addition to their significant social and political impact, CR groups have served as an important mental health resource for women. (Kravetz 1987, p. 55)

Increased self-esteem, reduction in passivity, and greater understanding of systemic dynamics involved in women's oppression are among the positive effects of these groups (Kirsh 1987; Kravetz 1987; Shreve 1989). In them women "learned that their individual experiences of shame, dependency, and anger were felt by others and that these experiences rested on shared conditions characterized by issues of dominance and power" (Unger and Crawford 1992, p. 603). Freeman observes that CR groups are "probably the most valuable contribution by the women's liberation movement to the tools for social change" (in Kirsh 1987, p. 46).

Conscientization attempts to understand how the public gives its tacit consent to the present social system. This phenomenon of consent and conformity achieved by persuasion rather than force is what Gramsci (1971) called cultural "hegemony." This concept, which has been the subject of many discussions in recent years (Femia 1981; Kiros 1985; Simon 1982), is well summarized by Boggs (1976):

> By hegemony Gramsci meant the permeation throughout civil society . . . of an entire system of values, attitudes, beliefs, morality, etc. that is in one way or another supportive of the established order and the class interests that dominate it. . . . To the extent that this prevailing consciousness is internalized by the broad masses, it becomes part of 'common sense'. (p. 39)

By challenging this "common sense," conscientization serves as the antithesis to the predominant ideological message. In other words, it challenges the notion that this social order is the best possible one.

As the main object of analysis for conscientization is awareness of the process whereby hegemony is attained, the following questions need to be addressed: How does hegemony work? What are its main components? How is it achieved? What psychological phenomena are involved? To these questions I now turn.

UNDERSTANDING HEGEMONY

The process of hegemony seems to be constituted by two main stages. The first entails the *definition* of a situation or a problem in such a way that its solution does not threaten the established order of things in society. The second involves the *inculcation* of these definitions to the public at large. First I will elaborate on these stages; then I will present some ideas about the contributions psychology can make to the process of conscientization.

Stage I: Definition

The way a problem is defined predetermines the means by which it is to be solved. The statement of the problem is therefore crucial. To attain hegemony, social conditions and problems are defined in such a way that they will not pose a threat to the status quo. Thus, the dominant ideology resorts to two sorts of explanations for social conditions: (a) "natural" causes; and (b) person-blame. They differ only in that the latter holds people responsible for their own fate, and the former places responsibility on biological factors. These explanations will be referred to as "hegemonic definitions."

Natural causes refers to the explanation of social phenomena on the basis of biological determinism. This version of ideology justifies power inequalities of class, race, and gender as being genetically originated (Rose, Lewontin, and Kamin 1984). The biological inevitability associated with these inequalities fosters fatalism, pessimism, and eventual resignation (cf. Alschuler 1986).

The person-blame definition of social circumstances attributes unequal distribution of wealth, income, and power to personality deficiencies. Laziness is frequently used as an example of this kind. Improvement of personal conditions, according to this concept, largely depends on modifications of character. This model views the individual as entirely responsible for his or her fate, and society as a conglomerate of individuals where there are opportunities for everybody to get ahead.

Hegemonic definitions strategically preclude systemic accounts of social problems. Systemic explanations are seldom admitted, and when they are, it is primarily as "lip service." The numerous system-preserving effects that can be derived from the above definitions of social problems have been documented by Caplan and Nelson (1973), Rose, Lewontin, and Kamin (1984), and W. Ryan (1971), among others.

Stage II: Inculcation

If hegemony is to be established, its definitions must be propagated. I shall refer to this process as "inculcation." In analyzing the psychological phenomena involved in that process, psychology can help in discerning why people give their tacit consent to the prevalent ideology. As will be shown, classic psychological paradigms can illuminate mechanisms involved in inculcation.

Figure 1 is a schematic representation of some influential psychological phenomena involved in the interaction between hegemony agents and hegemony targets during the process of inculcation. The

FIGURE 1
Some Psychological Phenomena Involved in the Process of Hegemony

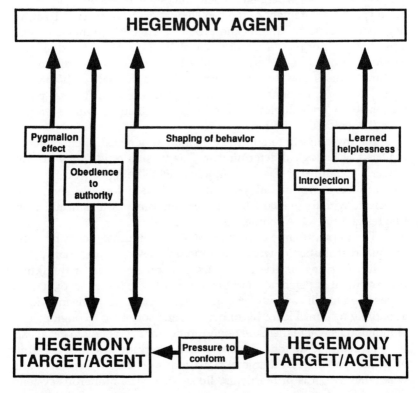

different psychological processes (to be described below) are named along the vertical interactive arrows. Power is the main variable distinguishing the primary hegemony agent (upper part) from the hegemony target and secondary hegemony agent (bottom part). The primary hegemony agent has the power to define a situation or problem according to his or her interests (usually in terms of person-blame or natural causes); the targets are subjected to these definitions. The bottom part shows hegemony targets also in their roles as secondary agents. Once a target has internalized some of the worldviews prescribed by an agent, he or she also starts functioning as an hegemony agent by exerting pressure to conform at the peer level.

As Gramsci (1971) pointed out, hegemony is propagated by institutions such as the government, schools, churches, community clubs, families, the media, and the workplace. Each of these institutions has its chief hegemony agents: politicians, teachers, parents, ministers, employers, and so on; and their primary hegemony targets: students, employees, constituents, and such. While the former have the *power to define a situation or problem* in their own interests (usually in terms of person-blame or natural causes), the latter are subjected to these definitions. The role of the agents is fulfilled through a number of psychological mechanisms. In isolation, each of the psychological phenomena to be examined would account for only a portion of inculcation, but their compounded effect is likely to be very powerful in the diffusion of hegemonic definitions. Understanding how these operate is a first step in counteracting some of their undesirable results. The list of mechanisms presented below is by no means exhaustive. Other potential psychological processes involved in inculcation include group pressure and social learning.

Subtle Inculcation: The Effects of Self-Fulfilling Prophecies

Self-fulfilling prophecy is the occurrence of certain behavioral phenomena as a result of the mere expectation that such events will take place. When expectations favor a certain individual or population, that person or group is likely to benefit from these predictions (Cooper and Good 1983; Dusek and Gail 1983; Rosenthal and Jacobson 1968). Conversely, when the prophecies are negative, the people are adversely affected (Babad, Inbar, and Rosenthal 1982; Rosenhan 1973).

Inasmuch as (a) hegemony agents create expectations (conscious or unconscious) about the behavior of hegemony targets based on hegemonic definitions, and (b) since it has been shown that expectations are likely to influence the course of events in the direction predicted by such prophecies, (c) it is probable that hegemony agents as well as targets behave according to, and ratify, the expectations prescribed by the former.

Those who suffer the harsh consequences of the internalization of negative expectations attached to them in our culture include women (Baker Miller 1986; Bartky 1990; Brittan and Maynard 1984; Burden and Gottlieb 1987; Chesler 1989; Collins 1991; Hyde and Rosenberg 1980; Miller and Mothner 1981; Unger and Crawford 1992), homosexuals, disabled individuals, aboriginal people, and other minorities (Abberley 1987; Adam 1978; Archibald 1978; Bennett 1987; Brittan and Maynard 1984; Kallen 1989; Zuniga 1988). Similar experiences can be related by the poor (Huber and Form 1973; Kluegel and Smith 1986; Sennet and Cobb 1972) and the colonized (Bulhan 1985; Fanon 1965).

Kallen (1989) postulates that the internalization by the powerless of the degrading attributes imposed on them by the powerful contributes to the perpetuation of the self-fulfilling cycle. By accepting "genetic inferiority" or "person-blame" factors as the main cause of their misfortune, the powerless lose confidence and hope in their ability to prosper. As a result, their attempts to transform discriminatory social structures are severely hampered, and the majority-dominated social order remains largely unchallenged.

Blatant Inculcation: The Effects of Obedience to Authority and Shaping of Behavior

Psychological research shows that people not merely obey authority figures but will even perform acts deemed by them to be immoral simply because they are asked to do so by a person of higher perceived status (Kelman and Hamilton 1989). This is one of the most alarming lessons to be learned from Milgram's studies on obedience (Milgram 1963).

Milgram's research on obedience to authority may be regarded as the strongest experimental support for the Gramscian notion of hegemony. Blind obedience occurs not only in the laboratory, but in real life as well, where people kill innocent others in response to an authority's command (Kelman and Hamilton 1989; A. Miller 1986, chap. 7). Through a successful process of indoctrination, the executors come to blame the victims for their own deaths. The latter are viewed as less than human and therefore deserving of their fate.

If subordinates execute orders to harm and kill defenseless individuals, it can be argued that they would have a much easier time obeying and imposing social rules that do not call for murdering civilians but merely require accepting the dominant ideology. Hence, prejudice, racism, and other discriminatory practices in society are reproduced.

Inculcation is also greatly facilitated by shaping the behavior of hegemony targets. This is accomplished through the use of behavior modification principles. Although behaviorism professes the need for social (as opposed to individual) changes, as we saw in chapter 7, many use it to uphold the status quo. In applying behavior modification principles, hegemony agents "accept the victim-blaming definitions which [actually] serve power and attempt to fix, not environments, but the inner nature of individuals" (J. G. Holland 1977, p. 203).

Based on the popularity and wide acceptance of behavior modification techniques in settings like schools, hospitals, and industries, it may well be argued that this efficacious method of behavior control is highly instrumental in attaining hegemony.

Resigned Inculcation: The Effects of Learned Helplessness

Learned helplessness may be regarded as a state of passivity developed in response to exposure to repeated failure (Seligman 1975). The dominant ideology defines failure in terms of personal inadequacies, and individuals who attribute failure to internal factors tend to develop more learned helplessness than those who blame external circumstances (Mikulincer 1988), so it may well be argued that hegemonic definitions tend to promote learned helplessness.

This picture is not inconceivable. Research on the reasons people give for poverty, for instance, lends support to such an assumption (Huber and Form 1973; Sennett and Cobb 1972). In their investigation on the relationship between income and ideology, Huber and Form (1973) concluded that "individualistic factors were thought much more important than structural . . . factors in explaining why people were poor" (p. 101). Similarly, a recent study of unemployed managers in the United States found that although they are the victims of a national economic trend, they blame themselves for not having a job. They readily embrace hegemonic definitions of success and failure and apply them to themselves and others in similar situations (Newman 1988).

Hence, if person-blame definitions are successfully conveyed, as the research reviewed above suggests, then it is not unlikely that many people do not challenge their personal or societal status quo, simply because they have acquired a learned helplessness attitude toward it. This proposition gains further support from observations on the behavior of some colonized people who, by accepting the colonizers' definitions of their problems (e.g., laziness, genetic inferiority), ceased to oppose domination (Bulhan 1985; Fanon 1965).

COUNTERACTING HEGEMONY

Now that the roles of definition and inculcation have been briefly reviewed, the following question may be posed: How can psychology help conscientization? One way psychology can be of assistance is through research on the natural processes of counteracting hegemony.

Some of that research provided the basis for figure 2, which shows some important steps to be followed in counteracting hegemony, which I describe below.

FIGURE 2
Counteracting Hegemony

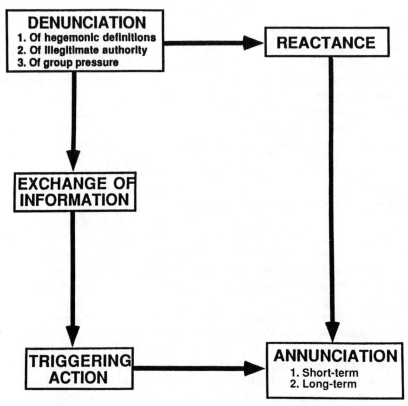

Denunciation

The first and most crucial stage of the process of counteracting hegemony is denunciation. Denunciation is the act of making explicit the mechanisms implicated in preventing an understanding of social problems that may lead to systemic changes. Three such essential mechanisms are these: (1) Hegemonic definitions. These preclude systemic considerations in problem definition. (2) Illegitimate authority. This is the moral stature ascribed to hegemonic agents by virtue of their being regarded as experts, or holding positions of power. Power and expertise are not necessarily a source of moral virtue, yet it has been found that people tend to change their attitudes on social issues in the direction expressed by individuals whose expertise and qualifications lie in fields unrelated to the issue at hand (McGuire 1985). (3) Group pressure. This is a potent source of conformity. Schneiderman (1988) posited that conformity and balance "can be preserved only so long as the individual is incapable of questioning the legitimacy of norms from an independent ethical perspective" (p. 70). Walker and Heyns (1962) clearly pointed out that if conformity is to be achieved, the person "need not be aware" of the effects of group pressure (p. 98). Conversely, if reduction of hegemonic conformity is desired, the person needs be aware of these effects.

The denunciation of these three mechanisms may be conducive to three simple realizations:

1. That a certain unsatisfactory condition may be the result not of personal, but rather of systemic, deficiencies.
2. That people who might have tried to convince one to take personal blame may be wrong.
3. That although groups may pressure one to conform, it is not necessarily beneficial to follow the majority.

Exchange of Information

Exchange of information is the next step in counteracting hegemony. As Gamson, Fireman, and Rytina (1982) report, sharing views with group members about erroneous, unjust, or immoral aspects of a situation may prepare the ground for remedial action. This is exemplified in a variation of the Milgram experiment. When three research participants, two of whom were confederates instructed to rebel against the experimenter who had requested that they deliver the shocks, were in charge of punishing the person for making errors the remaining participant of the investigation tended to rebel as well. Whereas in the original condition (only one participant) about 63 percent of the participants shocked to the limit, only 10 percent did so when two other people also rebelled against the experimenter (A. Miller 1986).

Similarly, in Asch's (1981) paradigm the presence of one supporting partner who did not go along with the rest of the group "depleted the majority of much of its power. Its pressure on the dissenting individual was reduced to one-fourth: that is, subjects answered incorrectly only one-fourth as often as under the pressure of unanimous majority" (p. 34).

Exchange of information, then, is important not only in alerting other people about crucial aspects of a situation but also in motivating them to do something about it, that is, resist group pressure or rebel against circumstances perceived as unfair or unjust.

Triggering Action

The next step in counteracting hegemony is triggering action. Gamson, Fireman, and Rytina (1982) contend that it is not enough to exchange information. Groups require the presence of one or more individuals with adequate knowledge and experience to activate the rest of the members. Otherwise, even though a group may perceive a situation as immoral, they will not take action. "Lack of know-how means the critical mobilizing acts are unlikely to occur" (p. 146). In other words, the absence of a person with previous political or activist experience of some sort may paralyze a group.

Reactance

Reactance has been defined by Gergen and Gergen (1981) as "a negative emotional state that may result when a person's freedom of choice is reduced" (p. 498); "reactance can be a source of independence" (p. 498). Such a reaction is likely to emerge from the denunciation process. When people realize that hegemonic definitions, for instance, have been designed in large part to constrict their perception of social conditions and consequently their freedom of choice, they may experience reactance. And "the individual who experiences reactance will attempt to reduce it by trying to reclaim the lost freedom" (p. 368). Inasmuch as reactance may lead to action to remediate a situation, as some of the research reviewed by Gergen and Gergen (1981) suggests, it is also instrumental in counteracting hegemony. In figure 2, reactance is placed at the same level as denunciation because it is more a parallel than a subsequent stage.

Annunciation

In figure 2 the vertical and horizontal arrows converge at the annunciation box. In simple terms, this is the stage where the question, What can be done? is posed. Short-term annunciation pertains to immediate social action designed to improve a specific condition. Long-term annunciation involves a conception of a utopian or ideal society where human welfare may be maximized. These are by no means easy projects. This, however, should not prevent those dissatisfied with the present state of affairs from trying to provide at least tentative answers.

What of annunciation within the realm of psychology? How can psychology become part of the short- and long-term annunciation processes? At the short-term level of annunciation, suggestions can be divided along the lines of psychologists as practitioners, teachers, and scientists.

PSYCHOLOGISTS AS AGENTS OF SOCIAL CHANGE

Practitioners

As practitioners (i.e., therapists and counselors) psychologists come in contact with people at all levels of the social ladder. In that capacity they have the opportunity to make the process of hegemony *explicit*. At the same time, they can make an effort to seriously bear in mind systemic variables affecting the behavior of their clients, not only in explaining their behavior but also in suggesting treatment.

> The psycho-therapist, social worker or social reformer, concerned only with his *[sic]* own clients and their grievance against society, perhaps takes a view comparable to the private citizen of Venice who concerns himself only with the safety of his own dwelling and his own ability to get about the city. But if the entire republic is slowly being submerged, individual citizens cannot afford to ignore their collective fate because, in the end, they all drown together if nothing is done; and again, as with Venice, what needs to be done is far beyond the powers of any one individual. In such circumstances . . . the therapist can no longer afford the luxury of ignoring everything that is going on outside the consulting room. (Badcock 1983, pp. 74-75)

As Caplan and Nelson (1973), Albee (1981, 1986) and Sarason (1981a, 1981b, 1982b) have eloquently argued, mainstream psychology has not yet overcome its predominant individualistic bias, either in diagnosis or in therapy. The exception is feminist therapy (Hare-Mustin 1991; S. Holland 1992; Watson and Williams 1992). Feminist therapists have become, as I have shown in chapter 10, painfully aware of the wounds inflicted on women by patriarchal cultural practices.

Educators

As educators, and particularly as educators of teachers, psychologists are presented with the opportunity to challenge their students to question the very definition of problems that constitutes the first step in obtaining hegemony. Freire envisioned this task as a *pedagogy of the question*. In my view Freire is quite right in his assessment that "educators are using more a pedagogy of answers than one of questions . . . no matter whether we teach in the primary school, secondary school, or at the university" (Bruss and Macedo 1985, p. 8). Contrary to a pedagogy of the answer, "which reduces learners to mere receptacles of prepackaged knowledge" (Bruss and Macedo 1985, p. 8), Freire's approach stimulates students to doubt, challenge, and reject preconceived notions about the social sphere. As Shore put it, this type of education has the potential "to penetrate the enormous myths that we're all surrounded with and socialized into" (in Martin 1986, p. 6). Among these myths are the person-blame and natural-causes definitions of political, cultural, and economic affairs.

But this is not enough. In addition, it is essential to provide people with some tools that will enable them to scrutinize the ideology implicated in the definition of social problems. To begin with, the language in which these definitions are presented is to be examined. According to K. J. Hughes (1986), in order to do that, it should first be realized that "there is no neutral language or discourse of Truth: there are simply different forms of discourse, employed for different purposes" (p. 18). Students will then be in a better position to read a text always "as a constructed TEXTUAL WORLD distinct from the EMPIRICAL WORLD" (p. 18). Hughes's appraisal of the current state of education indicates that "despite the massive amounts of money spent on teaching language . . . students are not taught the theory and practice of discourse in our schools" (p. 18).

Undermining conformity and mass thinking is another task that psychologists, as teachers, can undertake. Lessing (1986) has envisioned what an educator's message for independent thinking would or should be like:

> You are going to be pressured all through your life to join mass movements, and if you can resist this, you will be, every day, under pressure from various types of groups, often of your closest friends, to conform to them. . . . But you are going to be taught how to examine these mass ideas, these apparently irresistible pressures, taught how to think for yourself, and to choose for yourself. (p. 73)

Researchers

As researchers, psychologists can facilitate conscientization by exposing the limitations of individualistic and reductionist research rooted in the Cartesian mode of thinking (Capra 1982) and by offering alternate paradigms (cf. Thibault 1981). Bateson (1972) has been influential in furthering a conceptual integration between individual, social, and ecological variables in understanding human behavior. Along the lines proposed by Bateson, a systemic approach for the study of behavior in cultural and political contexts has been outlined by E. V. Sullivan (1984).

The underlying dynamics of hegemonic consent should continue to be explored. Research by Gamson, Fireman, and Rytina (1982) and Kelman and Hamilton (1989) provides a sound basis for that. Their analyses help elucidate the processes involved in the acceptance and rejection of unjust social arrangements.

Professionals

As professionals committed to the promotion of human welfare, all psychologists, I believe, would benefit from undergoing constant self-conscientization. If psychologists are to be vehicles of conscientization for other people, they should be the first ones to subject themselves to this very process. Otherwise, scrutiny of the society of which they are a constituent part will be seriously hindered. Psychologists are not, and cannot, be insulated from inculcation. Yet it would seem as if we were operating under the premise that we can exclude ourselves from the ubiquitous nature of the hegemonic process (e.g., Larsen 1986b; Prilleltensky 1989).

In my opinion, it would be advantageous to have some built-in mechanisms for self-conscientization in the training of psychologists. One systematic way of evaluating psychology's functions in either promoting or impeding beneficial societal changes is through courses dealing with ethics. Such courses, which were very rare in the social sciences a decade and a half ago (Warwick 1980), provide an opportunity to discuss how the discipline might impact upon the advent of the good society. But this is only one possible route. Workshops, study groups, conferences, and so forth are alternative ways.

There still remains the question of long-term annunciation: How do we make progress in delineating the ideal society? Conceiving a social arrangement where the well-being of the population could be advanced is a task psychologists have begun to study, but they are not yet well prepared to undertake it on their own (Fox 1985). Such an assignment would be greatly facilitated by collaborating with moral philosophers.

At least two foreseeable barriers would have to be overcome to foster this interdisciplinary dialogue. The first has to do with the belief that the psychologist, as scientist, contributes to social betterment by making progress in his or her area of specialty, regardless of how remote this field may be from the social arena. This assumption is rooted in the following syllogism: "Social science is science; science contributes to human welfare; therefore social science contributes to human welfare" (Warwick 1980, p. 31). As I have argued elsewhere, "unless psychologists extricate themselves from this moral naivete, the advent of annunciation will remain an illusion" (Prilleltensky 1989, p. 800).

The second source of resistance to be encountered will be psychology's historical quest for independence from philosophy. One can only hope that psychology has matured enough that a dialogue with philosophy no longer poses a threat.

CONCLUSION

When the social preconditions for the existence of the good society and the advancement of human welfare are conspicuously deficient, it is morally incumbent upon psychologists to engage in activities that would bring about a state of affairs more conducive to the well-being of the entire population. Yet, in contrast to its considerable efforts to insure proper ethical behavior toward individual clients, psychology has almost neglected its moral obligations toward society at large. Psychology can no doubt contribute to the advent of social change by making explicit the process by which people come to accept the current social order as the best possible one, and by proposing strategies to counteract this pervasive phenomenon. This chapter illustrated how well-established psychological research, as well as psychologists—as teachers, practitioners, and investigators—can play a significant role in the transformation of social structures that are presently incapable of promoting human welfare for all sectors of society.

Chapter 15

Empowerment in Mainstream Psychology

Empowerment is generally understood as interventions and policies intended to enhance the degree of control vulnerable individuals exercise over their lives (Rappaport 1981, 1987). Hitherto, this concept has been largely denied a respectable place in mainstream academic and applied psychology (Joffe and Albee 1988; Sarason 1982b, 1988). With the notable exception of community psychologists (e.g., Florin and Wandersman 1990; Wolff 1987; Zimmerman and Rappaport 1988) and some primary preventionists (Albee, Joffe, and Dusenbury 1988), psychologists have neglected to view empowerment research and practice as legitimate activities. In a recent edition of the *Journal of Social Issues* (Spacapan and Thompson 1991), "Perceived Control in Vulnerable Populations," no references could be found to the concept of empowerment. Similarly, no specific mention of this concept could be seen in the book *The Psychology of Human Control* (Friedman and Lackey 1991). A recent special issue of the *Canadian Journal of Behavioural Science* (P. T. Young 1992), "The Psychology of Control," contains only one reference on empowerment. These are only a few examples of missed opportunities for control researchers to take advantage of studies on empowerment (e.g., Rappaport, Swift, and Hess 1984; Zimmerman 1990). If research on empowerment and policies designed to empower individuals are to reach beyond community psychology and have an impact in other, more traditional areas such as clinical, school, personality, and social psychology, then it is incumbent upon community psychologists to assert the legitimacy of these endeavors. I will argue that the ethical, psychological, and therapeutic foundations of empowerment provide ample legitimacy for its vigorous pursuit in the discipline.

This chapter is designed to promote cross-fertilization between research on empowerment and mainstream psychological theories and practices. The concept of explanatory style advanced by Seligman (1990) and the four models of helping and coping identified by Brickman et al. (1982) will be instrumental in demonstrating the connections between empowerment, theories of control, and counseling approaches.

The chapter is divided into four parts. The first section presents a conceptual model of empowerment. The second section elaborates on the legitimate ethical and psychological foundations of empowerment. The third section deals with obstacles to be encountered in promoting empowerment in mainstream psychology, and the last offers some directions to facilitate this integration.

A DESCRIPTIVE AND PRESCRIPTIVE
MODEL OF EMPOWERMENT

The purpose of the model to be presented is twofold: (a) to clarify the various meanings of the term *empowerment* by delineating empowerment's multifaceted nature, and (b) to provide a framework for the advancement of research and action in this area. In other words, the model will describe the constitutive elements of empowerment and serve as a basis for its prescription in psychology.

The circular representation of the model found in figure 3 highlights the three main elements of empowerment as discussed in the literature. These are values, processes, and agents/stakeholders. Each third of the model is subdivided into three sections. The outer circle denotes the main components of empowerment at their most abstract level. The middle circle specifies the questions to be asked of values, processes, and agents/stakeholders. The inner circle details in concrete form the meaning of the key constitutive elements. The values of empowerment—self-determination, distributive justice, and collaborative and democratic participation—inform and guide the process as well the agents/stakeholders of empowerment. This influence is repre-

FIGURE 3
A Descriptive and Prescriptive Model of Empowerment

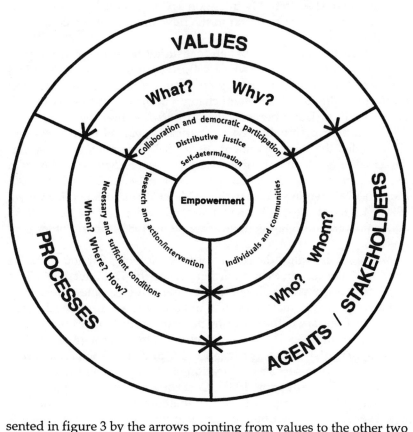

sented in figure 3 by the arrows pointing from values to the other two sections. These values are incorporated by researchers as well as by human services providers. The arrows pointing from processes to agents/stakeholders and vice versa represent the dynamic relationship between the people who conduct research and interventions and the processes involved. I will now discuss each section of the model in more detail.

Values

Values play a central role in empowerment research and actions. Empowerment studies and empowering interventions are explicitly concerned with, and guided by, three principal moral values: self-determination, distributive justice, and collaborative and democratic participation. The ethical foundations of these values will be articulated in the next section. My intention at this juncture is to show that these values have been central in the development of the concept of empowerment.

Against a background of paternalistic attitudes in social and psychological interventions (Swift 1984), Rappaport (1981, 1986, 1987) advanced the concept and practice of empowerment in psychology as means for individuals in need of changes in their lives to achieve self-determination. The inherent value of persons choosing a course of action on their own is indeed a constitutive part of what Riessman (1986) called the "empowerment ethos." Self-determination, as a fundamental principle in human services, has been recognized not only in psychology, but also in social work (Breton 1989; McDermott 1975; Moreau 1990), feminist theory (Baker Miller 1986), social policy (Boyte 1990; McKnight 1989; Wineman 1984), education (Freire 1971, 1985), and even agriculture and engineering (Ovitt 1989), among other professions.

The second value, distributive justice, promotes fair and equitable distribution of resources and burdens in society (D. Miller 1978). This value derives from the realization that misery and happiness are largely dictated by the way material goods and access to services are allocated in society. Contrary to the enduring belief in North America that equality of opportunity exists, the promoters of empowerment assert that the unequal distribution of wealth and power in society severely restricts access to services, education, and employment (Boyte and Riessman 1986; Rappaport 1984). Consequently, empowerment calls for interventions designed to rectify this imbalance of opportunities wherever it exists. Distributive justice applies at the microsocial level, where people and small groups negotiate the fair allocation of resources, as well as at the macrosocial sphere, where advocacy and social and political action are called for.

The third fundamental value underpinning the notion of empowerment is collaborative and democratic participation. This value reflects best the ideal that persons affected by individual and social interventions should be part of the decision-making process (cf. Habermas 1990). This principle, also identified by Riessman (1986) as a key element of the empowerment ethos, is a defining characteristic of empowering scientific and sociopolitical processes (Rappaport 1990).

These three constitutive moral values inform the actions of researchers, therapists, and social interventionists identified with the tenets of empowerment. In the next two sections we shall see how these principles are expressed in the people and processes involved in empowerment.

Agents/Stakeholders

The process of empowerment may take place either as a result of the natural actions of people desirous of attaining higher degrees of control over their affairs, or as a consequence of social interventions coming from outside the setting. Agents are the people whose actions empower themselves and/or others. Stakeholders are persons or groups invited to participate in the process. The ideal is for the stakeholders to become agents of empowerment themselves as soon as possible. As Lerner (1991) recently showed in his work with individuals, families, and entire communities, empowerment may occur at any of these levels. Similar conclusions can be arrived at by reviewing the work of S. Holland (1992) with poor women, many of them single parents, living in a large multiethnic community in West London, England. Briefly stated, this third of the model describes the people involved in and affected by empowering interventions. Their actions are expected to uphold the values described in the previous section. Whereas Serrano-Garcia (1984), Wolff (1987), and Chavis and Wandersman (1990) demonstrate how these values are incorporated into research and interventions with entire communities, Dunst, Trivette, and Deal (1988) illustrate the fusion of empowerment values with clinical practice.

Processes

This section of the model represents the variety of actions and processes taking place in studying and promoting empowerment. These may be best understood by posing the following questions: How, when, and where does empowerment occur? and What are the necessary and sufficient conditions for it to develop? The inner circle of figure 3 shows the two main processes of empowerment: research and action. Actions take many forms. They may be the result of powerless individuals initiating social action, or they may come from professionals involved in community organizing, or from therapists empowering women to leave abusive relationships.

What defines an intervention as empowering is not its specific content but rather its adherence to the values of empowerment. In one case political action may be called for in order to improve the housing conditions of a community. In another case empowerment may take the form of helping a person deflect blame for problems from internal sources to external oppressive conditions. As noted earlier, self-determination, distributive justice, and collaborative and democratic participation should predominate at all levels of human coexistence. Therefore, depending upon the situation, empowering processes may be necessary to advance the interests and rights of vulnerable persons in the context of relationships, families, occupational settings, educational institutions, social and political structures, and practically every other realm of human endeavor.

The complex nature of social settings where empowerment is called for necessitates that psychologists be more versatile and creative in their interventions. Greater degrees of control for vulnerable people cannot always be attained by counseling and therapy. Social policy recommendations and political actions may have to be incorporated into the psychologist's repertoire.

The analysis of empowerment along the dimensions of values, agents/stakeholders, and processes furnishes a systematic understanding of the field at the same time that it serves to guide research and action. Although other models of empowerment have been proposed before (e.g., Wolff 1987), I believe the present one to be unique in its explicit emphasis on moral principles. In addition, the model advanced here may prove to be (a) of heuristic value in interpreting and organizing the field of empowerment, and (b) useful in disseminating this concept in mainstream psychology.

LEGITIMACY

The model of empowerment described above rests on philosophical as well as psychological foundations. Both aspects are necessary to attain an integrative and holistic understanding of empowerment. Moreover, they are mutually complementary. While the moral philosophical basis provides the justification for pursuing empowerment, the psychological ground facilitates its promotion.

Moral Foundations

Although the prevailing discourse on empowerment is marked by ethical connotations (Rappaport 1990), its moral foundations have not yet been fully explicated. In the present atmosphere of so-called pluralism and ethical relativism, there is a risk of misinterpreting moral imperatives as moral predilections (Burman 1990; Halberstam 1993; C. Taylor

1991; Wolfe 1989). As a result, mainstream psychologists may continue to regard advocacy and empowerment as activities that are largely dictated, not by ethics, but by personal worldviews and preferences. I contend that a compelling argument for empowerment can and should be made on the basis of the ethical obligations of psychologists toward society in general and vulnerable populations in particular (O'Neill 1989; Steininger, Newell, and Garcia 1984). Otherwise, mainstream psychologists will continue to regard empowerment as a matter of personal choice and not as a matter of moral duty. Following a discussion of the ethical principles of empowerment, I will attempt to show how these values resonate in the professional ethics literature.

Ethical Principles. The three fundamental pillars of empowerment are self-determination, distributive justice, and collaborative and democratic participation. As noted earlier, these principles are widely promulgated by empowerment practitioners. Each of these values has a respectable tradition in moral philosophy.

Following Olson's (1978) analysis of freedom, self-determination may be thought of as "the individual's ability to pursue chosen goals without excessive frustration" (p. 45). The capacity to carry out one's objectives in life is, according to Rawls (1972), "perhaps the most important primary good" (p. 440). This constituent element of self-respect, Rawls claims, "implies a confidence in one's ability . . . to fulfill one's intentions" (p. 440). Ortega y Gasset (1983), who wrote extensively about self-determination (Ramos Mattei 1987), captured the human essence of this value in his remark that "to live is to constantly decide what we are to become" (Ortega y Gasset 1983, p. 190, my translation).

The primary good inherent in a sense of autonomy, personal freedom, and self-determination may be threatened by at least two sources: (a) a restrictive psychosocial environment, and (b) paternalism. Concerning the former, Aboulafia (1986) states that it is clear that "other[s] and the social-economic system can inhibit and prevent the realization of such a self. . . . The obstacle I speak of is the relationship of dominance versus subordinance" (Aboulafia 1986, p. 104). The interpersonal and societal barriers to self-determination identified by Aboulafia have also been widely recognized by the proponents of empowerment (Lerner 1991; Serrano-Garcia 1984) and feminism (Baker Miller 1986).

The second obstacle to self-determination has to do with paternalistic attitudes toward people in need of assistance. Many so-called benevolent interventions to help the disadvantaged have infringed upon their sense of self-respect and effectively curtailed their aspirations for self-determination (Gaylin et al. 1981). Among applied ethicists, R. Young (1982) contends that "opposition to paternalistic interference with adults, whether it involves the intervention of the state (legal paternalism) or another adult individual, has usually been based on a concern to preserve human autonomy or self-determination" (p. 47). The many converging critiques on paternalism coalesced to create alternate, empowering strategies (Boyte and Riessman 1986; Rappaport 1981, 1987; Swift 1984).

The needs and rights of individuals promoted and protected by self-determination should be complemented with values designed to preserve the needs and rights of fellow community members. This ensures a balance between personal fulfillment and communal well-being. As seen earlier in chapter 13, distributive justice is the value invoked to guide the fair and equitable allocation of burdens and resources in society. Proponents of empowerment in psychology and social services have asserted the need to redistribute resources in a more equitable fashion (Albee, Joffe, and Dusenbury 1988; Bennett 1987; Rappaport 1984; McKnight 1989). In differing degrees, legal, ideological, and social interventions have been launched in an effort to reallocate wealth and power in accordance with the precepts of distributive justice.

The intrinsic beneficial qualities of self-determination and distributive justice are brought forth by the collaborative and democratic process. The belief in the inherent capacity of individuals to select their goals and defend their interests is recognized in the value of democracy (Addams 1902). As Swift noted (1984), "The concept of democracy and its embodiment in our political institutions are based on the principle of empowering citizens to participate in decisions affecting their welfare" (p. xiii). A commitment to treating persons fairly, equitably, and with respect demands that a collaborative approach be used. This is in opposition to paternalistic models of intervention, which have traditionally operated from an expert-knows-best point of view.

While the importance of collaboration and democracy may be publicly upheld by psychologists, an in-depth examination of psychological theories and practices reveals that these values are not always at the forefront of their priorities (Sampson 1991; Walsh 1988). Proponents of empowerment in psychology endeavor to make collaboration and democratic participation one of the first items of their scientific and social agenda (Rappaport 1986, 1990). As we shall see next, applied moral philosophers attempt to incorporate primary values into the modus operandi of the professions.

Professional Ethics and Empowerment. Professional ethical behavior calls for efforts to promote the welfare of the community as a whole (Kultgen 1988). Reeck (1982) said it well when he claimed that the moral guide of the professional should be the *"devotion of professional skills to meeting the needs of client groups and, ultimately, to the common good"* (p. 38; italics in the original). Reflecting on the same topic, Lebacqz (1985) commented: "If the professional's relationship to society is seen as a matter of entrusting of power, then the professional will be bound by obligations to society. . . . It is really a matter of justice—of repaying a debt" (p. 85).

Reeck (1982) argues for the legitimacy of empowerment in the professions. He contends that "an ideal that seems common to the moral heritage of the professions is that of *enablement"* (p. 38), which is understood as the empowering of individuals for the purpose of helping themselves. Feminist therapists Smith and Douglas (1990) regard empowerment as an ethical imperative. According to them, "empowerment forms the core definition of feminist therapy, together with a continual analysis of the societal inequities that dictate unequal access to resources (power) for oppressed groups" (p. 43). Consistent with the philosophy of empowerment, Lebacqz claims that meaningful improvement in the life of many citizens cannot be attained without fundamental social changes—changes that require a more equitable distribution of political power.

Kultgen (1988), Lebacqz (1985), and Reeck (1982), as well as Smith and Douglas (1990) explicitly advance the precepts of empowerment in the professions. They support the process by which individuals acquire control over their lives and the power to enhance their personal and communal welfare. Professions can accelerate this process. However, in establishing their moral duties, professions have traditionally sought to secure only the welfare of their immediate clients and neglected to consider the welfare of the community at large and the need to change damaging societal structures (Lebacqz 1985; Reeck 1982; Wilding 1982). Psychology has not escaped this proclivity (Rowe 1987). The "Obstacles" section of this chapter will outline in some detail why psychology has been reluctant to embrace empowering paradigms and social change propositions.

Psychological Foundations

Psychology has much to offer, as well as to gain from, the field of empowerment. The potential of this mutually beneficial relationship will be explored in this section. The psychology of personal control can definitely inform empowerment research (Friedman and Lackey 1991; Langer and Rodin 1976; Seligman 1990; Spacapan and Thompson 1991; Zimmerman 1990; Zimmerman and Rappaport 1988). Control investigators, in turn, can learn a great deal from observing the experience of empowerment in real-life settings (Chavis and Wandersman 1990; Dobyns, Doughty, and Lasswell 1971; Lerner 1991). I will review next a number of studies that bear directly on the relationship between issues of personal control, coping, helping, and empowerment. These will show some of the psychological foundations of empowerment, as well as the therapeutic and protective aspects of empowering processes.

Research. Studies concerning issues of control and empowerment at the individual level of analysis will be reviewed first, followed by research dealing with communities. There are long-term beneficial repercussions for the early experiences of task mastery and control (Chess and Thomas 1984; Rolf et al. 1990). Indeed, as Cowen (1991) recently noted, "the rooting of relevant life competencies may be the single most important precondition for the young child's development of an early phenomenological sense of empowerment and having control over one's fate" (p. 406). Moreover, important positive effects can be derived from the perception of control, not the least of which is physical health (Lord and Farlow 1990). In their review of the literature, Thompson and Spacapan (1991) mention improved (a) emotional well-being, (b) ability to cope with stress, (c) health, (d) motor and intellectual performance, and (e) capacity to make desired behavioral changes, as resulting from perceptions of control.

A sense of personal control contributes also to the development of psychosocial resilience (Garmezy 1984; Rutter 1987; Seligman 1990; Zimmerman 1990). That is to say, experiences of control act as buffers against future adversities. On the other hand, experiences of helplessness across the life span render people vulnerable to a range of emotional problems (Seligman 1990).

It has been well documented that the experience of helplessness is mediated by cognitive style. Seligman (1990) contends that individuals who explain bad events in terms of external, specific, and temporary causes, what he calls "optimistic explanatory style," will show greater attempts at control when they encounter adversities in the future. Those who attribute failure to personal, permanent, and pervasive factors will likely not assume control when faced with the next setback. Although the degree of helplessness people manifest is moderated by their attributions, an optimistic explanatory style can go only so far in protecting people facing severe or chronic stressors. Recurring or acute life stressors may teach their victims that, no matter what they do, their lot in life does not improve. If the adverse effects of these experiences subside, children "will develop the theory that bad events can be changed and conquered. But if they are, in fact, permanent and pervasive, the seeds of hopelessness have been deeply planted" (Seligman 1990, p. 135).

To overcome the deeply planted seeds of hopelessness, individuals growing up in permanent and pervasive depriving conditions need more than a change in attributions and perceptions to cope with misfortune. They need real experiences of control to change real-life stressors. Research on empowerment can show how this can be attained (Zimmerman and Rappaport 1988; Zimmerman 1990). The present dominant focus on attributions and perceptions of control should be complemented by research on the increase of actual power in real-life settings. This is the main potential contribution of empowerment research in this area.

Research on the empowerment of communities shows the gains derived from a sense of group cohesion and collective action around specific goals and problems. Florin and Wandersman (1990) describe the empowering effects of citizen participation, voluntary organizations, and community development. Chavis and Wandersman (1990), for example, illustrated how a sense of community may generate social action and enhance the participants' perception and actual control over their environment. Given the action-research nature of community empowerment, more will be said about it in the next section.

Action/Intervention. As in the research section, I will examine empowering interventions at the individual and community levels separately. A useful theoretical framework for understanding and appreciating the need for empowerment at the personal level is provided by Brickman and his associates (1982). They made a comparative analysis of four models of helping and coping and their effects on clients. The techniques they explored were examined in terms of two dimensions: (a) attribution to self of responsibility for the problem, and (b) attribution to self of responsibility for the solution. Each variable was divided into high or low. This resulted into four models of helping: (a) *medical* (people are not held responsible for problems or solutions), (b) *compensatory* (people are not held responsible for problems but are held responsible for solutions), (c) *moral* (people are held responsible for problems and solutions), and (d) *enlightenment* (people are not held responsible for solutions but are held responsible for problems). Their comparison of helping methodologies falling into the four categories led them to the conclusion that the compensatory model, the one that advocates empowerment, is generally the preferred one, particularly with disadvantaged populations. In this approach people are not held responsible for their problems but are expected to be active in the solutions, a philosophy that is congruent with the tenets of empowerment. Brickman et al. (1982) prefer the compensatory model because it avoids blaming the victim at the same time as it benefits from the advantages associated with holding individuals responsible for improving their lives. Knowing that change is within their ability and control provides suffering people with an empowering feeling.

Lord and Farlow (1990) discuss the implications of the compensatory paradigm for health promotion. According to them, the "individuals who achieved the greatest degree of control in their lives" were those who resisted blaming themselves and adopted an active stance with respect to their future aspirations (p. 3). An application of the compensatory model by Rose and Black (1985) helped discharged psychiatric patients adjust to the community. They found that through the externalization of blame, and through "seizing command of some aspect (however minute) of their lives," individuals attained a degree of dignity and self-respect that could not have been obtained otherwise (p. 90).

Finally, empirical evidence for the positive results associated with the compensatory mode of helping comes from the work of Lerner (1991). Based on the assumption that occupational stress derives primarily from self-blaming, Lerner launched interventions designed to (a) reduce personal blame and (b) modify oppressive working conditions. He found that

> with a decrease in self-blaming comes an increase in ability to cope with stress at home and at work. This is partly explained by the increased sense of personal power that comes from being able to focus anger at oppressive work conditions. But it is also explained by the fact that once people are no longer totally disempowered by self-blaming, they are in a better position to formulate plans for how to engage in concrete struggles to change their environments. (p. 44)

The therapeutic aspects of the compensatory model can also be seen at the community level. A prime example of its powerful impact is furnished by the women's movement. The social action psychotherapy project with women carried out by S. Holland (1992) was most successful: "The therapeutic effect on the women involved was to enhance their self-esteem and empower them collectively" (p. 72). In elucidating systemic (as opposed to personal) conditions of oppression and facilitating control over their own affairs, Kravetz (1987) noted that "consciousness-raising groups have served as an important mental health resource for women" (p. 55). Grassroots associations (Boyte 1990; Burgess 1990), students' and seniors' groups (Wolff 1987), Native American (O'Sullivan, Waugh, and Espeland 1984), and poor rural communities (Serrano-Garcia 1984), among others, have been helped by the tools of social action advocated by empowerment theory.

To summarize, this section dealt with the moral and psychological foundations of empowerment in mainstream psychology. Next, I will examine some of the barriers to be encountered in promoting a wider acceptance for the concept of empowerment.

OBSTACLES

In spite of the fact that professional ethics call for the enablement and empowerment of vulnerable populations, most professions, in actuality, have either rejected these endeavors as illegitimate or paid little attention to them. What follows is an analysis of the main obstacles and arguments obstructing the introduction of empowering practices in psychology.

Professionalism

Social action, a key empowerment strategy, has been historically perceived as undermining the credibility of the social sciences. In the social sciences, the conflict between "academics" and "reformers" dates back to 1865, when the American Social Science Association was formed. This conflict is very well documented in Furner's book *Advocacy and Objectivity* (1975). According to her, the "academics" had no trouble winning the struggle for recognition as "professionals." Unfortunately, the monopoly over *professionalism* exerted by the academics had rather adverse consequences. As Furner (1975) noted: "As professionalization proceeded, most social scientists stopped asking ethical questions" (p. 8).

The fear of reformers is associated with the intrusion of values in what is supposed to be a value-free enterprise (Wilding 1982). The claim is made that social action, and its concomitant values, diminish the scientific status of psychology (Robinson 1984). This argument neglects to consider two points. First, nonepistemic values, that is, social and political values, are an inherent part of psychology, whether we like it or not (Howard 1985). And second, claiming to be value-neutral is in itself a value-laden position, one that upholds the societal status quo. Failure or neglect to challenge predominant values translates into indirect support for them (Prilleltensky 1989).

Empowerment, advocacy, and social action are not presented here for the pursuit of the narrow private interests of professionals, in which case the credibility of the profession may be jeopardized. On the contrary, empowerment is advanced as a means to fulfill our ethical commitment to the vulnerable (Hillerbrand 1987).

Individual versus Social Ethics

The study of social ethics in the social sciences in general and in psychology in particular has not received as much attention as it probably should (Tymchuk 1989; Warwick 1980). This error of omission led to a narrow preoccupation with individual, as opposed to social, ethics (for examples of this proclivity, see American Psychological Association 1987; Cabot 1926; Carroll, Schneider, and Wesley 1985; Clarke and Lawry 1988). As a result, the ethical dimensions of social action, power structures, domination, and oppression do not receive the attention they merit.

A commitment to the individual client, or what may be considered *individual ethics*, dominates the professional and psychological ethics literature. Few references are made in that literature to the need to promote a *social ethics*—an ethics that is directed toward enhancing the quality of life for large and vulnerable segments of society (Addams 1902; Chambers 1992).

The negative effects of this neglect are strongly felt in the helping professions. Human services in general (McKnight 1989), and medicine (Waitzkin 1989), social work (Carniol 1990; Gil 1990), and psychology in particular (Nelson 1983; Walsh 1988), provide examples of professional practices where, paradoxically, preoccupation with the single "case" may ultimately hurt the "case." This is simply because, in searching for solutions for a particular client, attention is diverted from pervasive social forces that may have caused, contributed to, or perpetuated the nature of the problem.

This was well illustrated in a program reported by Halpern in 1988. Attempts to minimize infants' diarrhea by psychoeducational measures were severely hindered by an overbearing environmental condition: lack of access to uncontaminated water. This is an incident where medical or psychological interventions should be accompanied by social and ecological change. In the context of psychotherapy, Lerner (1991) also shows the debilitating effects of focusing exclusively on the individual. "Lacking a sense of social causality, most therapists interpret the frustrations of family and personal life as individual failings . . . therapists implicitly suggest that the problems are individual in scope" (p. 323). In spite of the ill effects of this implicit message, therapies and therapists continue to reinforce the notion that it is only the client who needs to be changed, not the social conditions (Halleck 1971, Jacoby 1975; Lerner 1991; Nahem 1981). Such bias is prevalent in most social and medical services (McKnight 1989; Waitzkin 1989). If professionals are entrusted by society to enhance the quality of life for the population at large, then social ethics should be as important as individual ethics. Yet the former continue to be overshadowed by the latter.

Meritocracy

Another reason why professionals have not regarded collective empowerment as vital is because of their fundamental belief that the answer to social problems lies in individual merit (Bledstein 1976; Hall 1983; Kultgen 1988; Perkin 1990; Reiff 1974; Wilding 1982). By embracing the ideology of meritocracy, whereby success and failure are explained in person-centered terms, professionals proceed to change individuals and not social structures. Professionals project onto society their own experience of success due to so-called talent and merit, thereby expecting their clients to improve their fortune not by social action but by personal effort.

Power

Empowerment calls for equitable distribution of power between professionals and citizens (Lebacqz 1985; Lerman and Porter 1990b; Rappaport 1981, 1987; Riessman 1986), which is a departure from the customary practice of treating professionals with deference and ascribing them moral and intellectual superiority. Empowerment will not occur unless professionals consent to share power with the recipients of their services (Chavis and Wandersman 1990), which many observers consider unlikely under the dominant hierarchical professional ethos (Illich 1977; Kultgen 1988; Lieberman 1970; Perkin 1990; Reiff 1974; Wilding 1982).

Scientism

Psychologists are mostly trained and socialized into a professional problem-solving mentality that glorifies neat, sterile, lab-type methods and procedures, the kind that are not readily—if at all—applicable to social complexities (Sarason 1978). Psychology's adoption of natural science's experimental approach as its preeminent paradigm had unpropitious repercussions for the usefulness and applicability of psychological knowledge to human and social problems (cf. Kline 1988; E. V. Sullivan 1984). As Sarason (1981b) put it, since its early days

> psychology committed itself to the cult of standardization, i.e., to contrive situations that would be standard for all people. This seemed to meet the scientific requirements of objectivity, reliability, and validity but at the expense of recognizing or pursuing the following question: how does behavior in standardized situations relate to and illuminate behavior in naturally occurring situations. (p. 183)

Similarly, DeBoer (1983) wrote that "in nomothetic psychology . . . the human being is methodically stripped of his [sic] historicity. The test-person is ahistorical" (p. 6). This ahistorical stance has largely prevented a full and rich understanding of the dynamics involved in life in the community.

The empowerment of individuals and communities requires the management of unpredictable variables, political complications, and uncontrollable social events. Traditional training does not prepare applied psychologists for this kind of work. The few attempts by mental health specialists to launch community-wide interventions that we have seen in the last decade or so have been conducted almost exclusively by community psychologists (Albee, Joffe, and Dusenbury 1988; Rappaport, Swift, and Hess 1984), a professional group trained in a scientific approach that seeks to merge methodological rigor with real-life vicissitudes.

POSSIBILITIES

I have argued for the legitimacy of the concept of empowerment in mainstream psychology and outlined some of the obstacles to its inclusion in our profession. In this section I wish to discuss two areas of psychology that might particularly benefit from the values and theory of empowerment. The first has to do with ethics, the second with issues of control, power, and well-being.

Quotidian Ethics

Empowerment brings to the forefront of scientific and professional endeavors three values: self-determination, distributive justice, and collaborative and democratic participation. In fact, it may be argued that the main thrust of empowerment theory is the dissemination and permeation of ethical values into everyday activities. The term *quotidian ethics* refers to the recurrent application and promotion of moral values in the various services professionals provide. I offer this term to suggest that ethics are to be of prime concern in performing daily routines. Ethics become a matter of constant observance, and to a large degree determine the contents and procedures of the occupational realm. This is to be contrasted with the current attitude toward ethics. In the present atmosphere, professional ethics are essentially equated with rules and regulations to be upheld and called upon to discipline misconduct. Quotidian ethics proactively procure the enhancement of certain moral values in every aspect of the professional's life. In this sense, they are associated with the concept of everyday ethics recently advanced by Halberstam (1993).

Moral philosophy should be easily accessed and debated by professionals and consumers alike. Ethics should not remain exclusively in the hands of ethical boards or applied moral philosophers. For as long as the public feels excluded from the ethical decision-making process affecting professions, professionals, and citizens, the risk of nurturing an elitist kind of ethics is perpetuated.

The concept of quotidian ethics is evocative of J. Cohen's (1988) *discourse ethics*, "with its emphasis on the equal participation of all concerned in public discussions on contested norms" (p. 315). According to J. Cohen (1988), social policies and professional activities are to be regarded as legitimate only if all those possibly affected by them would have an equal opportunity to voice their concerns, and a vote on the final decision (cf. Habermas 1990). Discourse ethics, like quotidian ethics, are drawn from "the principles of democracy" (J. Cohen 1988, p. 315). This interpretation is congruent with Singer's (1993) opinion that ethical behavior ought to take into account the interests of all those affected by the agent's action or inaction.

Quotidian ethics attempt to incorporate moral values into the occupational realm and disseminate them among all individuals concerned, service providers as well as citizens/consumers. Proponents of empowerment have made some progress in translating these principles into action. As it was pointed out in this chapter, the values of empowerment are congruent with the values of professional ethics in general. The empowerment paradigm affords professionals an opportunity to actively pursue the fulfillment of their moral duties; primarily those concerned with the social welfare of the population at large, an area largely neglected in professional circles.

Quotidian ethics may be practiced at the university as well as in the community. Courses dealing with the social ethics and values of psychology may be introduced at both the undergraduate and the graduate levels. The degree of consistency between empowerment values and the contents and processes of psychology curricula could be the subject of discussions among students, staff, and faculty. In the community, psychologists can engage the public in debating service priorities. With limited resources, service providers struggle between giving immediate help to individuals in need and planning long-term interventions and prevention programs to enhance the welfare of the community at large. The ethical and social repercussions of each course of action need to be carefully examined, and input from consumers is vital in this process. An excellent illustration of how the ethical values of empowerment can be incorporated into counseling with individuals and families is provided by Dunst, Trivette, and Deal (1988). Their clinical work reaches a rarely attained integration of client participation, self-determination, and sensitivity to restrictive social circumstances and life events. These values are similarly reflected in the therapeutic work of Lerner (1991) with individuals and occupational stress groups, and in the social action psychotherapy approach of S. Holland (1992) with poor women. These authors attempt to operate from a clinical framework that would seem to be compatible with the philosophy of quotidian ethics.

In summary, the language of empowerment fosters public debate on moral issues; it vitalizes individual and social ethics. In applying the values of empowerment to their teaching, research, and interventions, psychologists would be advancing the practice of quotidian ethics.

Control, Power, and Well-Being

It has been argued that psychological well-being is generally enhanced by control over one's life events and circumstances. However, an important distinction must be made between the *perception* of control and *real experiences* of control and power. Research and interventions dealing exclusively with perceptions of control have serious limitations. Attempts to increase perceptions of control will have different effects depending on whether individuals live under relatively empowering or relatively disempowering conditions. Whereas in the former situation people may benefit from these efforts, in the latter people still have to contend with depriving living circumstances. At this point more than purely psychological help is needed. Individuals and groups facing disempowering life events and circumstances require assistance in changing not only their perceptions of power, but also, and more importantly, the real constellations of social power that deprive them of rights, goods, and services. For the psychological experience of control to occur, certain social circumstances need to obtain—specifically, distributive justice. Groups deprived of basic necessities cannot aspire to "feel in control," simply because these necessities are out of their reach. Consequently, under conditions of deprivation, distributive justice should take precedence over control. When minimal conditions of justice are met, and individuals can gratify their basic needs, the ground is more fertile for the emergence of positive experiences of control. These are severely curtailed, however, under conditions of oppression.

Since certain injurious systemic conditions remain present even after we adjust our cognitions, an optimistic explanatory style (Seligman 1990) may be considered only the first step in propelling people into changing demeaning and oppressive societal structures. Following a process of cognitive liberation equivalent to saying "It is not my fault," oppressed individuals need to be empowered to oppose structural configurations of power that precluded them from experiencing control in the past and perpetuate their misfortune in the present.

Furthermore, interventions designed to enhance the level of control people exercise over their affairs provide an insight into the real-life dynamics of power that can rarely be attained by the somewhat removed, laboratory-type of research on perceptions of control and attributional style. Hence, we might conclude that when dealing with depriving psychosocial environments, empowerment research and action are needed to complement psychological interventions dealing primarily with perceptions and cognitions.

CONCLUSION

The concept of empowerment brings to the forefront of research and action the unequal distribution of power among citizens and its concomitant personal and societal repercussions. Problems deriving from excessive and unjustified use of power are endemic in families, classrooms, industry, business, religious settings, and governments. In almost every sphere of our lives there is the potential for psychological damage caused by some people oppressively controlling others. The model of empowerment presented here offers mainstream psychology a value-based argument for exploring and intervening in situations of power inequality.

The importance of control and self-determination notwithstanding, these should never undermine the value of *interdependence* that is so essential for communal living. For control not to devolve into a new version of individualism, it should be tempered with the values of distributive justice, collaboration, and democratic participation in public affairs. A sense of community and peaceful coexistence cannot possibly flourish when all that its members desire is more control. The value of collaboration means, in daily practice, compassionate caring, mutual respect, and sensitivity to the interdependence of community members (Addams 1902). The predominant discourse on empowerment risks emphasizing control at the expense of justice, collaboration, compassion, and democracy. If psychologists, social scientists, and concerned citizens want to advance a social agenda of control that means more than a new version of individualism, attention will have to be paid to issues of justice and reciprocal social relations.

REFERENCES

Abberley, P. (1987). The concept of oppression and the development of a social theory. *Disability, Handicap, and Society, 2*(1), 5-19.

Abercrombie, N. (1980). *Class, structure, and knowledge: Problems in the sociology of knowledge.* New York: New York University Press.

Aboulafia, M. (1986). *The mediating self: Mead, Sartre, and self-determination.* New Haven: Yale University Press.

Abramson, J. B. (1984). *Liberation and its limits: The moral and political thought of Freud.* New York: Free Press.

Ackerman, F., & Zimbalist, A. (1986). Capitalism and inequality in the United States. In R. C. Edwards, M. Reich, & T. E. Weisskopf (Eds.), *The capitalist system* (3d ed., pp. 217-27). Englewood Cliffs, NJ: Prentice-Hall.

Adam, B. D. (1978). *The survival of domination: Inferiorization and everyday life.* New York: Elsevier.

Addams, J. (1902). *Democracy and social ethics.* New York: Macmillan.

Agel, J. (Ed.). (1971). *The radical therapist.* New York: Ballantine.

Albee, G. W. (1970). The uncertain future of clinical psychology. *American Psychologist, 25,* 1071-80.

———. (1981). Politics, power, prevention, and social change. In J. M. Joffe & G. W. Albee (Eds.), *Prevention through political action and social change* (pp. 3-24). Hanover, NH: University Press of New England.

———. (1986). Toward a just society: Lessons from observations on the primary prevention of psychopathology. *American Psychologist, 41,* 891-98.

——— . (1990). The futility of psychotherapy. *Journal of Mind and Behavior*, *11*(3,4), 369-84.

Albee, G. W., Bond, L. A., & Cook Monsey, T. V. (Eds.). (1992). *Improving children's lives: Global perspectives on prevention*. London: Sage.

Albee, G. W., Joffe, J. M., & Dusenbury, L. A. (Eds.). (1988). *Prevention, powerlessness, and politics: Readings on social change*. Beverly Hills, CA: Sage.

Alinsky, S. D. (1971). *Rules for radicals*. New York: Vintage Books.

Allen, K. R., & Baber, K. M. (1992). Ethical and epistemological tensions in applying a post modern perspective to feminist research. *Psychology of Women Quarterly, 16*, 1-15.

Alpert, J. L. (1985). Change within a profession: Change, future, prevention, and school psychology. *American Psychologist, 40*, 1112-21.

Alschuler, A. S. (1986). Creating a world where it is easier to love: Counseling applications of Paulo Freire's theory. *Journal of Counseling and Development, 64*, 492-96.

Alvesson, M. (1985). A critical framework for organizational analysis. *Organization Studies, 6*(2), 117-38.

American Psychiatric Association. (1987). *Diagnostic and statistical manual of mental disorders* (3d ed., rev.). Washington, DC: Author.

American Psychological Association. (1987). *Casebook on ethical principles of psychologists* (rev. ed.). Washington, DC: Author.

——— . (1990). Ethical principles of psychologists. *American Psychologist, 45*, 390-95.

Andersen, T. (1992). Reflections on reflecting with families. In S. McNamee & K. J. Gergen (Eds.), *Therapy as social construction* (pp. 54-68). London: Sage.

Anderson, C. C., & Travis, L. D. (1983). *Psychology and the liberal consensus*. Waterloo, Ontario: Wilfrid Laurier University.

Anderson, H., & Goolishian, H. (1992). The client is the expert: A not-knowing approach to therapy. In S. McNamee & K. J. Gergen (Eds.), *Therapy as social construction* (pp. 25-39). London: Sage.

Andriessen, E. J. H., & Coetsier, P. L. (1984). Industrial democratization. In P. J. D. Drenth, H. Tierry, P. J. Willems, and C. J. de Wolff (Eds.), *Handbook of work and organizational psychology* (Vol. 2, pp. 955-77). New York: Wiley.

Anthony, E. J., & Cohler, B. J. (Eds.). (1987). *The invulnerable child*. New York: Guilford.

Apple, M. W. (1982). *Education and power*. London: Routledge & Kegan Paul.

Apple, M. W., & Weis, L. (1983). Ideology and practice in schooling: A political and conceptual introduction. In M. W. Apple & L. Weis (Eds.), *Ideology and practice in schooling* (pp. 3-34). Philadelphia: Temple University Press.

Archibald, W. P. (1978). *Social psychology as political economy*. Toronto: McGraw-Hill Ryerson.

Arditi, R., Brennan, P., & Cavrak, S. (Eds.). (1980). *Science and liberation*. Montréal: Black Rose.

Aristotle. (1978). Happiness is self fullfillment. In J. A. Gould (Ed.), *Classic philosophical questions* (3d ed., pp. 157-67). Columbus, OH: Merrill.

Armistead, N. (1974). (Ed.), *Reconstructing social psychology*. Harmondsworth, England: Penguin.

Asch, S. E. (1981). Opinions and social pressure. In E. Aronson (Ed.), *Readings about the social animal* (3d ed., pp. 13-22). San Francisco: W. H. Freedman.

Baars, B. J. (1986). *The cognitive revolution in psychology*. New York: Guilford.

Babad, E., Inbar, J., & Rosenthal, R. (1982). Pygmaleon, Galatea, and the Golem: Investigations of biased and unbiased teachers. *Journal of Educational Psychology, 74*(4), 459-74.

Babington Smith, B. (1988). Industrial relations. In A. Bullock, O. Stallybrass, & S. Trombley (Eds.), *The Fontana dictionary of modern thought* (2d ed., pp.418-19). London: Fontana Press.

Back, K. W. (1978). An ethical critique of encounter groups. In G. Bermant, H. C. Kelman, & D. P. Warwick (Eds.), *The ethics of social intervention* (pp. 103-16). New York: Wiley.

Badcock, C. R. (1983). *Madness and modernity*. Oxford: Blackwell.

Baer, D. M., Wolf, M. M., & Risley, T. R. (1987). Some still-current dimensions of applied behavior analysis. *Journal of Applied Behavior Analysis, 20*(4), 313-27.

Baier, K. (1969). What is value? An analysis of the concept. In K. Baier & N. Ressler (Eds.), *Values and the future* (pp. 33-67). New York: Free Press.

Baker Miller, J. (1986). *Toward a new psychology of women* (2d ed.). Boston: Beacon Press.

———. (1990). The development of women's sense of self. In C. Zanardi (Ed.), *Essential papers on the psychology of women* (pp. 437-54). New York: University of New York Press.

Baritz, L. (1974). *The servants of power: A history of the use of social science in American industry.* Westport, CT: Greenwood.

Barling, J. (1988). Industrial relations: A "blind" spot in the teaching, research, and practice of I/O psychology. *Canadian Psychology, 29*(1), 103-8.

Bartky, S. L. (1990). *Femininity and domination: Studies in the phenomenology of domination.* New York: Routledge.

Bartlett, F. (1939). The limitations of Freud. *Science and Society, 3*(1), 64-105.

———. (1945). Recent trends in psychoanalysis. *Science and Society, 9*(3), 214-31.

Bass, M. B., & Drenth, P. J. D., (Eds.). (1987). *Advances in organizational psychology.* London: Sage.

Bassuk, E. L., & Gerson, S. (1985). Deinstitutionalization and mental health services. In P. Brown (Ed.), *Mental health care and social policy* (pp. 127-44). London: Routledge & Kegan Paul.

Bassuk, E. L., & Rubin, L. (1987). Homeless children: A neglected population. *American Journal of Orthopsychiatry, 57*(2), 279-86.

Bateson, G. (1972). *Steps to an ecology of mind.* New York: Ballantine.

Bateson, G., Jackson, D. D., Haley, J., & Weakland, J. (1956). Toward a theory of schizophrenia. *Behavioral Science, 1*, 251-64.

Bayer, R. (1981). *Homosexuality and American psychiatry: The politics of diagnosis.* New York: Basic Books.

Bechtel, R. B. (1984). Patient and community: The ecological bond. In W. A. O'Connor & B. Lubin (Eds.), *Ecological approaches to clinical and community psychology* (pp. 216-31). New York: Wiley.

Beck, A. T. (1976). *Cognitive therapy and the emotional disorders.* New York: International Universities Press.

———. (1982). Techniques of cognitive therapy. In D. Goleman & K. R. Speeth (Eds.), *The essential psychotherapies* (pp. 171-86). New York: New American Library.

Beit-Hallahmi, B. (1977). Humanistic psychology: Progressive or reactionary? *Self and Society, 5*, 97-103.

Bell, L., & Schniedewind, N. (1989). Realizing the promise of humanistic education: A reconstructed pedagogy for personal and social change. *Journal of Humanistic Psychology, 29*, 200-223.

Bellah, R. N., Madsen, R., Sullivan, W. M., Swidler, A., & Tipton, S. M. (1985). *Habits of the heart: Individualism and commitment in American life.* New York: Harper & Row.

Benne, R. (1981). *The ethic of democratic capitalism: A moral reassessment.* Philadelphia: Fortress.

Bennett, E. M. (Ed.). (1987). *Social intervention: Theory and practice.* Queenston, Ontario: Edwin Mellen.

Benson, J. K. (1977). Organizations: A dialectical view. *Administrative Science Quarterly, 22*(1), 1-21.

Berger, P. L., & Luckmann, T. (1967). *The social construction of reality.* New York: Anchor.

Berman, M. (1981). *The reenchantment of the world.* New York: Bantam.

Bermant, G., Kelman, H. C., & Warwick, D. P. (Eds.). (1978). *The ethics of social intervention.* New York: Wiley.

Bermant, G., & Warwick, D. P. (1978). The ethics of social intervention: Power, freedom, and accountability. In G. Bermant, H. C. Kelman, & D. P. Warwick (Eds.), *The ethics of social intervention* (pp. 377-417). New York: Wiley.

Berrueta-Clement, J. R., Schweinhart, L. J., Barnett, W. S., & Weikart, D. P. (1987). The effects of early educational intervention on crime and delinquency in adolescence and early adulthood. In J. D. Burchard & S. N. Burchard (Eds.), *Prevention of delinquent behavior* (pp. 220-40). Newbury Park, CA: Sage.

Bertalanffy, L. V. (1968). *General system theory: Foundations, development, applications.* New York: George Braziller.

Bethlehem, D. (1987). Scolding the carpenter. In S. Modgil and C. Modgil (Eds.), *B. F. Skinner: Consensus and controversy* (pp. 89-97). New York: Falmer Press.

Bevan, W. (1982). A sermon of sorts in three plus parts. *American Psychologist, 37,* 1303-22.

Billig, M. (1979). *Psychology, racism, and fascism.* Birmingham, England: Searchlight.

————. (1982). *Ideology and social psychology.* Oxford: Blackwell.

Blanshard, B. (1961). *Reason and goodness.* New York: Macmillan.

Bledstein, B. J. (1976). *The culture of professionalism.* New York: Norton.

Bocock, R. (1983). *Sigmund Freud.* London: Tavistock.

Boggs, C. (1976). *Gramsci's Marxism.* London: Pluto Press.

Bond, L. A., & Compas, B. E. (Eds.). (1989). *Primary prevention and promotion in the schools*. Newbury Park, CA: Sage.

Bowen, M. (1978). *Family therapy in clinical practice*. New York: Jason Aronson.

Bowlby, J. (1988). Developmental psychiatry comes of age. *American Journal of Psychiatry, 145*(1), 1-10.

Bowles, S., Gordon, D. M., & Weisskopf, T. E. (1986). The politics of long economic swings. In R. C. Edwards, M. Reich, & T. E. Weisskopf (Eds.), *The capitalist system* (3d ed., pp. 373-79). Englewood Cliffs, NJ: Prentice-Hall.

Boyte, H. C. (1990, Spring). Politics as education. *Social Policy*, pp. 35-42.

Boyte, H. C., & Riessman, F. (Eds.). (1986). *The new populism: The politics of empowerment*. Philadelphia: Temple University Press.

Braginsky, B. M., & Braginsky, D. D. (1974). *Mainstream psychology: A critique*. New York: Holt, Rinehart & Winston.

———. (1976). The myth of schizophrenia. In P. A. Magaro (Ed.), *The construction of madness* (pp. 66-90). New York: Pergamon Press.

Braginsky, D. D. (1985). Psychology: Handmaiden to society. In S. Koch & D. E. Leary (Eds.), *A century of psychology as science* (pp. 880-91). New York: McGraw-Hill.

Bramel, D., & Friend, R. (1981). Hawthorne, the myth of the docile worker, and class bias in psychology. *American Psychologist, 36*, 867-78.

———. (1982). The theory and practice of psychology. In B. Ollman & E. Vernoff (Eds.), *The left academy* (pp. 166-201). New York: McGraw-Hill.

———. (1987). The work group and its vicissitudes in social and industrial psychology. *Journal of Applied Behavioral Science, 23*(2), 233-53.

Braswell, L., & Kendall, P. (1988). Cognitive-behavioral methods with children. In K. S. Dobson (Ed.), *Handbook of cognitive behavioral therapies* (pp. 167-213). New York: Guilford.

Breggin, P. R. (1990). Brain damage, dementia, and persistent cognitive dysfunction associated with neuroleptic drugs: Evidence, etiology, implications. *Journal of Mind and Behavior, 11*(3-4), 425-64.

Breton, M. (1989). Liberation theology, group work, and the right of the poor and oppressed to participate in the life of the community. *Social Work with Groups, 12*(3), 5-18.

Brickman, P., Rabinowitz, V. C., Karuza, J., Coates, D., Cohn, E., & Kidder, L. (1982). Models of helping and coping. *American Psychologist, 37*, 368-84.

Brittan, A., & Maynard, M. (1984). *Sexism, racism, and oppression.* New York: Blackwell.

Brooks, K. (1973). Freudianism is not a basis for a Marxist psychology. In P. Brown (Ed.), *Radical psychology* (pp. 315-74). New York: Harper & Row.

Brown, J. A. C. (1954). *The social psychology of industry.* Harmondsworth, England: Penguin.

Brown, J. F. (1936). *Psychology and the social order.* New York: McGraw-Hill.

Brown, P. (Ed.). (1973). *Radical psychology.* New York: Harper & Row.

———. (1981). Anti-psychiatry and the left. *Psychology and Social Theory, 2,* 19-28.

———. (Ed). (1985). *Mental health care and social policy.* London: Routledge & Kegan Paul.

Bruss, N., & Macedo, D. P. (1985). Toward a pedagogy of the question: Conversations with Paulo Freire. *Journal of Education* (Boston), *167*(2), 7-21.

Buck-Morss, S. (1979). Socioeconomic bias in Piaget's theory: Implications for cross-cultural studies. In A. R. Buss (Ed.), *Psychology in social context* (pp. 349-63). New York: Irvington.

Bulhan, H. A. (1985). *Franz Fanon and the psychology of oppression.* New York: Plenum Press.

Burchard, J. D. (1987). Social policy and the role of the behavior analyst in the prevention of delinquent behavior. *Behavior Analyst, 10*(1), 83-88.

Burden, D. S., & Gottlieb, N. (1987). Women's socialization and feminist groups. In C. M. Brody (Ed.), *Women's therapy groups* (pp. 24-39). New York: Springer.

Burgess, L. (1990). A block association president's perspective on citizen participation and research. *American Journal of Community Psychology, 18,* 159-61.

Burman, E. (1990). Differing with deconstruction: A feminist critique. In I. Parker & J. Shotter (Eds.), *Deconstructing social psychology* (pp. 208-20). New York: Routledge.

Burston, D. (1991). *The legacy of Erich Fromm.* Cambridge: Harvard University Press.

Burstow, B., & Weitz, D. (1988). (Eds.). *Shrink resistant.* Vancouver: New Star Books.

Busfield, J. (1974). Family ideology and family pathology. In N. Armistead, (Ed.), *Reconstructing social psychology* (pp. 157-73). Harmondsworth, England: Penguin.

Buss, A. R. (1975). The emerging field of the sociology of psychological knowledge. *American Psychologist, 30,* 988-1002.

———. (1979a). Humanistic psychology as liberal ideology. *Journal of Humanistic Psychology, 19,* 43-55.

———. (Ed.). (1979b). *Psychology in social context.* New York: Irvington.

Butcher, E. (1983). Evolution or revolt? Role of the change agent in psychology. *Counseling and Values, 27*(4), 229-41.

Cabot, R. C. (1926). *Adventures on the borderlands of ethics.* New York: Harper & Brothers.

Campbell, E. (1984). Humanistic psychology: The end of innocence. *Journal of Humanistic Psychology, 24,* 6-29.

Canadian Psychological Association. (1991). *A Canadian code of ethics for psychologists.* Quebec: Author.

Caplan, N., & Nelson, S. (1973). On being useful: The nature and consequences of psychological research on social problems. *American Psychologist, 28,* 199-211.

Capponi, P. (1985). How psychiatric patients view deinstitutionalization. In Canadian Council on Social Development (Ed.), *Deinstitutionalization: Costs and effects* (pp. 7-10). Ottawa: Author.

———. (1992). *Upstairs in the crazy house: The life of a psychiatric survivor.* Toronto: Viking.

Capra, F. (1982). *The turning point: Science, society, and the rising culture.* New York: Bantam.

Carniol, B. (1990). *Case critical: Challenging social work in Canada* (2d ed.). Toronto: Between the Lines.

Carroll, M. A., Schneider, H. G., & Wesley, G. R. (1985). *Ethics in the practice of psychology.* Englewood Cliffs, NJ: Prentice-Hall.

Caruso, I. A. (1964). How social is psychoanalysis? In H. M. Ruitenbeek (Ed.), *Psychoanalysis and contemporary culture* (pp. 263-81). New York: Delta.

Castilla del Pino, C. (1981). *Psicoanalisis y Marxismo* [Psychoanalysis and Marxism]. Madrid: Alianza Editorial.

Catalano, R. (1991). The health effects of economic insecurity. *American Journal of Public Health, 81,* 1148-52.

Catano, V. M., & Tivendell, J. (1988). Industrial/Organizational psychology in Canada [Special issue]. *Canadian Psychology, 29*(1).

Cereseto, S., & Waitzkin, H. (1986). Economic development, political-economic system, and the physical quality of life. *American Journal of Public Health, 76*(6), 661-65.

Chamberlin, J. (1990). The ex-patients' movement: Where we've been and where we're going. *Journal of Mind and Behavior, 11*(3-4), 323-36.

Chambers, R. R. (1992). *Political theory and societal ethics.* Buffalo, NY: Prometheus Books.

Chavis, D. M., & Wandersman, A. (1990). Sense of community in the urban environment: A catalyst for participation and community development. *American Journal of Community Psychology, 18*, 55-81.

Chavis, D. M., & Wolff, T. (1993, June). *Public hearing: Community psychology's failed commitment to social change: Ten demandments for action.* Public meeting held at the biennial conference of the Society for Community Research and Action, Division 27 of the APA, Williamsburg, Virginia.

Chesler, P. (1989). *Women and madness.* New York: Harcourt Brace Jovanovich.

Chess, S., & Thomas, A. (1984). *Origins and evolution of behavior disorders: From infancy to adult life.* New York: Brunner/Mazel.

Chin, R., & Benne, K. D. (1985). General strategies for effecting changes in human systems. In W. Bennis, K. D. Benne, & R. Chin (Eds.), *The planning of change* (4th ed., pp. 22-45). New York: Holt, Rinehart & Winston.

Chodorow, N. J. (1978). *The reproduction of mothering: Psychoanalysis and the sociology of gender.* Berkeley: University of California Press.

————. (1990). Gender, relation, and difference in psychoanalytic perspective. In C. Zanardi (Ed.), *Essential papers on the psychology of women* (pp. 420-36). New York: New York University Press.

Chomsky, N. (1988). *Media, propaganda, and democracy.* The 1988 Massey Lectures. Lectures broadcast by Canadian Broadcasting Corporation Radio, Toronto.

Chorover, S. L. (1985). Psychology in cultural context. In S. Koch & D. E. Leary (Eds.), *A century of psychology as science* (pp. 870-79). New York: McGraw-Hill.

Clark, K. B. (1974). *Pathos of power.* New York: Harper & Row.

Clarke, R. W., & Lawry, R. P. (Eds.). (1988). *The power of the professional person.* New York: University Press of America.

Cohen, C. I. (1986). Marxism and psychotherapy. *Science and Society, 50*(1), 4-24.

Cohen, C. P., & Naimark, H. (1991). United Nations convention on the rights of the child: Individual rights concepts and their significance for social scientists. *American Psychologist, 46,* 60-65.

Cohen, D. (Ed.). (1990). Challenging the therapeutic state: Critical perspectives on psychiatry and the mental health system [Special issue]. *Journal of Mind and Behavior, 11*(3-4).

Cohen, D., & McCubbin, M. (1990). The political economy of tardive dyskinesia: Asymmetries in power and responsibility. *Journal of Mind and Behavior, 11*(3-4), 465-88.

Cohen, J. (1988). Discourse ethics and civil society. *Philosophy and Social Criticism, 14*(3-4), 315-37.

Collins, P. H. (1991). *Black feminist thought: Knowledge, consciousness, and the politics of empowerment.* New York: Routledge.

Commission on Prevention of Mental-Emotional Disabilities. (1987). Report of the Commission on Prevention of Mental-Emotional Disabilities. *Journal of Primary Prevention, 7*(4), 175-234.

Comunidad Los Horcones (1989). Walden two and social change: The application of behavior analysis to cultural design. *Behavior Analysis and Social Action, 7*(1-2), 35-41.

Connerton, P. (Ed.). (1976). *Critical sociology.* Harmondsworth, England: Penguin.

Conoley, J. C. (1981). Advocacy consultation: Promises and problems. In J. C. Conoley (Ed.), *Consultation in schools* (pp. 157-78). New York: Academic Press.

Conrad, P. (1981). On the medicalization of deviance and social control. In D. Ingleby (Ed.), *Critical psychiatry: The politics of mental health* (pp. 102-19). New York: Penguin.

Cooper, H. M., & Good, T. L. (1983). *Pygmalion grows up.* New York: Longman.

Cosgrove, M. P. (1982). *B. F. Skinner's behaviorism.* Grand Rapids, MI: Zondervan.

Costall A., & Still, A. (Eds.). (1987). *Cognitive psychology: In question.* New York: St. Martin's Press.

Coulter, J. (1979). *The social construction of mind.* Totowa, NJ: Rowman & Littlefield.

Cowen, E. L. (1991). In pursuit of wellness. *American Psychologist, 46,* 404-8.

Cowen, E. L., Trost, M. A., Lorion, R. P., Dorr, D., Izzo, L. D., & Isaacson, R. V. (1975). *New ways in school mental health: Early detection and school maladaption.* New York: Human Sciences Press.

Cowen, E. L., Work, W. C., & Wyman, P. A. (1992). Resilience among profoundly stressed urban school children. In M. Kessler & S. E. Goldston (Eds.), *The present and future of prevention research: Essays in honor of George W. Albee.* San Francisco: Sage.

Cowen, E. L., Wyman, P. A., Work, W. C., & Parker, G. R. (1990). The Rochester Child Resilience Project: Overview and summary of first year findings. *Development and Psychopathology, 2,* 193-212.

Cushman, P. (1990). Why the self is empty: Toward a historically situated psychology. *American Psychologist, 45,* 599-611.

Danziger, K. (1979). The social origins of modern psychology. In A. R. Buss (Ed.), *Psychology in social context* (pp. 27-45). New York: Irvington.

————. (1990). *Constructing the subject: Historical origins of psychological research.* New York: Cambridge University Press.

Day, W. F. (1977). Ethical philosophy and the thought of B. F. Skinner. In J. E. Krapfl & E. A. Vargas (Eds.), *Behaviorism and ethics* (pp. 7-28). Kalamazoo, MI: Behaviordelia.

————. (1987). What is radical behaviorism? In S. Modgil & C. Modgil (Eds.), *B. F. Skinner: Consensus and controversy* (pp. 13-40). New York: Falmer Press.

de Alberdi, L. (1990). *People, psychology, and business.* New York: Cambridge University Press.

Dean, A. (1976). Issues of deviance, labeling, and social control. In A. Dean, A. M. Kraft, & B. Pepper (Eds.), *The social setting of mental health* (pp. 187-95). New York: Basic Books.

Dean, A., Kraft, A. M., & Pepper, B. (Eds.). (1976). *The social setting of mental health.* New York: Basic Books.

DeBoer, T. (1983). *Foundations of a critical psychology.* Pittsburgh: Duquesne University Press.

Declaration of principles. (1985). *Phoenix Rising, 5*(2-3), 33A-34A.

Deese, J. (1985). *American freedom and the social sciences.* New York: Columbia University Press.

Deutsch, M. P. (1964). The disadvantaged child and the learning process. In F. Riessman, J. Cohen, & A. Pearl (Eds.), *Mental health of the poor* (pp. 172-87). New York: Free Press.

Dewey, J. (1900). Psychology and social practice. *Psychological Review, 7*(2), 105-24.

Di Giuseppe, R. A. (1981). Cognitive therapy with children. In G. Emery, S. D. Hollon, & R. C. Bedrosian (Eds.), *New directions in cognitive therapy: A casebook* (pp. 50-67). New York: Guilford.

Dinnerstein, D. (1976). *The mermaid and the minotaur*. New York: Harper.

Dobyns, H. F., Doughty, P. L., & Lasswell, H. D. (Eds.). (1971). *Peasants, power, and applied social change*. London: Sage.

Domhoff, W. (1986). Capitalist control of the state. In R. C. Edwards, M. Reich, & T. E. Weisskopf (Eds.), *The capitalist system* (3d ed., pp. 191-200). Englewood Cliffs, NJ: Prentice-Hall.

Doyle, J. (1986). The political process: Working statement. In T. Greening (Ed.), *Politics and innocence: A humanistic debate* (pp. 203-6). Dallas: Saybrook.

Dreyfus, H. L., & Dreyfus, S. E. (1987). The mistaken psychological assumption underlying belief in expert systems. In A. Costall & A. Still (Eds.), *Cognitive psychology: In question* (pp. 17-31). New York: St. Martin's Press.

Dunst, C., Trivette, C., & Deal, A. (1988). *Enabling and empowering families*. Cambridge, MA: Brookline.

Durlak, J. (1985). Primary prevention of school maladjustment. *Journal of Consulting and Clinical Psychology, 53*(5), 622-30.

Dusek, J., & Gail, J. (1983). The bases of teacher expectancies: A meta-analysis. *Journal of Educational Psychology, 75*(3), 327-46.

Eacker, J. N. (1975). *Problems of philosophy and psychology*. Chicago: Nelson-Hall.

Edwards, D., & Potter, J. (1992). *Discursive psychology*. London: Sage.

Edwards, R. C., Reich, M., & Weisskopf, T. E. (Eds.). (1986). *The capitalist system* (3d ed.). Englewood Cliffs, NJ: Prentice-Hall.

Elder, G. H., & Caspi, A. (1988). Economic stress in lives: Developmental perspectives. *Journal of Social Issues, 44*(4), 25-45.

Elliot, A. (1992). *Social theory and psychoanalysis in transition*. Cambridge, MA: Blackwell.

Ellis, A. (1982). The essence of rational emotive therapy. In D. Goleman & K. R. Speeth (Eds.), *The essential psychotherapies* (pp. 157-70). New York: New American Library.

————. (1985). Expanding the ABC's of rational emotive therapy. In M. J. Mahoney & A. Freeman (Eds.), *Cognition and psychotherapy* (pp. 313-24). New York: Plenum Press.

Ellis, A., & Harper, R. A. (1961). *A guide to rational living*. Hollywood, CA: Wilshire.

Emerson, E., & McGill, P. (1989). Normalization and applied behaviour analysis: Values and technology in services for people with learning difficulties. *Behavioural Psychotherapy, 17*(2), 101-17.

Emery, G., Hollon, S. D., & Bedrosian, R. C. (Eds.). (1981). *New directions in cognitive therapy: A casebook*. New York: Guilford.

Englert, E. H., & Suarez, A. (Eds.). (1985). *El psicoanalisis como teoria critica y la critica politica al psicoanalisis* [Psychoanalysis as critical theory and the political critique of psychoanalysis]. Madrid: Siglo Veintiuno.

Eriksson, B. (1975). *Problems of an empirical sociology of knowledge*. Stockholm: Uppsala.

Facione, P. A., Scherer, D., & Attig, T. (1978). *Values and society: An introduction to ethics and social philosophy*. Englewood Cliffs, NJ: Prentice-Hall.

Fagan, T. K. (1989). School psychology: Where next. *Canadian Journal of School Psychology, 5*(1), 1-8.

Fairbairn, G., & Fairbairn, S. (1987). Introduction: Psychology, ethics, and change. In S. Fairbairn & G. Fairbairn (Eds.), *Psychology, ethics, and change* (pp. 1-30). New York: Routledge & Kegan Paul.

Fanon, F. (1965). *Los condenados de la tierra* [Wretched of the earth]. Mexico: Fondo de cultura economica.

Fawcett, S. B., Bernstein, G. S., Czyzewski, M. J., Greene, B. F., Hannah, G. T., Iwata, B. A., Jason, L. A., Matthews, R. M., Morris, E. K., Otis-Wilborn, A., Seekins, T., & Winnett, R. A. (1988). Behavior analysis and public policy. *Behavior Analyst, 11*(1), 11-25.

Femia, J. V. (1981). *Gramsci's political thought: Hegemony, consciousness, and the revolutionary process*. Oxford: Clarendon.

Feminist Therapy Institute (1990). Code of ethics. In H. Lerman & N. Porter (Eds.), *Feminist ethics in psychotherapy* (pp. 37-40). New York: Springer.

Ferguson, M. (1983). Transformation as rough draft. *Journal of Humanistic Psychology, 23*, 16-18.

Field, T. (1987). Interaction and attachment in normal and atypical infants. *Journal of Consulting and Clinical Psychology, 55*(6), 853-59.

Fine, M., & Gordon, S. M. (1991). Effacing the center and the margins: Life at the intersection of psychology and feminism. *Feminism and Psychology, 1*(1), 19-27.

Fireside, H. (1979). *Soviet psychoprisons*. New York: Norton.

Florin, P., & Wandersman, A. (1990). An introduction to citizen participation, voluntary organizations, and community development: Insights for empowerment through research. *American Journal of Community Psychology, 18*, 41-53.

Foucault, M. (1961/1965). *Madness and civilization* (R. Howard, Trans.). New York: Random House. (Original work published 1961)

——. (1985). *Un dialogo sobre el poder* [A dialogue on power]. Madrid: Alianza Editorial.

——. (1954/1987). *Mental illness and psychology* (A. Sheridan, Trans.). Berkeley: University of California Press. (Original work published 1954)

Fox, D. R. (1985). Psychology, ideology, utopia, and the commons. *American Psychologist, 40*, 48-58.

——. (1993). Psychological jurisprudence and radical social change. *American Psychologist, 48*, 234-41.

Frankena, W. K. (1963). *Ethics*. Englewood Cliffs, NJ: Prentice-Hall.

Freedman, A. E. (1972). *The planned society: An analysis of Skinner's proposals*. Kalamazoo, MI: Behaviordelia.

Freeman, A. (1987). Cognitive therapy: An overview. In A. Freeman & V. Greenwood (Eds.), *Cognitive therapy: Applications in psychiatric and medical settings* (pp. 19-35). New York: Human Sciences Press.

Freeman, A., & Greenwood, V. (Eds.). (1987). *Cognitive therapy: Applications in psychiatric and medical settings*. New York: Human Sciences Press.

Freire, P. (1971). *Pedagogia del oprimido* [Pedagogy of the oppressed]. Buenos Aires: Siglo XXI.

——. (1975). Cultural action for freedom. *Harvard Educational Review Monograph, 1*.

——. (1985). *The politics of education: Culture, power, and liberation*. South Hadley, MA: Bergin & Garvey.

Freud, S. (1940/1949). *An outline of psychoanalysis* (J. Strachey, Trans.). New York: Norton. (Original work published 1940)

——. (1930/1961). *Civilization and its discontents* (J. Strachey, Trans.). New York: Norton. (Original work published 1930)

——. (1927/1964). *The future of an illusion* (W. D. Robson-Scott, Trans.). New York: Anchor. (Original work published 1927)

Friedman, M. I., & Lackey, G. H. (1991). *The psychology of human control.* New York: Praeger.

Fromm, E. (1955). *The sane society.* New York: Holt, Rinehart & Winston.

———. (1965). *Escape from freedom.* New York: Avon.

Frosh, S. (1987). *The politics of psychoanalysis.* New Haven: Yale University Press.

Fuller, R. C. (1986). *Americans and the unconscious.* New York: Oxford University Press.

Fuller Torrey, E. (1992). *Freudian fraud: The malignant effect of Freud's theory on American culture.* New York: Harper Collins.

Furby, L. (1979). Individualistic bias in studies of locus of control. In A. R. Buss (Ed.), *Psychology in social context* (pp. 169-90). New York: Irvington.

Furner, M. O. (1975). *Advocacy and objectivity: A crisis in the professionalization of American social science.* Lexington: University Press of Kentucky.

Gamson, W., Fireman, B., & Rytina, S. (1982). *Encounters with unjust authority.* Homewood, IL: Dorsey.

Gardner, H. (1985). *The mind's new science: A history of the cognitive revolution.* New York: Basic Books.

Garmezy, N. (1984). Stress-resistant children: The search for protective factors. In J. E. Stevenson (Ed.), *Recent research in developmental psychopathology* (pp. 213-33). New York: Pergamon Press.

Gaylin, W., Glasser, I., Marcus, S., & Rothman, D. J. (1981). *Doing good: The limits of benevolence.* New York: Pantheon.

Geiser, R. (1976). *Behavior mod and the managed society.* Boston: Beacon Press.

George, V., & Wilding, P. (1976). *Ideology and social welfare.* Boston: Routledge & Kegan Paul.

Gergen , K. J. (1973). Social psychology as history. *Journal of Personality and Social Psychology, 26*(2), 309-20.

———. (1985). Social psychology and the phoenix of unreality. In S. Koch., & D. E. Leary (Eds.), *A century of psychology as science* (pp. 529-57). New York: McGraw-Hill.

———. (1990). Therapeutic professions and the diffusion of deficit. *Journal of Mind and Behavior, 11,* 353-68.

———. (1992). Toward a postmodern psychology. In S. Kvale (Ed.), *Psychology and postmodernism* (pp. 17-31). London: Sage.

Gergen, K. J., Comer-Fisher, D., & Hepburn, A. (1986). Hermeneutics of personality description. *Journal of Personality and Social Psychology, 50*(6), 1261-70.

Gergen, K. J., & Gergen, M. M. (1981). *Social psychology*. New York: Harcourt Brace Jovanovich.

Gergen, K. J., & Gigerenzer, G. (Eds.). (1991). Cognitivism and its discontents [Special issue]. *Theory and Psychology, 1*(4).

Gesten, E. L., & Jason, L. A. (1987). Social and community interventions. *Annual Review of Psychology, 38*, 427-60.

Geuss, R. (1981). *The idea of a critical theory: Habermas and the Frankfurt school*. New York: Cambridge University Press.

Geyer, R. F., & Schweitzer, D. (Eds.). (1981). *Alienation: Problems of meaning, theory,and method*. London: Routledge & Kegan Paul.

Gholson, B., & Rosenthal, T. L. (Eds.). (1984). *Applications of cognitive developmental theory*. New York: Academic Press.

Giddens, A. (1979). *Central problems in social theory*. New York: Macmillan.

Gil, D. G. (1990). Implications of conservative tendencies for practice and education in social welfare. *Journal of Sociology and Social Welfare, 17*(2), 5-27.

Gilligan, C. (1982). *In a different voice: Psychological theory and women's development*. Cambridge: Harvard University Press.

―――. (1990). Remapping the moral domain: New images of the self in relationship. In C. Zanardi (Ed.), *Essential papers on the psychology of women* (pp. 480-95). New York: New York University Press.

Ginsburg, H. (1972). *The myth of the deprived child*. Englewood Cliffs, NJ: Prentice-Hall.

Giroux, H. A. (1985). Critical pedagogy, cultural politics, and the discourse of experience. *Journal of Education* (Boston), *167*(2), 22-41.

Glenn, M., & Kunnes, R. (1973). *Repression or revolution*. New York: Harper & Row.

Goble, F. G. (1970). *The third force: The psychology of Abraham Maslow*. Markham, Ontario: Simon & Schuster.

Goffman, E. (1981). The insanity of place. In O. Grusky & M. Pollner (Eds.), *The sociology of mental illness* (pp. 179-201). New York: Holt, Rinehart & Winston.

Goldenberg, I., & Goldenberg, H. (1985). *Family therapy: An overview*. (2d ed.). Monterey, CA: Brooks/Cole.

Goldstein, M. J. (1990). Family relations as risk factors for the onset and course of schizophrenia. In J. Rolf, A. S. Masten, D. Cicchetti, K. H. Nuechterlein, & S. Weintraub (Eds.), *Risk and protective factors in the development of psychopathology* (pp. 408-23). New York: Cambridge Universtiy Press.

Graham, H. (1986). *The human face of psychology: Humanistic psychology in its historical, social, and cultural context.* Philadelphia: Open University Press.

Gramsci, A. (1971). *Selections from the prison notebooks.* London: Lawrence & Wishart.

Greening, T. (Ed.). (1986). *Politics and innocence: A humanistic debate.* Dallas: Saybrook.

Gross, B. (1980). *Friendly fascism.* Montréal: Black Rose.

Grusky, O., & Pollner, M. (Eds.). (1981). *The sociology of mental illness.* New York: Holt, Rinehart & Winston.

Guareschi, P. (1982). Teoria e ideologia em psicologia [Theory and ideology in psychology]. *Psico, 5*(2), 5-17.

Gurin, P., Gurin, G., & Morrison, B. M. (1978). Personal and ideological aspects of internal and external control. *Social Psychology, 41*(4), 275-96.

Habermas, J. (1990). *Moral consciousness and communicative action.* Cambridge: MIT Press.

Halberstam, J. (1993). *Everyday ethics.* New York: Viking.

Hall, P. M. (1983). Individualism and social problems: A critique and an alternative. *Journal of Applied Behavioral Science, 19*(1), 85-94.

Halleck, S. (1971). *The politics of therapy.* New York: Science House.

Halpern, R. (1988). Action research for the late 1980s. *Journal of Community Psychology, 16,* 249-60.

Hamilton, J. (1989, March). Poverty and nutrition: Health time bomb. *Canada and the World,* pp. 16-17.

Harding, S. (1991). *Whose science? Whose knowledge?.* Ithaca, NY: Cornell University Press.

Hare-Mustin, R. T. (1991). Sex, lies, and headaches: The problem is power. *Journal of Feminist Family Therapy, 3*(1/2), 39-61.

Hare-Mustin, R. T., & Marecek, J. (1988). The meaning of difference: Gender theory, postmodernism, and psychology. *American Psychologist, 43,* 455-64.

———. (Eds.). (1990). *Making a difference: Psychology and the construction of gender.* New Haven: Yale University Press.

Harris, B., & Brock, A. (1991). Otto Fenichel and the left opposition in psycho-analysis. *Journal of the History of the Behavioral Sciences, 27,* 157-65.

Harsthouse, R. (1986). Aristotle, Nichomachean ethics. In G. Vesey (Ed.), *Philosophers ancient and modern* (pp. 35-53). New York: Cambridge University Press.

Hart, S. N. (1987). Psychological maltreatment in schooling. *School Psychology Review, 16*(2), 169-80.

――――. (1989). NASP at Thirty: A vision for children. *School Psychology Review, 18*(2), 221-24.

Hartman, H. (1976). Capitalism, patriarchy, and job segregation by sex. *Signs, 1*(3), 137-68.

Hartmann, H. (1960). *Psychoanalysis and moral values.* New York: International University Press

Haru, T. T. (1987). Basic sociologies of knowledge: On the nature of possible relationships between ideas and social contexts. *Sociological Focus, 20*(1), 1-12.

Haverman, E. (1957). *The age of psychology.* New York: Simon & Schuster.

Health and Welfare Canada. (1988). *Mental health for Canadians: Striking a balance.* Ottawa: Author.

Heber, F. R. (1984). Sociocultural mental retardation: A longitudinal study. In J. M. Joffe, G. W. Albee, & L. D. Kelly (Eds.), *Readings in primary prevention of psychopathology* (pp. 329-47). Hanover, NH: University Press of New England.

Heller, K., & Monahan, J. (1977). *Psychology and community change.* Homewood, IL: Dorsey.

Heller, K., Price, R. H., Reinharz, S., Riger, S., & Wandersman, A. (Eds.). (1984). *Psychology and community change.* Pacific Grove, CA: Brooks/Cole.

Henriques, J., Hollway, W., Urwin, C., Venn, C., & Walkerdine, V. (Eds.). (1984). *Changing the subject: Psychology, social regulation, and subjectivity.* London: Methuen.

Herman, E., & Chomsky, N. (1988). *Manufacturing consent.* New York: Pantheon.

Heshusius, L. (1989). The Newtonian mechanistic paradigm, special education, and contours of alternatives: An overview. *Journal of Learning Disabilities, 22*(7), 403-15.

Hillerbrand, E. (1987). Philosophical tensions influencing psychology and social action. *American Psychologist, 42,* 111-18.

Hjelle, L. A., & Ziegler, D. J. (1981). *Personality theories: Basic assumptions, research, and applications.* Tokyo: McGraw-Hill.

Hoffman, L. (1981). *Foundations of family therapy: A framework for systems change.* New York: Basic Books.

———. (1992). A reflexive stance for family therapy. In S. McNamee & K. J. Gergen (Eds.), *Therapy as social construction* (pp. 7-24). London: Sage.

Hofstadter, R. (1955). *Social Darwinism in American thought.* Boston: Beacon Press.

Holland, J. G. (1977). Is institutional change necessary? In J. E. Krapfl & E. A. Vargas (Eds.), *Behaviorism and ethics* (pp. 201-16). Kalamazoo, MI: Behaviordelia.

———. (1978). Behaviorism: Part of the problem or part of the solution? *Journal of Applied Behavior Analysis, 11,* 163-74.

Holland, S. (1992). From social abuse to social action: A neighbourhood psychotherapy and social action project for women. In J. M. Ussher & P. Nicolson (Eds.), *Gender issues in clinical psychology* (pp. 68-77). New York: Routledge.

Hollway, W. (1984). Fitting work: Psychological assessment in organizations. In J. Henriques, W. Hollway, C. Urwin, C. Venn., & V. Walkerdine (Eds.), *Changing the subject: Psychology, social regulation, and subjectivity* (pp. 26-59). London: Methuen.

———. (1991). The psychologization of feminism or the feminization of psychology. *Feminism and Psychology, 1*(1), 29-37.

Honig, A. S. (1986a, May). Stress and coping in children (Part 1). *Young Children,* pp. 50-63.

———. (1986b, July). Stress and coping in children (Part 2). *Young Children,* pp. 47-59.

Horney, K. (1937). *The neurotic personality of our time.* New York: Norton.

Howard, G. S. (1985). The role of values in the science of psychology. *American Psychologist, 40,* 255-65.

Howitt, D. (1991). *Concerning psychology.* Philadelphia: Open University Press.

Huber, J., & Form, W. H. (1973). *Income and ideology.* New York: Free Press.

Hughes, G. R. (1991, June). *B. F. Skinner's radical behaviorism: Past, present, and future.* Paper presented at the annual convention of the Canadian Psychological Association, Calgary, Alberta.

Hughes, K. J. (1986). *Signs of literature: Language, ideology, and the literary text*. Vancouver: Talonbooks.

Huszczo, G. E., Wiggins, J. G., & Currie, J. S. (1984). The relationship between psychology and organized labor. *American Psychologist, 39*, 432-40.

Hyde, J. S., & Rosenberg, B. G. (1980). *Half the human experience: The psychology of women* (2d ed.). Toronto: D. C. Heath.

Iaroshevskii, M. G. (1950). The eclipse of consciousness in contemporary psychology. *Benjamin Rush Bulletin, 1*(4), 32-42.

Ibanez Gracia, T. (1983). Los efectos politicos de la psicologia social [The political effects of social psychology]. *Cuadernos de Psicologia, 2*, 95-106.

Illich, I. (1977). Disabling professions. In I. Illich (Ed.), *Disabling professions* (pp. 11-40). London: Marion Boyars.

Ingleby, D. (1972). Ideology and the human sciences: Some comments on the role of reification in psychology and psychiatry. In T. Pateman (Ed.), *Counter course* (pp. 51-81). Baltimore: Penguin.

———. (1974). The job psychologists do. In N. Armistead (Ed.), *Reconstructing social psychology* (pp. 314-28). Harmondsworth, England: Penguin.

———. (Ed.). (1981a). *Critical psychiatry: The politics of mental health* (pp. 72-101). New York: Penguin.

———. (1981b). Introduction. In D. Ingleby (Ed.), *Critical psychiatry: The politics of mental health* (pp. 7-19). New York: Penguin.

———. (1981c). The politics of psychology: Review of a decade. *Psychology and Social Theory, 2*, 4-18.

———. (1981d). Understanding mental illness. In D. Ingleby (Ed.), *Critical psychiatry: The politics of mental health* (pp. 23-71). New York: Penguin.

Israel, J. (1979). From level of aspiration to dissonance: Or, what the middle class worries about. In A. R. Buss (Ed.), *Psychology in social context* (pp. 239-57). New York: Wiley.

Jacoby, R. (1975). *Social amnesia*. Boston: Beacon Press.

———. (1983). *The repression of psychoanalysis*. New York: Basic Books.

Jahoda, M. (1988). Economic recession and mental health: Some conceptual issues. *Journal of Social Issues, 44*(4), 13-23.

James, K., & McIntyre, D. (1983). The reproduction of families: The social role of family therapy? *Journal of Marital and Family Therapy, 9*(2), 119-29.

Jason, L. A. (1982). Community-based approaches in preventing adolescent problems. *School Psychology Review, 11*(4), 417-24.

Jason, L. A., & Glenwick, D. S. (1984). Behavioral community psychology. In M. Hersen, R. M. Eisler, & P. M. Miller (Eds.), *Progress in behavior modification* (Vol. 18, pp. 85-121). New York: Academic Press.

Jewell, L. N. (1985). *Contemporary industrial/organizational psychology.* New York: West.

Joffe, J. M., & Albee, G. W. (Eds.). (1981a). *Prevention through political action and social change.* Hanover, NH: University Press of New England.

————. (1981b). Powerlessness and psychopathology. In J. M. Joffe & G. W. Albee (Eds.), *Prevention through political action and social change* (pp. 321-25). Hanover, NH: University Press of New England.

————. (1988). Powerlessness and psychopathology. In G. W. Albee, J. M. Joffe, & L. A. Dusenbury (Eds.), *Prevention, powerlessness, and politics: Readings on social change* (pp. 53-56). Beverly Hills, CA: Sage.

Johnson, H. M. (1968). Ideology and the social system. In D. L. Sills (Ed.), *International encyclopedia of the social sciences* (pp. 76-85). New York: Macmillan & Free Press.

Johnston, N. S. (1990). School consultation: The training needs of teachers and school psychologists. *Psychology in the Schools, 27*(1), 51-56.

Johnstone, L. (1989). *Users and abusers of psychiatry: A critical look at traditional psychiatric practice.* New York: Routledge.

Joint Commission on Mental Health of Children. (1973). *Social change and the mental health of children.* New York: Harper & Row.

Jones, E. (1955). *The life and work of Sigmund Freud* (Vol. 2). New York: Basic Books.

————. (1986). The critique of ideology: Psychology and social theory. In K. S. Larsen (Ed.), *Dialectics and ideology in psychology* (pp. 245-56). Norwood, NJ: Ablex.

Josephson, E., & Josephson, M. (Eds.). (1962). *Man alone: Alienation in modern society.* New York, NY: Dell.

Kallen, E. (1989). *Label me human: Minority rights of stigmatized Canadians.* Toronto: University of Toronto Press.

Kamin, L. (1974). *The science and politics of IQ.* Potomac, MD: Erlbaum.

Kanuha, V. (1990). The need for an integrated analysis of oppression in feminist therapy ethics. In H. Lerman & N. Porter (Eds.), *Feminist ethics in psychotherapy* (pp. 24-36). New York: Springer.

Kaplan, M. S., & Kaplan, H. E. (1985). School psychology: Its educational and societal connections. *Journal of School Psychology, 23*(4), 319-25.

Karpel, M. A., & Strauss, E. S. (1983). *Family evaluation.* New York: Gardner Press.

Kavanagh, M. J., Borman, W. C., Hedge, J. J. W., & Gould, R. B. (1987). Performance measurement quality. In M. B. Bass & P. J. D. Drenth (Eds.), *Advances in organizational psychology* (pp. 43-57). London: Sage.

Kelly, G. A. (1971). Man's construction of his alternatives. In E. A. Southwell & M. Merbaum (Eds.), *Personality: Readings in theory and research* (pp. 291-317). Belmont, CA: Brooks/Cole.

Kelman, H. C., & Hamilton, V. L. (1989). *Crimes of obedience: Toward a social psychology of authority and responsibility.* New Haven: Yale University Press.

Kendall, P. C., & Braswell, L. (1984). *Cognitive behavior therapy for impulsive children.* New York: Guilford.

Kessler, R. C., Price, R. H., & Wortman, C. B. (1985). Social factors in psychopathology. *Annual Review of Psychology, 36,* 531-72.

Kipnis, D. (1987). Psychology and behavioral technology. *American Psychologist, 42,* 30-36.

Kiros, T. (1985). *Toward the construction of a theory of political action: Antonio Gramsci: Consciousness, participation, and hegemony.* New York: Lanham.

Kirsh, B. (1987). Evolution of consciousness-raising groups. In C. M. Brody (Ed.), *Women's therapy groups: Paradigms of feminist treatment* (pp. 43-54). New York: Springer.

Kitzinger, C. (1991a). Feminism, psychology, and the paradox of power. *Feminism and Psychology, 1*(1), 111-29.

———. (1991b). Politicizing psychology. *Feminism and Psychology, 1*(1), 49-54.

Klein, D. (1985). Some notes on the dynamics of resistance to change: The defender role. In W. Bennis, K. D. Benne, & R. Chin (Eds.), *The planning of change* (4th ed., pp. 98-105). New York: Holt, Rinehart & Winston.

Kline, P. (1988). *Psychology exposed.* New York: Routledge.

Kluegel, J. R., & Smith, E. R., (1986). *Beliefs about inequality.* New York: Aldine de Gruyter.

Knitzer, J. (1990, June). *At the school house door: The challenge of prevention.* Paper presented at the Vermont Conference on the Primary Prevention of Psychopathology: Improving Children's Lives—Global Perspectives on Prevention, Burlington.

Koch, S. (1980). Psychology and its human clientele: Beneficiaries or victims? In R. A. Kaschau & F. S. Kessel (Eds.), *Psychology and society: In search of symbiosis* (pp. 30-53). New York: Holt, Rinehart & Winston.

Koch, S., & Leary, D. E. (Eds.). (1985). *A century of psychology as science.* New York: McGraw-Hill.

Kolvin, I., Miller, F. J. W., Fleeting, M., & Kolvin, P. A. (1988). Risk/protective factors for offending with particular reference to deprivation. In M. Rutter (Ed.), *Studies of psychosocial risk* (pp. 77-95). New York: Cambridge University Press.

Kovaleski, J. F. (1988). Paradigmatic obstacles to reform in school psychology. *School Psychology Review, 17*(3), 479-84.

Kovel, J. (1981a). *The age of desire.* New York: Pantheon.

———. (1981b). The American mental health industry. In D. Ingleby (Ed.), *Critical psychiatry: The politics of mental health* (pp. 72-101). New York: Penguin.

———. (1988). *The radical spirit: Essays on psychoanalysis and society.* London: Free Association Books.

Krasner, L. (1976). Behavior modification: Ethical issues and future trends. In H. Leitenberg (Ed.), *Handbook of behavior modification and behavior therapy* (pp. 627-49). Englewood Cliffs, NJ: Prentice-Hall.

Krasner, L., & Houts, A. C. (1984). A study of the "value" systems of behavioral scientists. *American Psychologist, 39,* 840-50.

Kravetz, D. (1987). Benefits of consciousness-raising groups for women. In C. M. Brody (Ed.), *Women's therapy groups: Paradigms of feminist treatment* (pp. 55-66). New York: Springer.

Kultgen, J. (1988). *Ethics and professionalism.* Philadelphia: University of Pennsylvania Press.

Kvale, S. (1985). Skinner's radical behaviorism and behavior therapy—an outline for a Marxist critique. *Revista Mexicana del Analisis de la Conducta, 11*(3), 239-53.

———. (Ed.). (1992). *Psychology and postmodernism.* London: Sage.

Labedz, L. (1988). Reification. In A. Bullock, O. Stallybrass, & S. Trombley (Eds.), *The Fontana dictionary of modern thought* (p. 735). London: Fontana.

Lacayo, N., Sherwood, G., & Morris, J. (1981). Daily activities of school psychologists: A national survey. *Psychology in the Schools, 18,* 184-90.

Lafferty, J. (1981). Political responsibility and the human potential movement. *Journal of Humanistic Psychology, 21,* 69-75.

Laing, R. D. (1967). *The politics of experience and the bird of paradise.* Harmondsworth, England: Penguin.

———. (1969). *The politics of the family.* Toronto: Canadian Broadcasting Corporation Publications.

———. (1972). *Esquizofrenia y presion social* [Schizophrenia and social pressure]. Barcelona: Tusquets.

———. (1980). *Los locos y los cuerdos: Entrevista de Vincenzo Caretti* [The crazy and the normal: Interview by Vincenzo Caretti]. Barcelona: Editorial Critica.

———. (1985). *Wisdom, madness, and folly.* Toronto: McGraw-Hill.

Laing R. D., & Esterson, A. (1974). *Sanity, madness, and the family.* London: Tavistock.

Lamal, P. A. (1989). The impact of behaviorism on our culture: Some evidence and conjectures. *Psychological Record, 39,* 529-35.

Lamb, H. R., & Zusman, J. (1979). Primary prevention in perspective. *American Journal of Psychiatry, 136,* 12-17.

Landy, F. L. (1989). *Psychology of work behavior* (4th ed.). Pacific Grove, CA: Brooks/Cole.

Langer, E. J., & Rodin, J. (1976). The effects of choice and enhanced personal responsibility for the aged: A field experiment in an institutional setting. *Journal of Personality and Social Psychology, 34,* 191-98.

Larrain, J. (1979). *The concept of ideology.* London: Hutchinson.

Larsen, K. S. (1986a). Development of theory: The dialectic in behaviorism and humanism. In K. S. Larson (Ed.), *Dialectics and ideology in psychology* (pp. 219-28). Norwood, NJ: Ablex.

———. (Ed.). (1986b). *Dialectics and ideology in psychology.* Norwood, NJ: Ablex.

Lasch, C. (1984). *The minimal self.* New York: Norton.

Lebacqz, K. (1985). *Professional ethics: Power and paradox.* Nashville: Abingdon Press.

Lee, V. L. (1988). *Beyond behaviorism.* Hillsdale, NJ: Erlbaum.

Leibowitz, I. (1985). *Sichot al mada vearachim* [Science and values]. Tel Aviv: Ministry of Defense.

Leifer, R. (1990). The medical model as the ideology of the therapeutic state. *Journal of Mind and Behavior, 11*(3-4), 247-58.

Lerman, H. (1986). From Freud to feminist personality theory: Getting here from there. *Psychology of Women Quarterly, 10,* 1-18.

Lerman, H., & Porter, N. (1990a). The contribution of feminism to ethics in psychotherapy. In H. Lerman & N. Porter (Eds.), *Feminist ethics in psychotherapy* (pp. 5-13). New York: Springer.

————. (Eds.). (1990b). *Feminist ethics in psychotherapy.* New York: Springer.

Lerner, M. (1991). *Surplus powerlessness.* London: Humanities Press International.

Lessing, D. (1986). *Prisons we choose to live inside.* Toronto: CBC Enterprises.

Levant, R. (1984). *Family therapy: A comprehensive overview.* Englewood Cliffs, NJ: Prentice-Hall.

Levine, M. (1981). *The history and politics of community mental health.* New York: Oxford University Press.

Levine, M., & Levine, A. (1970). *A social history of helping services: Clinic, court, school, and community.* New York: Appleton-Century-Crofts.

Levine, M., & Perkins, D. V. (1987). *Principles of community psychology.* New York: Oxford University Press.

Levinson, E. M. (1990). Actual/desired role functioning, perceived control over role functioning, and job satisfaction among school psychologists. *Psychology in the Schools, 27*(1), 64-70.

Lichtenberg, P. (1969). *Psychoanalysis: Radical and conservative.* New York: Springer.

Lieberman, J. K. (1970). *The tyranny of the experts.* New York: Walker.

London, P. (1969). Morals and mental health. In S. C. Plog & R. B. Edgerton (Eds.), *Changing perspectives in mental illness* (pp. 32-47). New York: Holt, Rinehart & Winston.

————. (1986). *The modes and morals of psychotherapy* (2d ed.). New York: Hemisphere.

Lord, J., & Farlow, D. M. (1990, Fall). A study of personal empowerment: Implications for health promotion. *Health Promotion,* pp. 2-8.

Lozoff, B. (1989). Nutrition and behavior. *American Psychologist, 44,* 231-36.

Lundin, R. W. (1972). *Theories and systems of psychology.* Toronto: D. C. Heath.

Machan, T. R. (1974). *The pseudo science of B. F. Skinner.* New Rochelle, NY: Arlington House.

Macpherson, C. B. (1969). Models of society. In T. Burns (Ed.), *Industrial man* (pp. 24-34). Baltimore: Penguin.

Magaro, P. A., Gripp, R., McDowell, D. J., & Miller, I. W., III. (1978). *The mental health industry: A cultural phenomenon.* New York: Wiley.

Mahoney, M. J. (1977). Reflections on the cognitive learning trend in psychotherapy. *American Psychologist, 32,* 5-13.

Mahoney, M. J., & Freeman, A. (Eds.). (1985). *Cognition and psychotherapy.* New York: Plenum Press.

Maier, N. R. F. (1946). *Psychology in industry.* Boston: Houghton Mifflin.

Malagodi, E. F. (1986). On radicalizing behaviorism: A call for cultural analysis. *Behavior Analyst, 9*(1), 1-17.

Mannheim, K. (1936). *Ideology and utopia.* New York: Harcourt Brace Jovanovich.

Mannino, F. V., & Shore, M. F. (1984). An ecological perspective on family intervention. In W. A. O'Conner & B. Lubin (Eds.), *Ecological approaches to clinical and community psychology* (pp. 75-93). New York: Wiley.

Marcatillo, A. J. M., & Nevin, J. A. (1986). The threat of nuclear war: Some responses. *Behavior Analyst, 9*(1), 61-70.

Marcuse, F. L. (1980). Behaviour—when? *Ontario Psychologist, 12,* 36-37.

————. (1983, February). Threads of prejudice—Canadian. *Jewish Currents,* pp. 16-19.

Marcuse, H. (1966). *Eros and civilization: A philosophical inquiry into Freud.* Boston: Beacon Press.

Marien, M. (1983). The transformation as sandbox syndrome. *Journal of Humanistic Psychology, 23,* 7-15.

Marmor, J. (1988). Psychiatry in a troubled world. *American Journal of Orthopsychiatry, 58*(4), 484-91.

Martin, R. (1977). *Historical explanation.* Ithaca: Cornell University Press.

————. (1986). A conversation with Ira Shore. *Literacy Research Center, 2*(1), 1-7.

Marx, K. (1964). *Selected writings in sociology and social philosophy.* New York: McGraw-Hill.

Marx, M. H., & Hillix, W. A. (1979). *Systems and theories in psychology* (3d ed.). New York: McGraw-Hill.

Maslow, A. H. (1965). *Eupsychian management.* Homewood, IL: Irwin.

———. (1968). *Toward a psychology of being* (2d ed.). New York: Van Nostrand.

———. (1970a). *Motivation and personality* (2d ed.). New York: Harper & Row.

———. (1970b). *Religions, values, and peak experiences.* New York: Viking.

———. (1971). *The farther reaches of human nature.* New York: Penguin.

———. (1979). Politics 3. *Journal of Humanistic Psychology, 17,* 5-20.

Masten, A. S., & Garmezy, N. (1985). Risk, vulnerability, and protective factors in developmental psychopathology. In B. B. Lahey & A. E. Kazdin (Eds.), *Advances in child clinical psychology* (Vol. 8, pp. 1-52). New York: Plenum Press.

Maughan, B. (1988). School experiences as risk/protective factors. In M. Rutter (Ed.), *Studies of psychosocial risk* (pp. 200-220). New York: Cambridge University Press.

McCannell, K. (1986). Family politics, family policy, and family practice: A feminist perspective. *Canadian Journal of Community Mental Health, 5*(2), 61-72.

McDermott, F. E. (Ed.). (1975). *Self-determination in social work.* London: Routledge & Kegan Paul.

McDowell, J. (1989, March). Children and poverty: The endless cycle. *Canada and the World,* pp. 18-19.

McGuire, W. (1985). Attitudes and attitude change. In G. Lindzey & E. Aronson (Eds.), *The handbook of social psychology: Vol. 2. Special fields and applications* (3d ed., pp. 233-346). New York: Random House.

McKnight, J. (1989). Do no harm: Policy options that meet human needs. *Social Policy,* (Summer) 5-15.

McLean, A. A. (1985). One hundred years of occupational mental health. In P. A. Carone, S. N. Kieffer, S. E. Yolles, & L. W. Krinsky (Eds.), *History of mental health and industry: The last hundred years* (pp. 30-53). New York: Human Sciences Press.

McManus, J. L. (1986). Students as paraprofessionals in school psychology: Practices and possibilities. *School Psychology Review, 15*(1), 9-23.

McNamee, S., & Gergen, K. J. (Eds.). (1992). *Therapy as social construction.* London: Sage.

Medvedev, Z., & Medvedev, R. (1971). *A question of madness.* New York: Vintage Books.

Melton, G. B. (1987). Children, politics, and morality: The ethics of child advocacy. *Journal of Clinical Child Psychology, 16*, 357-67.

———. (1991). Socialization in the global community: Respect for the dignity of children. *American Psychologist, 46*, 66-71.

Michael, J. (1984). Behavior analysis: A radical perspective. In B. L. Hammond (Ed.), *Master lecture series: Vol. 4. Psychology of learning* (pp. 99-121). Washington, DC: American Psychological Association.

Mikulincer, M. (1988). Reactance and helplessness following exposure to unsolvable problems: The effects of attributional styles. *Journal of Personality and Social Psychology, 4*(4), 679-86.

Milgram, S. (1963). Behavioral study of obedience. *Journal of Abnormal and Social Psychology, 67*(4), 371-78.

Miller, A. G. (1986). *The obedience experiments.* New York: Praeger.

Miller, D. (1978). *Social justice.* Oxford: Clarendon.

Miller, J. B., & Mothner, I. (1981). Psychological consequences of sexual inequality. In E. Howell & M. Bayes (Eds.), *Women and mental health* (pp. 41-51). New York: Basic Books.

Mills, C. W. (1943). The professional ideology of social pathologists. *American Journal of Sociology, 49*(2), 165-180.

Mills, J. A. (1982). Some observations on Skinner's moral theory. *Journal for the Theory of Social Behavior, 12*, 141-60.

Minton, H. L. (1993, May). *Toward an emancipatory psychology: Lessons from the construction of sexual identities.* Invited address presented at the symposium "Psychology in the 21st Century," York University, Toronto.

Mirowsky, J., & Ross, C. E. (1989). *Social causes of psychological distress.* New York: Aldine de Gruyter.

Mishra, R. (1977). *Society and social policy: Theoretical perspectives on welfare.* London: Unwin.

Mitchell, J. (1974). *Psycho-analysis and feminism.* New York: Vintage Books.

Morawski, J. G. (1990). Toward the unimagined: Feminism and epistemology in psychology. In R. T. Hare-Mustin & J. Marecek (Eds.), *Making a difference: Psychology and the construction of gender* (pp. 150-83). New Haven: Yale University Press.

Moreau, M. J. (1990). Empowerment through advocacy and consciousness-raising: Implications of a structural approach to social work. *Journal of Sociology and Social Welfare, 17*(2), 53-67.

Morgan, R. F. (Ed.). (1983). *The iatrogenics handbook.* Toronto: IPI Publishing.

Mullaly, R. P. (1980). *A calculus for social planning: Rawls' theory of justice.* Toronto: University of Toronto.

Mulvey, A. (1988). Community psychology and feminism: Tensions and commonalities. *Journal of Community Psychology, 16,* 70-83.

Munsterberg, H. (1913). *Psychology and industrial efficiency.* Boston: Houghton Mifflin.

Murchland, B. (1984). *Humanism and capitalism: A survey of thought on morality.* Washington, DC: American Enterprise Institute.

Nahem, J. (1981). *Psychology and psychiatry today.* New York: International Publishers.

Napoli, D. S. (1981). *Architects of adjustment: A history of the psychological profession in the United States.* Port Washington, NY: National University Publications.

Nelson, G. (1983). Community psychology and the schools: From iatrogenic illness to prevention. In R. F. Morgan (Ed.), *The iatrogenics handbook* (pp. 385-436). Toronto: IPI Publishing.

Nelson, G., Potasznik, H., & Bennett, E. M. (1985). Primary prevention: Another perspective. In E. M. Bennett & B. Tefft (Eds.), *Theoretical and empirical advances in community mental health* (pp. 11-20). Queenston, Ontario: Edwin Mellen.

Nevid, J. S., & Morrison, J. (1980). Attitudes toward mental illness: The construction of the libertarian mental health ideology scale. *Journal of Humanistic Psychology, 20*(2), 71-85.

Nevin, J. A. (1982). On resisting extinction [Review of Jonathan Schell's *The fate of the earth*]. *Journal of Experimental Analysis of Behavior, 38,* 349-53.

————. (1985). Behavior analysis, the nuclear arms race, and the peace movement. In S. Oskamp (Ed.), *Applied Social Psychology Annual* (Vol. 6, pp. 27-44). Beverly Hills, CA: Sage.

Newman, K. S. (1988). *Falling from grace: The experience of downward mobility in the American middle class.* New York: Vintage Books.

Nicholson, M. (1957). *A dictionary of American English usage.* New York: Signet.

Nicol A. R. (Ed.). (1985). *Longitudinal studies in child psychology and psychiatry: Practical lessons from research experience.* New York: Wiley.

Nietzel, M., Bernstein, D. A., & Milich, R. (1991). *Introduction to clinical psychology* (3d ed.). Englewood Cliffs, NJ: Prentice-Hall.

Nietzel, M., & Himelein, M. J. (1987). Crime prevention through social and physical environmental change. *Behavior Analyst, 10*(1), 69-74.

Nisbet, R. A. (1969). *The quest for community.* New York: Oxford University Press.

Nord, W. (1977). A Marxist critique of humanistic psychology. *Journal of Humanistic Psychology, 17,* 75-83.

Norman, R. (1983). *The moral philosophers.* Oxford: Clarendon.

Notterman, J. M. (1985). *Forms of psychological inquiry.* New York: Columbia University.

O'Conner, W. A., & Lubin, B. (Eds.). (1984). *Ecological approaches to clinical and community psychology.* New York: Wiley.

O'Donohue, W. T., Hanley, G. L., & Krasner, L. (1984). Toward the explication of the value contexts of the community psychologies. *Journal of Community Psychology, 12,* 199-205.

Olson, R. B. (1978). *Ethics.* New York: Random House.

O'Neill, P. (1989). Responsible to whom? Responsible for what? Some ethical issues in community intervention. *American Journal of Community Psychology, 17,* 323-41.

Ortega y Gasset, J. (1983). *Que es filosofia?* [What is philosophy?]. Madrid: Alianza.

O'Sullivan, M. J., Waugh, N., & Espeland, W. (1984). The Fort McDowell Yavapai: From pawns to powerbrokers. *Prevention in Human Services, 3*(2/3), 73-98.

Ovitt, G. (1989). Appropriate technology: Development and social change. *Monthly Review, 40*(9), 22-32.

Pappenheim, F. (1959). *The alienation of modern man.* New York: Monthly Review Press.

Parker, I. (1989). *The crisis in modern social psychology and how to end it.* New York: Routledge.

——— . (1992). *Discourse dynamics: Critical analysis for social and individual psychology.* New York: Routledge.

Parker, I., & Shotter, J. (Eds.). (1990). *Deconstructing social psychology.* New York: Routledge.

Patterson, G. R., DeBarsyshe, B. D., & Ramsey, E. (1989). A developmental perspective on antisocial behavior. *American Psychologist, 44,* 329-35.

Pearson, G. (1974). The reification of the family in family therapy. In N. Armistead (Ed.), *Reconstructing social psychology* (pp. 137-56). Harmondsworth, England: Penguin.

———. (1975). *The deviant imagination: Psychiatry, social work, and social change.* New York: Holmes & Meier.

Penfold, P. S. (1992). Sexual abuse by therapists: Maintaining the conspiracy of silence. *Canadian Journal of Community Mental Health, 11*(1), 5-15.

Perkin, H. (1990). *The rise of professional society.* New York: Routledge.

Perkins, R. (1992). Working with socially disabled clients: A feminist perspective. In J. M. Ussher & P. Nicolson (Eds.), *Gender issues in clinical psychology* (pp. 171-93). New York: Routledge.

Pianta, R. C. (1990). Widening the debate on educational reform: Prevention as a viable alternative. *Exceptional Children, 4,* 306-313.

Pitt, J. C. (1987). On why technology can't improve society. *Behaviorism, 15*(1), 51-56.

Plas, J. M. (1986). *Systems psychology in the schools.* New York: Pergamon Press.

Poster, M. (1978). *Critical theory of the family.* New York: Seabury.

Pransky, J. (1991). *Prevention: The critical need.* Springfield, MO: Burrell Foundation.

Price, R. H., Cowen, E. L., Lorion, R. P., & Ramos-McKay, J. (1988). *Fourteen ounces of prevention: A casebook for practitioners.* Washington, DC: American Psychological Association.

———. (1989). The search for effective prevention programs: What we learned along the way. *American Journal of Orthopsychiatry, 59*(1), 49-58.

Prilleltensky, I. (1989). Psychology and the status quo. *American Psychologist, 44,* 795-802.

———. (Chair). (1993, June). *Understanding and overcomming oppression: The political sphere of primary prevention.* Symposium conducted at the biennial conference of the Society for Community Research and Action, Division 27 of the American Psychological Association, Williamsburg, VA.

Prilleltensky, I., & Gonick, L. (1993, June). The discourse of oppression: Towards an emancipatory social science praxis. In I. Prilleltensky (Chair), *Understanding and overcomming oppression: The political sphere of primary prevention.* Symposium conducted at the biennial conference of the Society for Communuty Research and Action, Division 27 of the American Psychological Association, Williamsburg, VA.

Ralph, D. (1983). *Work and madness.* Montréal: Black Rose.

Ramos Mattei, C. (1987). *Ethical self-determination in Don Jose Ortega y Gasset.* New York: Peter Lang.

Rand, A. (1967). *Capitalism: The unknown ideal.* New York: New American Library.

Rappaport, J. (1977). *Community psychology.* New York: Holt, Rinehart & Winston.

———. (1981). In praise of paradox: A social policy of empowerment over prevention. *American Journal of Community Psychology, 9*(1), 1-25.

———. (1984). Seeking justice in the real world: A further explication of value contexts. *Journal of Community Psychology, 12,* 208-16.

———. (1986). Collaborating for empowerment: Creating the language of mutual help. In H. C. Boyte & F. Riessman (Eds.), *The new populism: The politics of empowerment* (pp. 64-79). Philadelphia: Temple University Press.

———. (1987). Terms of empowerment/exemplars of prevention: Toward a theory for community psychology. *American Journal of Community Psychology, 15,* 121-48.

———. (1990). Research methods and the empowerment social agenda. In P. Tolan, C. Keys, F. Chertok, & L. Jason (Eds.), *Researching community psychology* (pp. 51-63). Washington, DC: American Psychological Association.

Rappaport, J., Swift, C., & Hess, R. (Eds.). (1984). *Studies in empowerment: Steps toward understanding and action.* New York: Haworth Press.

Raven, B. H. (1990). Political applications of the psychology of interpersonal influence and social power. *Political Psychology, 11*(3), 493-520.

Rawls, J. (1972). *A theory of justice.* New York: Oxford University Press.

Reading, P. (1977). *Dictionary of the social sciences.* London: Routledge & Kegan Paul.

Reeck, D. (1982). *Ethics for the professions.* Minneapolis: Augsburg.

Reich, M. (1986). The political-economic effects of racism. In R. C. Edwards, M. Reich, & T. E. Weisskopf (Eds.), *The capitalist system* (3d ed., pp. 305-11). Englewood Cliffs, NJ: Prentice-Hall.

Reich, M., & Edwards, R. C. (1986). Liberal democracy, political parties, and the capitalist state. In R. C. Edwards, M. Reich, & T. E. Weisskopf (Eds.), *The capitalist system* (3d ed., pp. 200-11). Englewood Cliffs, NJ: Prentice-Hall.

Reiff, R. (1974). The control of knowledge: The power of the helping professions. *Journal of Applied Behavioral Science, 10,* 451-61.

Reinharz, S. (1992). *Feminist methods in social research.* New York: Oxford University Press.

Reinherz, H. Z. (1982). Primary prevention of emotional disorders in school settings. In H. C. Schulberg & M. Killilea (Eds.), *The modern practice of community mental health* (pp. 445-66). San Francisco: Jossey-Bass.

Reiser, M. F. (1988). Are psychiatric educators "losing the mind"? *American Journal of Psychiatry, 145*(2), 148-49.

Reynolds, C. R., Gutkin, T. B., Elliot, S. N., & Witt, J. C. (1984). *School psychology: Essentials of theory and practice.* New York: Wiley.

Ricouer, P. (1978). Can there be a scientific concept of ideology? In J. Bien (Ed.), *Phenomenology and the social sciences: A dialogue* (pp. 44-59). Boston: Martinus Nijhoff.

Rieff, P. (1961). *Freud: The mind of the moralist.* New York: Anchor.

Riessman, F. (1986). The new populism and the empowerment ethos. In H. C. Boyte & F. Riessman (Eds.), *The new populism: The politics of empowerment* (pp. 53-63). Philadelphia: Temple University Press.

Riger, S. (1992). Epistemological debates, feminist voices: Science, social values, and the study of women. *American Psychologist, 47,* 730-40.

Roazen, P. (1986). *Freud: Political and social thought.* New York: Da Capo Press.

————— . (1990). *Encountering Freud: The politics and histories of psychoanalysis.* London: Transaction.

Robinson, D. N. (1984). Ethics and advocacy. *American Psychologist, 39,* 787-93.

————— . (1985). *Philosophy of psychology.* New York: Columbia University.

Roffe, M. W. (1986). Psychology and self reflection. In K. S. Larsen (Ed.), *Dialectics and ideology in psychology* (pp. 196-218). Norwood, NJ: Ablex.

Rogers, C. (1967). Toward a modern approach to values. In C. Rogers & B. Stevens (Eds.), *Person to person: The problem of being human* (pp. 4-21). Richmond Hill, Ontario: Simon & Schuster.

————— . (1972). Some social issues which concern me. *Journal of Humanistic Psychology, 12,* 45-60.

Rogers, C. B. (1977). Behaviorism, ethics, and the political arena. In J. E. Krapfl & E. A. Vargas (Eds.), *Behaviorism and ethics* (pp. 355-71). Kalamazoo, MI: Behaviordelia.

Rolf, J., Masten., A., Cicchetti, D., Nuechterlein, K. H., & Weintraub, S. (Eds.). (1990). *Risk and protective factors in the development of psychopathology.* New York: Cambridge University Press.

Rose, S., Lewontin, R. C., & Kamin, L. J. (1984). *Not in our genes.* New York: Viking Penguin.

Rose, S. M., & Black, B. L. (1985). *Advocacy and empowerment: Mental health care in the community.* Boston: Routledge & Kegan Paul.

Rosen, G. M. (1987). Self-help treatment and the commercialization of psychotherapy. *American Psychologist, 42,* 46-51.

Rosenhan, D. L. (1973). On being sane in insane places. *Science, 179,* 250-58.

Rosenthal, R., & Jacobson, L. (1968). *Pygmalion in the classroom: Teacher expectation and pupils' intellectual development.* New York: Holt.

Rosewater, L. B. (1990). Public advocacy. In H. Lerman & N. Porter (Eds.), *Feminist ethics in psycotherapy* (pp. 229-38). New York: Springer.

Ross, D. (1991). *The origins of American social sience.* New York: Cambridge University Press.

Rowe, D. (1987). Avoiding the big issues and attending to the small. In S. Fairbairn & G. Fairbairn (Eds.), *Psychology, ethics, and change* (pp. 231-43). New York: Routledge & Kegan Paul.

Rutter, M. (1985a). Family and school influences: Meanings, mechanisms, and implications. In A. R. Nicol (Ed.), *Longitudinal studies in child psychology and psychiatry: Practical lessons from research experience* (pp. 357-403). New York: Wiley.

———. (1985b). Resilience in the face of adversity: Protective factors and resistance to psychiatric disorders. *British Journal of Psychiatry, 147,* 598-611.

———. (1987). Psychosocial resilience and protective mechanisms. *American Journal of Orthopsychiatry, 57*(3), 316-31.

———. (1988). *Studies of psychosocial risk: The power of longitudinal data.* Oxford: Cambridge University Press.

Ryan, A. (1970). *The philosophy of the social sciences.* London: Macmillan.

Ryan, T. J. (Ed.). (1972). *Poverty and the child.* New York: McGraw-Hill.

Ryan, W. (1971). *Blaming the victim.* New York: Pantheon.

———. (1981). *Equality.* New York: Pantheon.

Sabia, D. R., & Wallulis, J. (Eds.). (1983). *Changing social science: Critical theory and other critical perspectives.* Albany: State University of New York Press.

Sahakian, W. S. (1977). *Psychology of personality: Readings in theory* (3d ed.). Chicago: Rand McNally.

Samelson, F. (1979). Putting psychology on the map: Ideology and intelligence testing. In A. R. Buss (Ed.), *Psychology in social context* (pp. 103-68). New York: Irvington.

Sampson, E. E. (1977). Psychology and the American ideal. *Journal of Personality and Social Psychology, 35*(11), 767-82.

———. (1978). Scientific paradigms and social values: Wanted—a scientific revolution. *Journal of Personality and Social Psychology, 36*(11), 1332-43.

———. (1981). Cognitive psychology as ideology. *American Psychologist, 36*, 730-43.

———. (1983). *Justice and the critique of pure psychology.* New York: Plenum Press.

———. (1991). The democratization of psychology. *Theory and Psychology, 1*, 275-98.

Sarason, S. B. (1978). The nature of problem solving in social action. *American Psychologist, 33*, 370-80.

———. (1981a). An asocial psychology and a misdirected clinical psychology. *American Psychologist, 36*, 827-36.

———. (1981b). *Psychology misdirected.* New York: Free Press.

———. (1982a). *The culture of the school and the problem of change* (2d ed.). Boston: Allyn & Bacon.

———. (1982b). *Psychology and social action.* New York: Praeger.

———. (1983). School psychology: An autobiographical fragment. *Journal of School Psychology, 21*(4), 285-95.

———. (1984a). Community psychology and public policy: Missed opportunity. *American Journal of Community Psychology, 12*(2), 199-207.

———. (1984b). If it can be studied or developed, should it be? *American Psychologist, 39*, 477-85.

———. (1986). And what is the public interest? *American Psychologist, 41*, 899-905.

———. (1988). *The making of an American psychologist: An autobiography.* San Francisco: Jossey-Bass.

———. (1990). *The predictable failure of educational reform.* San Francisco: Jossey-Bass.

Sarbin, T. R., & Mancuso, J. C. (1980). *Schizophrenia: Medical diagnosis or moral verdict?* New York: Pergamon Press.

Sargent, L. T. (1969). *Contemporary political ideologies.* Homewood, IL: Dorsey.

Sass, L. A. (1992). The epic of disbelief: The postmodernist turn in contemporary psychoanalysis. In S. Kvale (Ed.), *Psychology and postmodernism* (pp. 166-182). London: Sage.

Saulnier, K. (1985). Networks, change, and crisis: The web of support. In E. M. Bennett & B. Tefft (Eds.), *Theoretical and empirical advances in community mental health* (pp. 21-40). Queenston, Ontario: Edwin Mellen.

Savan, B. (1988). *Science under siege: The myth of objectivity in scientific research.* Montréal: CBC Enterprises.

Schacht, T. E. (1985). DSM-III and the politics of truth. *American Psychologist, 40,* 513-21.

Scheff, T. J. (1976). Schizophrenia as ideology. In A. Dean, A. M. Kraft, & B. Pepper (Eds.), *The social setting of mental health* (pp. 209-15). New York: Basic Books.

Schneider, M. (1975). *Neurosis and civilization.* New York: Seabury Press.

Schneiderman, L. (1988). *The psychology of social change.* New York: Human Sciences Press.

Schwartz, B. (1986). *The battle for human nature: Science, morality, and modern life.* New York: Norton.

Schwartz, M. (Ed.). (1987). *The structure of power in America: The corporate elite as a ruling class.* New York: Holmes & Meyer.

Sedgwick, P. (1974). Ideology in modern psychology. In N. Armistead (Ed.), *Reconstructing social psychology* (pp. 29-38). Harmondsworth, England: Penguin.

―――. (1982). *Psychopolitics.* New York: Harper & Row.

Seligman, M. E. P. (1975). *Helplessness: On depression, development, and death.* San Francisco: W. H. Freeman.

―――. (1990). *Learned optimism.* New York: Knopf.

Sennett, R., & Cobb, J. (1972). *The hidden injuries of class.* New York: Vintage.

Serrano-Garcia, I. (1984). The illusion of empowerment: Community development within a colonial context. *Prevention in Human Services, 3*(2/3), 173-200.

Seve, L. (1978). *Man in Marxist theory and the psychology of personality.* Sussex, England: Harvester.

Shackleton, V., & Anderson, N. (1987). Personnel recruitment and selection. In M. B. Bass & P. J. D. Drenth (Eds.), *Advances in organizational psychology* (pp. 68-82). London: Sage.

Shaw, R., & Colimore, K. (1988). Humanistic psychology as ideology: An analysis of Maslow's contradictions. *Journal of Humanistic Psychology, 28,* 51-74.

Shepard, P. T., & Hamlin, C. (1987). How not to presume: Toward a descriptive theory of ideology in science and technology controversy. *Science, Technology, and Human Values, 12*(2), 19-28.

Shields, S. A. (1975). Functionalism, Darwinism, and the psychology of women: A study in social myth. *American Psychologist, 30,* 739-54.

Shils, E. (1968). The concept and function of ideology. In D. L. Sills (Ed.), *International encyclopedia of the social sciences* (pp. 66-76). New York: Macmillan & Free Press.

Shimrat, I. (Ed.). (1992, January). *OPSAnews: The newsletter of the Ontario Psychiatric Survivors' Alliance.* (Available from OPSA, 3107 Bloor Street West, Suite 207, Etobicoke, Ontario, Canada, M8X 1E3).

Shore, R. P. (1982). Servants of power revisited. *American Psychologist, 37,* 334-35.

Shotter, J. (1991). Rhetoric and the social construction of cognitivism. *Theory and Psychology, 1*(4), 495-514.

Shreve, A. (1989). *Women together, women alone: The legacy of the consciousness-raising movement.* New York: Viking Penguin.

Sidgwick, H. (1922). *The methods of ethics* (7th ed.). London: Macmillan.

Sigmon, S. B. (1987). Present roles and future objectives for American school psychology. *Journal of Social Behavior and Personality, 2*(3), 379-82.

Silva, L. (1970). *La plusvalia ideologica* [Ideological surplus]. Caracas: Universidad Central de Venezuela.

Simon, R. (1982). *Gramsci's political thought.* London: Lawrence & Wishart.

Singer, P. (1993). *Practical ethics* (2d ed.). New York: Cambridge University Press.

Skinner, B. F. (1948). *Walden two.* New York: Macmillan.

——— . (1953). *Science and human behavior.* New York: Free Press.

——— . (1972). *Beyond freedom and dignity.* New York: Bantam/Vintage Books.

———. (1974). *About behaviorism*. New York: Vintage Books.

———. (1978). *Reflections on behaviorism and society*. Englewood Cliffs, NJ: Prentice-Hall.

———. (1985). Toward the cause of peace. In S. Oskamp (Ed.), *Applied social psychology annual* (Vol. 6, pp. 21-25). Beverly Hills, CA: Sage.

———. (1987). Whatever happened to psychology as the science of behavior? *American Psychologist, 42,* 780-86.

Smith, A. J., & Douglas, M. A. (1990). Empowerment as an ethical imperative. In H. Lerman & N. Porter, (Eds.), *Feminist ethics in psychotherapy* (pp. 43-50). New York: Springer.

Smith, D. E. (1990). *The conceptual practices of power: A feminist sociology of knowledge*. Toronto: University of Toronto.

Smith, J. C. (1990). *Psychoanalytic roots of patriarchy*. New York: New York University Press.

Spacapan, S., & Thompson, S. C. (Eds.). (1991). Perceived control in vulnerable populations [Special issue]. *Journal of Social Issues, 47*(4).

Spence, J. T. (1985). Achievement American style. *American Psychologist, 40,* 1285-95.

Spiers, H. (1973, Winter). Psychiatric neutrality. *The Body Politic,* pp. 16-24.

Stagner, R., & Rosen, H. (1965). *Psychology of union-management relations*. Belmont, CA: Wadsworth.

Statistics Canada. (1987). *Canada year book 1988*. Ottawa: Author.

Steininger, M. (1983). Critical questions for the psychological foundations of value theory. *Zygon, 18*(2), 183-85.

Steininger, M., Newell, D. J., & Garcia, L. T. (1984). *Ethical issues in psychology*. Homewood, IL: Dorsey.

Sternberg, R. J. (1988). Applying cognitive theory to the testing and teaching of intelligence. *Applied Cognitive Psychology, 2,* 231-55.

Still, A., & Costall, A. (1987). Introduction: In place of cognitivism. In A. Costall & A. Still (Eds.), *Cognitive psychology: In question* (pp. 1-16). New York: St. Martin's Press.

Stolz, S. B. (1978). Ethical issues in behavior modification. In G. Bermant, H. C. Kelman, & D. P. Warwick (Eds.), *The ethics of social intervention* (pp. 37-60). New York: Wiley.

Stoppard, J. M. (1989). An evaluation of the adequacy of cognitive/behavioural theories for understanding depression in women. *Canadian Psychology*, *30*(1), 39-47.

Strauss, J. S. (1979). Social and cultural influences on psychopathology. *Annual Review of Psychology, 30*, 397-415.

Sullivan, E. V. (1984). *A critical psychology*. New York: Plenum Press.

Sullivan, H. S. (1953). *The interpersonal theory of psychiatry*. New York: Norton.

Svec, H. J. (1990). An advocacy model for the school psychologist. *School Psychology International, 11*(1), 63-70.

Swift, C. (1984). Foreword: Empowerment: An antidote for folly. *Prevention in Human Services, 3*(2/3), i-xi.

Szasz, T. (1963). *Law, liberty, and psychiatry*. New York: Collier.

———. (1965). *The ethics of psychoanalysis: The theory and method of autonomous therapy*. New York: Delta.

———. (1974). *The myth of mental illness* (rev. ed.). New York: Harper & Row.

———. (1984). *The therapeutic state*. Buffalo, NY: Prometheus.

Tageson, C. W. (1982). *Humanistic psychology: A synthesis*. Homewood, IL: Dorsey.

Task Force on Public Policy (1988). Recommendations of the task force on public policy. *Behavior Analyst, 11*(1), 27-32.

Taylor, C. (1991). *The malaise of modernity*. Toronto: CBC Productions.

Taylor, R. (1989, March). Poverty statistics. *Canada and the World*, pp. 13-15.

Therborn, G. (1980). *The ideology of power and the power of ideology*. London: Verso.

Thibault, A. (1981). Studying alienation without alienating people: A challange for society. In R. F. Geyer & D. Schweitzer (Eds.), *Alienation: Problems of meaning, theory, and method* (pp. 275-83). London: Routledge & Kegan Paul.

Thielman, S. B. (1985). Psychiatry and social values: The American Psychiatric Association and the immigration restriction, 1880-1930. *Psychiatry, 48*, 299-310.

Thomas, A., & Sillen, S. (1972). *Racism and psychiatry*. Seacaucus, NJ: Citadel.

Thompson, J. B. (1984). *Studies in the theory of ideology*. Cambridge, England: Polity Press.

Thompson, S. C., & Spacapan, S. (1991). Perceptions of control in vulnerable populations. *Journal of Social Issues, 47*(4), 1-22.

Tingstrom, D. H., Stewart, K. J., & Little, M. (1990). School consultation from a social psychological perspective. *Psychology in the Schools, 27*(1), 41-50.

Tomm, K. (1980). Towards a cybernetic systems approach to family therapy at the University of Calgary. In D. S. Freeman (Ed.), *Perspectives on family therapy* (pp. 3-18). Vancouver: Butterworth.

Toulmin, S., & Leary, D. E. (1985). The cult of empiricism in psychology, and beyond. In S. Koch & D. E. Leary (Eds.), *A century of psychology as science* (pp. 594-617). New York: McGraw-Hill.

Trachtman, G. M. (1990). Best practices in political activism. In A. Thomas & J. Grimes (Eds.), *Best practices in school psychology* (pp. 563-74). Washington, DC: National Association of School Psychologists.

Turkle, S. (1978). *Psychoanalytic politics.* New York: Basic Books.

————. (1981). French anti-psychiatry. In D. Ingleby (Ed.), *Critical psychiatry* (pp. 150-83). Harmondsworth, England: Penguin.

Tymchuk, A. J. (1989). Anticipatory ethical and policy decision making and community psychology. *American Journal of Community Psychology, 17,* 361-65.

Ulman, J. (1991). Towards a synthesis of Marx and Skinner. *Behavior and Social Issues, 1*(1), 57-70.

Unger, R., & Crawford, M. (1992). *Women and gender: A feminist psychology.* Toronto: McGraw-Hill.

Ussher, J. M. (1992). Science sexing psychology: Positivistic science and gender bias in clinical psychology. In J. M. Ussher & P. Nicolson (Eds.), *Gender issues in clinical psychology* (pp. 39-67). New York: Routledge.

Ussher, J. M., & Nicolson, P. (Eds.). (1992). *Gender issues in clinical psychology.* New York: Routledge.

Valsiner, J. (1991). Construction of the mental. *Theory and Psychology, 1*(4), 477-94.

Van Hoorn, W. (1984). The minimal meaningful context. *Revista de Historia de la Psicologia, 5*(1-2), 163-71.

Vatz, R. E., & Weinberg, L. S. (Eds.). (1983). *Thomas Szasz: Primary values and major contentions.* Buffalo, NY: Prometheus.

Vetere, A. (1992). Working with families. In J. M. Ussher & P. Nicolson (Eds.), *Gender issues in clinical psychology* (pp. 129-52). New York: Routledge.

Waitzkin, H. (1989). A critical theory of medical discourse: Ideology, social control, and the processing of social context in medical encounters. *Journal of Health and Social Behavior, 30,* 220-39.

Waldegrave, C. (1990). Just therapy. *Dulwich Centre Newsletter, 1,* 6-46.

Walker, E. L., & Heyns, R. W. (1962). *An anatomy for conformity.* Englewood Cliffs, NJ: Prentice-Hall.

Wallwork, E. (1991). *Psychoanalysis and ethics.* New Haven: Yale University Press.

Walsh, R. T. (1988). The dark side of our moon: The iatrogenic aspects of professional psychology. *Journal of Community Psychology, 16,* 244-48.

Walsh-Bowers, R. T., & Nelson, G. (1993, May). *An empowerment approach to community support for consumers/survivors.* Paper presented at the meeting of the Canadian Psychological Association, Montréal.

Walton, R. E. (1978). Ethical issues in the practice of organizational development. In G. Bermant, H. C. Kelman, & D. P. Warwick (Eds.), *The ethics of social intervention* (pp. 121-46). New York: Wiley.

Warwick, D. P. (1978). Moral dilemmas in organizational development. In G. Bermant, H. C. Kelman, & D. P. Warwick (Eds.), *The ethics of social intervention* (pp. 147-59). New York: Wiley.

————. (1980). *The teaching of ethics in the social sciences.* New York: Hastings Center.

Watson, G., & Williams, J. (1992). Feminist practice in therapy. In J. M. Ussher & P. Nicolson (Eds.), *Gender issues in clinical psychology* (pp. 212-36). New York: Routledge.

Watzlawick, P., Weakland, J. H., & Fisch, R. (1974). *Change: Principles of problem formation and problem resolution.* New York: Norton.

Webb, S., & Webb, B. (1923). *The decay of capitalist civilization.* New York: Harcourt, Brace.

Webster's third new international dictionary, unabridged: The great library of the English language. (1976). Springfield, MA: Merriam-Webster.

Weintraub, S., Winters, K. C., & Neale, J. N. (1986). Competence and vulnerability in children with an affectively disordered parent. In M. Rutter, C. E. Izard, & P. B. Read (Eds.), *Depression in young people: Developmental and clinical perspectives* (pp. 205-22). New York: Guilford.

Weisband, E. (Ed.). (1989). *Poverty amidst plenty: World political economy and distributive justice.* San Francisco: Westview Press.

Wells, D. M. (1987). *Empty promises: Quality of working life programs and the labor movement*. New York: Monthly Review Press.

Werner, E. E. (1985). Stress and protective factors in children's lives. In A. R. Nicol (Ed.), *Longitudinal studies in child psychology and psychiatry: Practical lessons from research experience* (pp. 335-55). New York: Wiley.

————. (1986). A longitudinal study of perinatal risk. In D. C. Farran & J. D. McKinney (Eds.), *Risk in intellectual and psychosocial development* (pp. 3-27). New York: Academic Press.

Wexler, P. (1983). *Critical social psychology*. Boston: Routledge & Kegan Paul.

Whyte, W. H. (1957). *The organization man*. New York: Anchor.

Wilding, P. (1981). *Socialism and professionalism*. London: Fabian Society.

————. (1982). *Professional power and social welfare*. London: Routledge & Kegan Paul.

Wilkinson, S. (1991). Feminism and psychology: From critique to reconstruction. *Feminism and Psychology, 1*(1), 5-18.

Williams, B. (1972). *Morality: An introduction to ethics*. New York: Harper & Row.

Wilson, G. T., & O'Leary, K. D. (1980). *Principles of behavior therapy*. Englewood Cliffs, NJ: Prentice-Hall.

Wilson, H. T. (1977). *The American ideology: Science, technology, and organization as modes of rationality in advanced industrial societies*. London: Routledge & Kegan Paul.

Wilson, J. R. (1991). Participation—a framework and a foundation for ergonomics? *Journal of Occupational and Organizational Psychology, 64*, 67-80.

Wineman, S. (1984). *The politics of human services*. Montréal: Black Rose.

Winett, R. A., & Winkler, R. C. (1972). Behavior modification in the classroom: Be still, be quiet, be docile. *Journal of Applied Behavior Analysis, 5*, 499-504.

Witt, J. C. (1986). Teachers' resistance to the use of school-based interventions. *Journal of School Psychology, 24*(1), 37-44.

Witt, J. C., & Martens, B. K. (1988). Problems with problem-solving consultation: A re-analysis of assumptions, methods, and goals. *School Psychology Review, 17*(2), 211-26.

Wolfe, A. (1989). *Whose keeper? Social science and moral obligation*. Los Angeles: University of California Press.

Wolff, T. (1987). Community psychology and empowerment: An activist's insight. *American Journal of Community Psychology, 15*, 151-66.

Wood, G. (1986). *The myth of neurosis: Overcoming the illness excuse.* New York: Harper & Row.

Woolfolk, R., & Richardson, F. C. (1984). Behavior therapy and the ideology of modernity. *American Psychologist, 39*, 777-86.

Wortis, J. (1945). Freudianism and the psychoanalytic tradition. *American Journal of Psychiatry, 101*, 814-20.

Young, M. (1991). *Justice and the politics of difference.* Princeton, NJ: Princeton University Press.

Young, P. T. P. (Ed.). (1992). The psychology of control [Special issue]. *Canadian Journal of Behavioural Science, 24*(2).

Young, R. (1982). Autonomy and paternalism. *Canadian Journal of Philosophy,* (Suppl. 8), 47-66.

Zanardi, C. (Ed.). (1990). *Essential papers on the psychology of women.* New York: New York University Press.

Zaretsky, E. (1986). *Capitalism, the family, and the personal life* (rev. ed.). New York: Harper & Row.

Zimbardo, P. (1984, January). Mind control in 1984. *Psychology Today,* pp. 68-72.

Zimmerman, M. A. (1990). Toward a theory of learned helpfulness: A structural model analysis of participation and empowerment. *Journal of Research in Personality, 24*, 71-86.

Zimmerman, M. A., & Rappaport, J. (1988). Citizen participation, perceived control, and psychological empowerment. *American Journal of Community Psychology, 16*, 725-50.

Zins, J. E., Conyne, R. K., & Ponti, C. R. (1988). Primary prevention: Expanding the impact of psychological services in schools. *School Psychology Review, 17*(4), 542-49.

Zins, J. E., & Forman, S. G. (1988). Primary prevention in the schools: What are we waiting for? *School Psychology Review, 17*(4), 539-41.

Zuniga, M. A. (1988). Chicano self-concept. In C. Jacobs & D. D. Bowles (Eds.), *Ethnicity & race: Critical concepts in social work* (pp. 71-85). Silver Spring, MD: National Association of Social Workers.

Author Index

Subject Index

A

Abnormal psychology models
asocial, 99, 100-104
medical-defect model, 19, 35-
36, 39, 67, 96, 99-103, 107,
109-11, 124, 152, 217
political implications of, 102-
103
and prevention, 103-104
shortcomings of, 101-102
macrosocial, 99, 113-15
community psychology, 34,
86, 99, 114-16, 121-22, 125,
127-29, 154-55, 188, 218
ecological perspective, 114-15
theory versus practice, 114-
15
macrosociopolitical, 99, 116-29
consumers/survivors move-
ment, 116, 122-25, 129
enacting macrosociopolitical
stance, 125-29
feminist psychology, 9, 12, 34,
36, 40, 116-122, 125, 199.
See also feminism
radical politics, 61, 116, 125

shortcomings of community
psychology, 116, 121-22,
125, 129. *See also* community psychology
microsocial, 99, 104-13
double bind theory, 109-10
labelling theory, 99, 104-109,
113
systems-family therapy, 37,
99, 105, 109-13
Author, background of, 5-7

B

Behaviorism, 9, 26, 81, 89, 194
behavior modification, 9, 70, 75-
76, 79, 194-95
ethics in, 73, 77
gaps between theory and practice, 74-76, 79
philosophy of adjustment, 71-74,
76
positive reinforcement, 72-73
and power, 77-79
in schools, 75-76
and social betterment, 70-74, 76-
78